Forecasting Methods for Management

WILEY SERIES ON SYSTEMS AND CONTROLS FOR FINANCIAL MANAGEMENT

Edited by Robert L. Shultis and Frank M. Mastromano

EDP Systems for Credit Management
Conan D. Whiteside

Profile for Profitability: Using Cost Control and Profitability Analysis
Thomas S. Dudick

Zero-Base Budgeting: A Practical Management Tool for Evaluating Expenses
Peter A. Pyhrr

Forecasting Methods for Management
Steven C. Wheelwright and Spyros Makridakis

Forecasting Methods for Management

STEVEN C. WHEELWRIGHT

Harvard University Graduate School of Business

SPYROS MAKRIDAKIS

*The European Institute of Business
Administration (INSEAD)*

A Wiley-Interscience Publication

JOHN WILEY & SONS, New York • London • Sydney • Toronto

The text of this book was initially prepared as teaching material for CESEA, Centro Superior de Estudios Aplicados, Madrid and is being published by authorization.

Library of Congress Cataloging in Publication Data:

Wheelwright, Steven C   1943–
    Forecasting methods for management.

    (Wiley series on systems and controls for financial management)
    "A Wiley-Interscience publication."
    Includes bibliographies.
    1.   Economic forecasting.   2.   Economic forecasting—Methodology.   3.   Business forecasting.   I.   Makridakis, Spyros G., joint author.   II.   Title.

HD69.F58W5   658.4'03   73–3071
ISBN 0–471–93769–X

Printed in the United States of America

10–9 8 7 6 5 4 3 2

SERIES PREFACE

No one needs to tell the reader that the world is changing. He sees it all too clearly. The immutable, the constant, the unchanging of a decade or two ago no longer represent the latest thinking—on *any* subject, whether morals, medicine, politics, economics, or religion. Change has always been with us, but the pace has been accelerating, especially in the postwar years.

Business, particularly with the advent of the electronic computer some 20 years ago, has also undergone change. New disciplines have sprung up. New professions are born. New skills are in demand. And the need is ever greater to blend the new skills with those of the older professions to meet the demands of modern business.

The accounting and financial functions certainly are no exception. The constancy of change is as pervasive in these fields as it is in any other. Industry is moving toward an integration of many of the information gathering, processing, and analyzing functions under the impetus of the so-called systems approach. Such corporate territory has been, traditionally, the responsibility of the accountant and the financial man. It still is, to a large extent—but times are changing.

Does this, then, spell the early demise of the accountant as we know him today? Does it augur a lessening of influence for the financial specialists in today's corporate hierarchy? We think not. We maintain, however, that it is incumbent upon today's accountant and today's financial man to learn *today's* thinking and to *use today's* skills. It is for this reason the Wiley Series on Systems and Controls for Financial Management is being developed.

Recognizing the broad spectrum of interests and activities that the series title encompasses, we plan a number of volumes, each representing the latest thinking, written by a recognized authority, on a particular facet of the financial man's responsibilities. The subjects contemplated for discussion within the series range from production accounting systems to planning, to corporate records, to control of cash. Each book is an in-depth study of one subject within this group. Each is intended to be a practical, working tool for the businessman in general and the financial man and accountant in particular.

ROBERT L. SHULTIS
FRANK M. MASTROMANO

PREFACE

The past decade has seen a number of developments in the area of forecasting methods that can be used in business. These advances in theory and practice have been the result largely of the increasing complexity and competitiveness of the business environment. Companies of all sizes now find it essential to make forecasts for a number of uncertain quantities that affect their decisions and their performance.

As in the development of most management science techniques, the application of these methods has lagged behind their theoretical formulation and verification. Thus, although most managers are aware of the need for improved forecasting methods, few managers are familiar with the range of techniques that has been developed and the characteristics that must be known in order to select the most appropriate technique for a given situation.

Unfortunately the literature on forecasting methods has done little to solve the problem of what is technically known and what the manager can actually understand and apply. When we examine the existing forecasting literature, we find a handful of excellent books, but these books have actually been written by the individuals who have performed the theoretical formulation and verification of specific techniques; for example, we can find authors such as Box and Jenkins who have produced a book that certainly describes the technique they have developed for forecasting but fails to cover a wide range of alternative forecasting methods. Thus the manager seeking to understand what alternative forecasting techniques are available must read not a single book but several books, with each one describing a single method or a narrow class of methods. In addition to this problem, we find that the literature describing these individual methods is generally more concerned with theoretical development and verification than with the practical application of the method. Most managers are not directly concerned with these theoretical aspects (they have experts in the company who can examine the method's validity) and they have neither the time nor perhaps the inclination to study the details of each forecasting method. Thus what seems to be needed is a book that covers a wide range of forecasting methods, is accurate in describing their essential characteristics and how they can be applied in practice, but does not dwell on the theoretical questions behind their development.

For such a forecasting book to be helpful to management it must not only describe the many available techniques and their application but it must also deal with the forecasting function in the organization. This function includes such things as data acquisition, data audits, links with formal planning procedures and other management systems, maintenance of existing applications, and identification and implementation of new applications. To have maximum effectiveness management must have guidelines for carrying out these functions and for assigning responsibility for them in the corporate organization.

Having been involved in both teaching and the application of forecasting methods in a wide range of situations, we are aware of the lack of suitable literature for meeting the needs of *managers* in the area of forecasting. The aim of this book is to begin to fill the gap by presenting in terms that can be easily understood by the manager (yet accurately describe the techniques), a wide range of forecasting methods that can be used by management and guidelines that relate to performance of the forecasting function within the organization. These materials have proved to be effective when we used them both in seminars for middle management and in classes at the graduate level of business education. It is our hope that by preparing these materials in the form of a book they will be of much more general use to the management community.

The material in this book has been organized into three parts. The first lays the groundwork for the remainder of the book in a discussion of the nature of forecasting problems, the types of technique developed for forecasting, and the criteria that can be used in matching specific techniques with specific problem situations. Thus Chapter 1 begins with an overview of our view of forecasting and where it fits in management decision making and corporate activity. In Chapter 2 a range of criteria that can be used in evaluating the application of alternative forecasting techniques is discussed. It is these criteria that are used in subsequent chapters in determining the appropriateness of various techniques for various applications.

The second part of the book is aimed at describing a number of different forecasting methods and their application in business. Chapters 3 through 8 describe many different methods that would commonly be categorized as quantitative forecasting techniques. This designation indicates that they base a forecast on quantitative data. Because data plays such an important role in the application of these methods, Chapter 9 focuses on the problems of data acquisition and the handling of data in the forecasting function. Obviously all situations that require a forecast do not have readily available substantial historical data. In some situations forecasts must be based on managerial judgment and subjective estimates. Chapter 10 describes this type of forecast and how it can be integrated into the decision-making process. The third type of forecasting technique described is that commonly referred to as qualitative approaches to forecasting. These approaches, discussed in Chapter 11, deal with aggregate changes in the environment and in the longer term needs of forecasts for which little historical data is available.

The final chapters deal with the forecasting function in the business organization and the procedures for handling that function. This discussion is broken into two parts, with Chapter 12 dealing with the relationship of forecasting to planning and controlling in the organization and Chapter 13 dealing with the selection and implementation of specific applications within the firm.

To keep this volume to a reasonable size we have had to make some trade-offs between technical completeness in the discussion of individual forecasting methods and a wide range of applications in the examples and in providing guidelines for implementation. Because other textbooks do a good job of describing individual techniques, we have chosen simply to reference them by including a list of references for additional study and to focus our efforts on those aspects of forecasting that are directly relevant to the practicing manager.

STEVEN C. WHEELWRIGHT
SPYROS MAKRIDAKIS

Dedicated to

MARGARET, MARIANNE,

MELINDA AND BARBARA

Contents

1 Forecasting and Management: An Introduction   **1**

The Role of Forecasting in Decision Making, 1
Types of Forecasting Techniques, 4
Selecting the Forecasting Technique, 6
Forecasting in the Firm, 10
Summary, 12
Appendix I   Notation for Quantitative Forecasting Techniques, 12

2 The Evaluation of Forecasting Techniques   **15**

The Underlying Pattern of the Data, 17
The Accuracy of Forecasting Techniques and the Measurement
    of Error, 20
The Type of Model Represented by Forecasting Techniques, 22
The Costs of a Forecasting Technique, 24
The Lead Time in Forecasting Methods, 25
Applicability, 26

3 Forecasting with Smoothing Techniques   **29**

Simple Moving Averages, 30
Exponential Smoothing, 36
Higher Forms of Smoothing, 39
References for Additional Study, 47

4 Forecasting with Adaptive Filtering   **48**

Forecasts Based on a Weighted Average of Historical
    Observations, 48
An Adaptive Process for Weighting Past Observations, 50

Using Adaptive Filtering in Practice, 55
References for Additional Study, 61
Appendix   Additional Guidelines to Forecasting with Adaptive
   Filtering, 61

5 Simple Regression and Correlation   **63**

Determining the Parameters of a Straight Line, 66
The Accuracy and Significance of a Regression Equation, 72
Simple Correlation, 77
The Regression Equation as a Model, 80
References for Additional Study, 82

**6 The Classical Decomposition Method of Time Series
    Forecasting**   **83**

Identifying the Different Factors in the Pattern, 84
Preparing a Forecast Based on the Decomposition Method for
   Time Series Analysis, 91
An Evaluation of Decomposition Forecasting, 95
Improved Methods of Decomposition Forecasting, 97
References for Additional Study, 99

7 Multiple Regression and Correlation   **100**

The Application of Multiple Regression Analysis, 103
Multiple Correlation and the Coefficient of Determination, 105
Tests of Significance, 106
Assumptions Inherent in Multiple Regression Analysis, 109
Using Multiple Regression Analysis in Practice, 113
Summary, 122
References for Additional Study, 122

8 Other Quantitative Methods of Forecasting   **123**

The Box-Jenkins Method of Forecasting, 123
Econometric Forecasting, 135
Input-Output Tables, 141
Inventory Control Theory, 143
References for Additional Study, 143

9 Data Acquisition and Handling in Forecasting   **144**

Definition and Specification of Variables in Forecasting, 144
Data Collection and Data Sources, 147

Problems of Accuracy in Data, 150
Use of a Data Base System in Forecasting, 153
Updating and Internal Audits, 160
References for Additional Study, 161

10 Forecasts Based on Subjective Estimates   **162**

Probability and Uncertainty in Decision Making, 162
Using Subjective Probabilities in Decision Making, 166
Obtaining Subjective Probabilities, 171
Limitations and Extensions, 174
References for Additional Study, 176

11 Qualitative Approaches to Forecasting   **177**

Logistic and S-Curve Approaches, 180
Time Independent Technological Comparisons, 183
Morphological Research Method, 185
The Delphi Method, 188
PATTERN: A Relevance Tree Method, 190
Recent Experience in Qualitative Forecasting, 193
References for Additional Study, 194

12 Matching the Forecasting Method with the Situation   **195**

Applying Evaluation Criteria in Selecting a Forecasting
    Method, 195
Designing a Forecasting System, 212
References for Additional Study, 219

**13 Organizing and Implementing a Corporate Forecasting
    Function**   **220**

Elements of an Ongoing Forecasting Procedure, 214
Forecasting Organization and Sponsorship, 224
The Implementation of Forecasting Requires Changing
    Behavior, 231
Characteristics of Successful Forecasting Situations, 233
References for Additional Study, 235

Index   **237**

CHAPTER 1

FORECASTING AND MANAGEMENT: AN INTRODUCTION

THE ROLE OF FORECASTING IN DECISION MAKING

In recent years a tremendous emphasis has been placed on improving decision making both in business and government. One aspect of this improvement has been the requirement that the steps taken be made more explicit than they have been in the past. By making these subparts of the decision-making process distinct they can then be focused on for purposes of individual improvement. Thus, although many managers 20 or 30 years ago were able to run their businesses, whether large or small, largely on their own feelings and intuition about the industry and their own situations, that kind of management is rapidly disappearing. In its place we hear more and more about the use of new management decision-making techniques: operations research, computers, and principles of organizational design.

A key aspect of any decision-making situation is being able to predict the circumstances that surround that decision and that situation. Such predictions, generally handled under the title of forecasting, have been identified as a key subpart of the decision-making process. As a natural consequence of the increased emphasis placed on systematic management, the area of predicting and forecasting has been studied extensively, and methods of making predictions more objective and reliable have been developed. These techniques vary considerably in their sophistication and usefulness.

To appreciate the fact that no single forecasting method can meet the needs of all decision-making situations it is helpful to consider the range of problems that requires forecasting. A simple way of classifying these problems is in terms of the functional areas to which they relate. One of the reasons that this functional classification is extremely useful is that forecasting is merely a means of improving decision making and is not an end in itself.

1

Thus any discussion of forecasting methods must deal directly with the decision-making problems and processes to which they will be applied. Since these problems and processes are often grouped along functional lines (marketing, finance, or production), we shall examine the requirements of forecasts that use the same functional groupings.

In marketing there are a number of decisions that should be based on reliable forecasts of market size and market characteristics; for example, a company that produces and sells household appliances (washing machines, televisions, and refrigerators) must be able to forecast what the demand will be for each of its products by geographical regions and types of consumer. These forecasts can then be used by its marketing department in its plans for advertising, direct sales, and other promotional efforts. In addition, marketing requires forecasts on such things as market share, trends in prices, and new product development.

In production a major need for forecasting is in the area of sales by product so that the firm can plan its production schedule and inventories to meet that sales demand at a reasonable cost. In such a situation the manager needs a forecast by individual item for a specific period to help him with his decision making. Many of the other areas related to the production function that need forecasts are material requirements, trends in material and labor costs, trends in availability of material and labor, maintenance requirements, and plant capacity available for production.

Finance and accounting is an area in which forecasting has been most valuable. The finance department must be able to project cash flows and the rates of various expenses and revenues to keep the company liquid and operating efficiently. In making such cash-flow forecasts it will generally predict each of several elements that go into the net cash-flow computation. These projections will then be combined to form the cash-flow forecast. Finance also needs forecasts of interest rates to help in planning the timing of new capital acquisitions, of receipt of accounts receivable to help in controlling slow accounts and unusual increases in working capital, and of actual operations in order to perform the financial control function and identify detrimental trends early in their development.

Even the personnel department requires a number of forecasts to help in the major decisions of planning for the number of workers in each category to be hired and the need for additional training programs. Thus the personnel manager of a firm may ask for forecasts of the number of workers that will be needed in each job category, the turnover in each of those categories, changes in working hours and retirement age, and trends in absenteeism and lateness.

Because the general management function is central to the successful operation of a firm, the importance of forecasts that can be used as the basis for decision making at that level is perhaps most critical. Especially helpful in making better top-management decisions is the forecasting of economic factors that can serve as a basis in planning the timing and magnitude of expansion and the execution of strategic actions. Besides predictions of the general economy, general managers have found that projecting changes in prices, costs, growth of product lines and earnings, and the results of possible acquisition candidates are all areas in which recently developed forecasting methods can be most beneficial.

Although each of the functional areas of business clearly has its own requirements for forecasts, a number of forecasts also relate these various functional areas and are important in the overall decision-making framework of the company; for example, the planning of a new facility clearly demands decision-making contributions from marketing, production, finance, general management, and most of the other areas of business. Thus the forecasts that are needed for facilities planning must relate these different functions.

Although many managers often think that these examples of situations in which decisions must be made and in which a forecast may be helpful are different in nature, some elements are common to all. They are what make it possible to develop and use a single method of forecasting for a number of different situations. The *first* element that will be noticed is that all these situations deal with the future and time is directly involved. Thus a forecast must be made for some specific point in time, and changing that point generally affects what the forecast will be. A *second* element that is always present in forecasting situations is uncertainty. If management were certain about what circumstances would exist at a given time, the preparation of a forecast would be a trivial matter. Virtually all situations faced by management involve uncertainty, however, and judgments must be made and information must be gathered on which to base a forecast. The *third* element, present in varying degrees in all the situations described, is the reliance of a forecast on information that is contained in historical data. The term "data" is generally used to refer to any number or fact that may be available. The *amount of information* contained in such data is a measure of how relevant that data is to decision making. Thus we could have a tremendous amount of data without having much information on what will happen in the future and vice versa. Generally speaking, forecasts are based directly or indirectly on information that is obtained from historical data. Although other elements may be present in a number of forecasting situations, these three are the most important.

One point that deserves special attention here is the notion that planning and forecasting are different functions. Forecasting is generally used to describe what will happen (e.g., to sales demand, cash flow, or employment) in a given set of circumstances. The forecast provides an idea of what the results will be if the manager makes no changes in the way things are being done. Planning, on the other hand, involves use of forecasts to help make decisions about what circumstances will be most attractive for the company. Thus a forecast is based on the notion of describing what will happen for a set of decisions and events in a given situation, whereas a plan is based on the notion that by taking certain actions the decision maker can affect the subsequent events relating to a given situation. Thus, if a forecast is prepared which shows that demand is going to fall in the next month, management may want to prepare a plan of action that will help to prevent sales from falling. Generally speaking, forecasting and a forecast are only one input to the planning process.

An important point that should always be remembered by the manager is that as he makes decisions he has to consider how they will change his forecast. A forecast indicates what will happen if no action is taken, and thus when action *is* taken the forecast must be adjusted to reflect the impact of that action. If this is not done, the forecast can become misleading when used as a basis for making other decisions, and it will not be possible to evaluate the accuracy of the forecast after the fact.

FORECASTING TECHNIQUES

To fit the varied situations in which forecasts are required a number of methods or techniques, have been developed during the last two decades. These can be distinguished into two broad classes: quantitative techniques and qualitative techniques. This classification generally reflects the extent to which a forecast can be based directly on historical data in a mechanical fashion. Those techniques that start with a series of past data values and then, following a certain set of rules, develop a prediction of future values fall into the category of quantitative methods. Situations in which such data is not readily available or applicable and in which much more management judgment must be inserted are generally best suited to the application of qualitative forecasting methods.

In the area of quantitative forecasting methods we find a number of techniques whose common element is that the forecasts are based almost exclusively on historical data. Some of the more widely used techniques in this class include moving averages, exponential smoothing, and regression analysis. In these techniques a historical sequence of data (taken over a number of periods of time) is the starting point and this data is used to help predict what will happen in some future time; for example, a company that has selected a quantitative forecasting method to predict its monthly sales might begin by taking actual sales for each of the last 36 months and using a specific technique to forecast the next month's sales based on that historical pattern. (The appendix to this chapter outlines the general mathematical approach used in these quantitative techniques.)

Quantitative forecasting techniques have gained wide acceptance on the last decade for at least two reasons. One has been that they have developed a record of accuracy as a means of preparing forecasts. Thus managers have placed increasing confidence in them as an aid to decision making. A second important factor has been the development and adoption of computers by many companies. The computer can be used not only to make the many computations that quantitative forecasting methods require but also to store historical data and then retrieve that data rapidly and efficiently when it is needed for the preparation of a new forecast.

Although we refer to the second class of forecasting techniques as "qualitative," another term commonly used for these methods is "technological forecasting." The latter term is somewhat misleading, however, since these techniques can be used to forecast many things other than technological developments. The aim of qualitative methods is to forecast changes in a basic pattern as well as the pattern itself. These changes may be the result of several outside factors; for example, a company may feel that one of its consumer products is reaching a peak in its appeal and in its product life cycle. This turning point might well be forecast with some qualitative technique. Because of the difficulty (and cost) of working with qualitative methods of forecasting, they are generally applied only to long-term situations and to those of major importance to the firm.

Since in many situations in which qualitative forecasting is applied an attempt is made to predict a change in some historical pattern, the historical data is not itself generally sufficient to predict that change. What is required is some way of interpreting the historical data that will help in the prediction and perhaps to identify other leading indicators and causal or correlated factors that relate to the change in question. The interpretation of this related data under most qualitative forecasting techniques is done by "experts," those who may simply be individuals in the firm with the best understanding of the situation or a group of individuals from the company's industry who are well respected for their ability to predict changes of a similar nature and to understand the industry and its evolution.

It is safe to say that the state of the art in qualitative forecasting methods is not nearly so well developed as it is in quantitative forecasting methods. The qualitative techniques are still largely intuitive and have only recently begun to gain widespread acceptance in industry. (Even now, however, they are generally used only by large companies because of the costs involved.) As these methods build up a record of successful application they will undoubtedly become more widely used.

Obviously there are some forecasting methods that clearly do not fall in either the qualitative or quantitative category. One of the most important, discussed in Chapter 10, is subjective probabilistic forecasting. This method has gained particularly rapid acceptance in the last few years because it can easily be integrated with an entire approach to decision making (commonly called decision analysis), it uses the manager's judgment in preparing forecasts for his area, and it can be worked with in mathematical terms. This technique is particularly appropriate when considerable uncertainty is met in making a forecast and when the manager is in the best position to assimilate available data and to supply his judgment of the likelihood of different outcomes.

SELECTING THE FORECASTING TECHNIQUE

Any manager who has recently been concerned with the application of forecasting in his decision making is well aware of the importance of selecting the appropriate forecasting technique for his specific situation. Although a number of techniques have been made available to the manager, the appropriate set of guidelines that can be used in matching them with specific situations has not yet been developed because of the newness of these methods. Because of the importance of the selection process, we deal with it in depth in Chapter 12. At this point, however, it is important to mention three major related aspects.

The first relates to the *characteristics of the decision-making situation* for which a forecast is to be prepared. Six major characteristics deserve mention:

1. The Time Horizon.   The period of time over which a decision will have an impact and for which the manager must plan clearly affects the selection of the most appropriate forecasting method. Time horizons can generally be divided into immediate term (less than one month), short term (one to three months), medium term (three months to two years) and long term (more than two years). Although the exact length of time used to describe each of these four categories may vary by company, some set of guidelines is necessary so that the forecast will be appropriate for the planning horizon used by the decision maker.

2. Level of Detail.   The full range of decision-making tasks in most corporations, is generally subdivided for easy handling according to the level of detail required. Thus a firm may have a planning department that does aggregate planning, perhaps by product group or entire sales of the company, and at some other level in the organization, for example, the production department, another individual will plan on the basis of individual products and their individual styles. In selecting a forecasting technique for a specific situation one must be aware of the level of detail that will be required for that forecast to be useful in making decisions. The corporate planning department would see little value in having a forecast by individual items in the company's product line; similarly, the production foreman would find little value in having a general sales estimate of total corporate sales when he is trying to schedule his weekly production.

3. Number of Items. In situations in which the decisions made concern hundreds or even thousands of products companies have found it most effective to develop simple decision rules that can be applied mechanically to each of the items. The same general principle holds true in forecasting. In a situation in which only a single item is being forecast the rules used in preparing that forecast can be much more detailed and complex than they can in a situation in which hundreds or thousands of forecasts must be prepared. Clearly, an inventory control manager with 10,000 products would want to use a different forecasting method for meeting his requirements than would the corporate economics staff in its attempt to predict the general economy.

4. Control Versus Planning. The manager making a decision in the control area has requirements different from those of the manager making a decision in the planning area. In control management by exception is the general procedure. Thus what is needed is some way to determine as early as possible when a process is out of control (i.e., when the basic pattern has shifted in some undesirable direction). Thus a forecasting method in such situations should be able to predict and recognize changes in basic patterns at an early stage. On the planning side it is generally assumed that existing patterns will continue in the future and thus the major emphasis is on identifying those patterns and extrapolating them into the future.

5. Stability. The forecasting of situations that are extremely stable over time is a different proposition from the forecasting of situations that are in a state of flux. In the stable situation a forecasting method can be adopted and checked periodically to determine its appropriateness. In the uncertain case, however, what is needed is a method that can be adapted continually to the most recent results and the latest information.

6. Existing Planning Procedures. The institution of any forecasting method will generally involve the process of changing the company's planning and decision-making procedures. As managers are well aware, there is always built-in resistance to change in any organization. It is extremely important in the effective application of forecasting methods to start with those that are most closely related to existing procedures and then to go through an evolutionary approach of upgrading these methods and making improvements. In this way the changes can be made in a steplike fashion rather than all at once. Thus the manager needs to be aware of the existing procedure in use in a decision-making situation and the requirements for different forecasting methods in order to select the most appropriate method as a starting point.

A number of other characteristics of the situation are important in selecting a forecasting technique, but the six we have discussed briefly are the major ones. In addition to considering the situation, the decision maker must also consider the *characteristics of the various forecasting methods* in making his selection. Although there is clearly overlap in the characteristics of the situation and the characteristics of the different techniques, the two should be addressed separately as a part of the selection process. The six major factors that can be identified with forecasting techniques are the following:

1. The Time Horizon.   Two aspects of the time horizon relate to individual forecasting methods. First is the span of time into the future for which different forecasting methods are best suited. Generally speaking, qualitative methods of forecasting are used much more for longer term forecasts, whereas quantitative methods are more appropriate to the intermediate and shorter term. The second important aspect of time horizon is the number of periods for which a forecast is desired. Some techniques are appropriate only for forecasting one or two periods in advance, whereas other techniques can be used for several periods into the future.

2. The Pattern of Data.   Underlying the majority of forecasting methods is an assumption of the type of pattern found in the data to be forecast; for example, some series depict a seasonal as well as a trend pattern and others may simply consist of an average value with random fluctuations surrounding it. Because different forecasting methods vary in their ability to identify different patterns, it is important to match the presumed pattern in the data with the appropriate technique.

3. Type of Model.   In addition to assuming some basic underlying pattern in the data, most forecasting methods also assume some model of the situation being forecast. This model may be a series in which time is viewed as the important element in determining changes in the pattern or it may be statistical in nature—regression or correlation analysis. Others, such as causal models that represent the forecast as being dependent on the occurrence of a number of different events or mixed in which a number of different models are actually combined, are also available. The importance of the model is not so much that the decision maker must understand the mathematics of each one, but rather that the assumptions underlying each of them are different and the capabilities of different models in different decision making situations do vary.

4. Cost. Generally four elements of cost are involved in the application of a forecasting procedure: development, storage, actual operation, and opportunity in terms of other techniques that might have been applied. The variation in costs obviously has an impact on the attractiveness of different methods for different situations.

5. Accuracy. Closely related to the level of detail required in a forecast is the accuracy required. For some decision makers anywhere between plus or minus 10% may be sufficient for their purposes, but in other cases a variation of as much as 5% could spell disaster for the company.

6. Ease of Application. One general principle that has been found to hold in the application of scientific methods to management is that only those methods that are understood are actually used by the decision maker. This is particularly true in the area of forecasting, since the manager is held responsible for his decisions, and he is certainly not going to base them on forecasts that he does not understand or in which he has no confidence. Thus, in addition to meeting the requirements of the situation, the forecasting technique must fit with the particular manager who will use the forecast.

A consideration of the characteristics of the situation and also of the available techniques is a starting point for selecting a forecasting method. The basis on which the techniques and the situation are reconciled should be one of value versus cost. This requires that the manager develop his own judgment in order to be able to evaluate and make selections in his own situation. An approach that has generally been found useful as a guide in selecting a forecasting method considers four key areas. First is the item that is being forecast. This can be done by studying the characteristics of the situation. Particular attention should be paid to whether one is trying to predict the continuance of a historical pattern for a particular item or whether one is trying to predict a turning point for some change in the basic pattern. Second is the interaction of the situation with the characteristics of different forecasting methods. Here the manager should be aware not only of value and cost but also of the relative changes in value and cost when the level of accuracy changes. If a manager can use a more straightforward and less expensive forecasting method rather than the most sophisticated technique available and still achieve the required level of accuracy, he should do so. A third consideration is the amount of available historical data. Since different methods (particularly quantitative methods) are based on historical information, the manager must consider how much data is currently at hand, what information it contains, and what it would cost to gather additional data. Oftentimes it is most effective to start with a simple forecasting method that does not require much data until the manager can build up a set of records that can then be used as the basis for applying a more sophisticated method. Finally, the manager must consider the time allowed for preparing the forecast. The urgency in particular situations influences the selection of the method. Although some forecasts may not be prepared for several weeks or even months after historical data has been generated, others, particularly for short-term decision making, most be ready within a few days after the data has been generated. This urgency and the amount of time alloted for data gathering therefore must be factors in the selection of a forecasting method.

In all of what the manager does in terms of selecting a forecasting method it is of paramount importance that he deal with each step of the process so that he will understand the limitations and capabilities of what is being done and be able to apply them in his decision making. This generally means that it is much wiser initially to apply a straightforward, relatively unsophisticated method of forecasting and then gradually to upgrade to more sophisticated methods. The tendency to start with the most sophisticated method available generally leads to an expensive experiment that will have little impact on what the manager actually does.

The reader will note that in the main this book deals with the quantitative methods of forecasting. In fact, only a single chapter is devoted to qualitative methods. The main reason for this emphasis is that most managers wish to gain competence in the use of quantitative methods before adopting the more qualitative ones. In fact, most forecasting situations can be handled with these quantitative methods. Thus the emphasis herein is probably similar to the relative usefulness that these methods will have for the practicing manager.

FORECASTING IN THE FIRM

The preceding sections of this chapter have dealt mainly with the decision maker, his situation, and the interaction of these two factors with the forecasting method. Although they are important considerations, every manager knows he must also remember that decision making is done within the organizational environment and not on an isolated basis. Thus in any discussion of forecasting methods for management it is essential that these methods and their applications be related to the ongoing activity of the firm and the interactions among various organizational subunits. Because of the importance of this topic, Chapter 13 is devoted entirely to it. To complete our overview of forecasting for management we mention here some of the highlights of the discussion in Chapter 13.

In any given application of forecasting generally a number of organizational units must be included; for example, consider the case of a company whose marketing department has decided to forecast sales by product group. It may be the marketing manager who wants the forecast to use as a basis for planning advertising, pricing, and promotion. However, he will probably have assigned the details of obtaining that forecast to a member of his staff. This staff member must work with the accounting department in the company to obtain historical data on sales by product category, with the computer department to apply a given technique, and with the sales force to verify the possibility of future changes in product sales. As with any new management function, the development of a forecasting procedure must include an explicit statement of responsibility for its various aspects. Thus the head of the marketing department may want to outline his own responsibilities and those of his staff assistant in preparing the forecast as well as those of the accounting and computer departments in implementing that procedure. It is only when such responsibility assignments are made in detail and agreed on that such a procedure can work effectively.

One of the responsibilities that must always remain with the decision maker who will use the forecast is that of identifying and initiating new forecasting procedures. Although he may use a staff person to assist him in this task, it is his own commitment to its actual use that will determine its value in the end. This commitment can be developed much more effectively if the manager completes the identification and initial development steps himself rather than having them done by an outsider who must then do a "selling job" to the manager.

As in the marketing example given above, it frequently happens in a forecasting situation that the data required originates in another section of the company. Since the accuracy of the forecast is wholly dependent on the accuracy of that data, it is essential that cooperation be achieved and maintained at that level. This requires not only that people in the accounting department be motivated to collect the data accurately but also establishing a system of checks to verify that data and to build the manager's confidence in it. This might be done by using an internal audit group periodically to perform an audit on any data base being used in forecasting.

When another organizational unit is used for part of the data collection and data processing it can generally supply a number of insights into how the entire forecasting operation might be made more efficient and how that particular situation might be handled more effectively. Thus such support people should be viewed not merely in a mechanical fashion but also as a source of help in designing improvements in forecasting.

A typical problem that can develop when communication among organizational subunits is incomplete is that of improperly defining the data items to be collected. Even in the simple example of forecasting sales by product group it is necessary that those gathering the data understand exactly what constitutes each product group, the time period that is involved and the manner in which exceptions are to be handled. Resolving even such minor items is essential to a smooth-working forecasting system.

No consideration of forecasting for decision making would be complete without mention of the need for feedback and continuous evaluation. It is not enough simply to evaluate a forecasting technique when it is being adopted. A continuous review process must be established in order that the forecast may be compared with the actual results and improvements, and perhaps even changes in the technique itself can be made. When such an evaluation procedure is established, its results can then be used to guide further improvements. When no evaluation is performed, what happens is that managers rapidly become aware of the weaknesses in the forecast and thus begin to discount it, and eventually it is of no value in decision making. At that point, however, there is no record of actual versus forecast and other evaluation measures, and thus it is difficult if not impossible to determine where improvements are required.

SUMMARY

The purpose of this chapter has been to provide an overview of the management application of forecasting, those aspects of the decision-making situation that relate to forecasting, and some of the considerations in regard to forecasting within a business organization. The remaining chapters go into detail in these various areas to provide the manager with the information he needs to use recently developed forecasting methods effectively in his own situation.

In subsequent chapters the mathematics of various forecasting methods have been kept to a minimum, but they have not been avoided completely. The reason for this is our belief that managers can understand the basic concepts underlying different techniques and that an understanding of these fundamentals is essential to the most effective use of forecasting methods. It is only by understanding the underlying assumptions of each method that the manager can exercise his judgment in utilizing forecasts to improve decision making.

APPENDIX: NOTATION FOR QUANTITATIVE FORECASTING TECHNIQUES

In preparing a forecast with a quantitative technique one almost always has a number of historical *observations* or *observed values*. These observations may represent many things, from the actual number of units sold, to the cost of producing each unit, to the number of people unemployed. Since these observed values vary over time, they are generally represented by a *variable* such as x. A variable is simply the symbol of the value of some item. Thus x could be the number of washing machines sold in a month. The actual value of x would depend on the month in question, and for month 5 we might have $x = 320$ washing machines.

Since a variable that represents observations takes on different values depending on the time *period*, a way of identifying this period is also needed. This is usually done by assigning consecutive numbers to consecutive time periods. Thus the 24 months beginning with January 1969 would be referred to as time periods 1, 2, 3, . . ., 24. Obviously the length of the period has to be defined at the outset. Depending on the situation, we might call it one day, one week, one month, one year, or some other duration. Once the time periods have been established the observed values can be referred to with the use of *subscripts*; for example, x_{10} would refer to the observed value in period 10 and x_{13} would refer to the observed value in period 13. One thing to keep in mind with regard to time periods is that the decision maker can decide which to call number 1. Subsequent periods are then given consecutive numbers.

Although x or some other symbol generally identifies the actual (historical) observed values of a variable, a different symbol is often used to represent the *forecasted value* of that variable. In this book the symbol S denotes the forecasted value for time period t. As a summary of the relation between observed values over time and forecast values consider Figure 1-1 in which it can be seen that the desired forecast is for two periods into the future rather than one. This is done simply to illustrate the point that a forecast can be prepared for any number of periods in advance, although in the discussions in this book forecasts are generally made for only one period ahead.

A number of the forecasting techniques in widespread use are based on some kind of weighting of historical observations (see Chapters 3 and 4). These *weights* are used to multiply the observed values and the forecast is based on the sum of these weighted values. If the symbol w_i is the weight

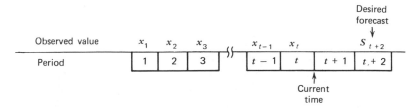

Figure 1-1.

given to the ith observed value and we want to weight the last three observations, we would write

$$S = w_1x_1 + w_2x_2 + w_3x_3.$$

Obviously any number of weights could be used as long as the observed values were available. An important property of such a set of weights is that the sum of the values of all the weights equals 1; that is,

$$w_1 + w_2 + \cdots + w_n = 1.0.$$

Since many forecasting techniques require the use of weights and the summing of several values, it is convenient to identify such a sum by a *summation* sign $\sum$. Thus the sum of the weights above can be written as

$$w_1 + w_2 + \cdots + w_n = \sum_{i=1}^{n} w_i,$$

which can be read as "the sum of the values of w_i taken from $i = 1$ to $i = n$ (inclusive)." With this summation sign the forecast of a weighted sum can be written as

$$w_1x_1 + w_2x_2 + w_3x_3 = \sum_{i=1}^{3} w_ix_i.$$

Whenever a forecast is prepared it is instructive to be able to compare that forecast with the observed value for the same period, once the observed value is available. This can be done by computing the *error* in the forecast e_i:

$$e_i = S_i - x_i.$$

As a forecasting method is used over several periods, a series of error values is obtained, one for each period. Now to summarize the accuracy of the forecasting technique for that situation is best done by using this series of error values. Obviously we could add these values together, divide by the number of error values, and call that the average error. Such an approach, however, might be misleading because negative errors would partly cancel out positive errors and thus the average error might be close to 0, even though there had been sizable errors in each forecast.

A better approach to an examination of the accuracy of a forecasting technique is a computation of the *mean square error*. This is done by first squaring the individual errors (i.e., e_i^2) which gives all positive values and then taking their average (mean value). This approach not only eliminates the canceling of positive and negative errors, but by the very nature of taking the square of a number large errors are given more importance in the mean-square-error computation than are small errors. (The reader may want to convince himself of this by working through a simple example.)

CHAPTER 2

THE EVALUATION OF
FORECASTING TECHNIQUES

One idea introduced in Chapter 1 is that certain characteristics of fore-casting methods can be used to distinguish the various techniques. For the manager who is going to use forecasting an understanding of these charac-teristics is essential for two main reasons. The first is that this understanding is the basis for understanding individual forecasting techniques and their properties. Thus we discuss characteristics first so that they can then be used as a framework on which the manager can develop his own knowledge of them.

The second important reason is that these characteristics can and should serve to evaluate alternative forecasting methods in a given situation. People often get the mistaken notion that accuracy is the only criterion required, but just as in any management situation there are usually several criteria whose trade-offs need to be considered in making a decision, so it is with forecasting. As we show later on, even the relatively straightforward calcu-lation of the error in a forecasting technique can be misleading when used as the only basis for evaluating that method.

Before launching our discussion of these characteristics, some general comments should be made on the fundamental idea on which any fore-casting method is built. The central theme of forecasting is the assumption that some pattern exists in what has gone before. This pattern generally takes one of two forms. First, it could be detectable simply by examining the historical values of the items to be forecast. Many of the techniques discussed in this book assume a pattern of this nature, which means that using related historical data is sufficient for detecting its existence and extrapolating it into the future. The alternative pattern often assumed to exist is one of some form of relationship between two or more variables. In this instance the historical data from a single variable does not contain all the information

15

about the underlying pattern. Rather it is necessary to have data on several variables to identify the relationship between them.

For purposes of forecasting the underlying pattern is assumed to be constant over at least two subsequent periods. In the first period data is collected and analyzed to identify the pattern; the second is in the future in which the identified pattern will be used as the basis for forecasting. Thus the notion of constancy in some basic pattern or relationship is fundamental to any forecasting method. This idea is discussed further in connection with some of the characteristics of forecasting methods.

Although many characteristics could be discussed as properties of forecasting techniques, we now consider a grouping that identifies six major areas.

1. The pattern of data that can be recognized.
2. The accuracy of the method.
3. The type of model.
4. The cost of using that method.
5. The lead time for which the method is most appropriate.
6. The applicability of the method.

To make our discussion of these characteristics more concrete let us consider first an example of a forecasting situation and a method of handling it that can then be related to each of the characteristics. Suppose that the

Table 2-1   Weekly Supermarket Sales

Week	Sales (in $000s)	Forecast
1	$ 9	—
2	8	9
3	9	8
4	12	9
5	9	12
6	12	9
7	11	12
8	7	11
9	13	7
10	9	13
11	11	9
12	10	11
13	?	10

manager of a large supermarket would like to forecast his sales one week in advance to help in planning his inventory level and the arrival of his shipments. As a starting point he has collected data on the weekly sales of his store for each of the preceding 12 weeks. These sales figures are shown in Table 2-1.

It is clear that the supermarket manager must expect fluctuations in his weekly sales. In forecasting for the coming week, however, he would like to have something better than a mere guess. We shall suppose that he has adopted a forecasting method commonly referred to as naïve. Specifically, we assume that he has used the preceding week's sales as his forecast for the coming week. Thus, looking at Table 2-1, his forecast for week 13 would be $10,000, the actual sales in week 12. Following this forecasting method, the third column in Table 2-1 shows what his forecast would have been for weeks 2 through 13. We can now examine the characteristics of this forecasting technique and of forecasting methods in general.

THE UNDERLYING PATTERN OF THE DATA

As already mentioned, all forecasting methods assume that some pattern or relationship exists that can be identified and used as the basis for preparing a forecast. For the qualitative methods of forecasting these patterns and/or relationships can take virtually any form and need not be identified explicitly. In quantitative methods of forecasting, however, each technique does make explicit assumptions about the type of underlying pattern. Therefore the ability of a given technique to forecast effectively in a specific situation depends largely on matching the pattern in that situation with a technique that can handle that pattern. The four types of pattern usually discussed are horizontal, trend, seasonal, and cyclical.

A horizontal pattern exists when there is no trend in the data. When such a pattern appears, the series is generally referred to as stationary; that is, it does not tend to increase or decrease in any systematic way. Thus it is equally likely that the next value of the series will be above the stationary value as below it. Figure 2-1 shows a typical horizontal pattern for a variable.

The kind of situation that generally exhibits a horizontal pattern would include products with stable sales, the number of defective items that occur in a stable production process, and perhaps the percentage of sales a company gets from each of several categories over a fairly short time period. The element of time is generally an important one in considering horizontal patterns, since in the short run even patterns that may exhibit a definite trend over several years might be assumed to be horizontal for purposes for short-term forecasting.

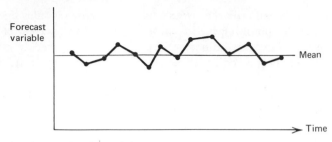

Figure 2-1   Horizontal data pattern.

A seasonal pattern exists when a series fluctuates according to some seasonal factor. The season may be a month or the four seasons of the year, but they could also be the days of the week or the days in a month. Seasonal patterns exist for a number of different reasons, varying from the way in which a firm has chosen to handle certain operations (internally caused seasons) to external factors such as the weather.

Some of the items that typically follow seasonal patterns include the sales of soft drinks, heating oil, and other items conditional on the weather; the receipt of revenues at a utility company, which may depend on the pattern used in sending out the bills and the pay period in that community; and the number of new cars sold, which may depend on the timing of style changes and even tradition. Figure 2-2 illustrates a pattern in which the seasons correspond to the four calendar quarters.

A cyclical pattern is similar to a seasonal pattern, but the length of a single cycle is generally longer than one year. Many series such as the number of housing starts, the price of some meat and agricultural products, and factory orders of a highly integrated company contain a cyclical pattern. (In an integrated firm the cycle may be induced by the company's own operating

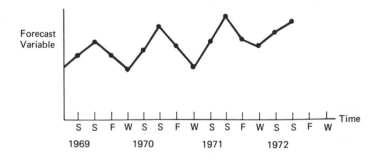

Figure 2-2   Seasonal data pattern.

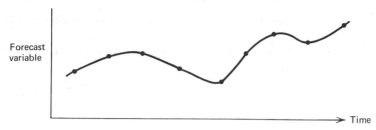

Figure 2-3   Cyclical data pattern.

procedures rather than by some outside influence.) Figure 2-3 is a cyclical pattern.

A trend pattern commonly exists when there is a general increase or decrease in the value of the variable over time. The sales of many companies, the gross national product, stock prices, and many other business and economic indicators follow a trend pattern like that shown in Figure 2-4 in their movements over time.

Although a number of other patterns can be found in specific series of data, the four we have discussed are the most important. These four patterns can often be found together as well as each alone. In fact, some series actually combine a trend, a seasonal pattern, and a cyclical pattern.

In our example of the weekly supermarket sales it can be seen that its pattern is most likely a horizontal, with random fluctuations occurring around the average value of weekly sales. As to the ability of the naïve forecasting method adopted by that manager to forecast a horizontal pattern, we can see that his method actually assumes that the most recent value is the best estimate of the next value. This implies that the fluctuations are not random but rather represent some change in the value of weekly sales. Thus, if we do not feel that any change is taking place, the forecasting method being used will seem to be inappropriate. If a horizontal pattern does exist,

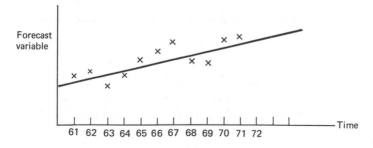

Figure 2-4   Trend data pattern.

use of an average of the last 12 weeks' sales would seem to be a much better approach to forecasting. This average would eliminate the random fluctuations around the horizontal pattern, thus avoiding over-reacting whenever such a fluctuation occurs.

THE ACCURACY OF FORECASTING TECHNIQUES AND THE MEASUREMENT OF ERROR

The basic assumption underlying the use of any forecasting technique is that the actual value observed will be determined by some pattern, plus some random influences. This can be written algebraically as

$$\text{actual} = \text{pattern} + \text{randomness}.$$

Because uncertainty always exists in any uncontrollable variable, randomness will always be present. This means that even when the exact pattern of the underlying data has been identified some deviation will still exist between the forecast values and the values actually observed. A common goal in the application of forecasting techniques is to minimize these deviations. This is generally done by first defining as the error in the forecast the difference between the actual value and what was predicted. This can be written as

$$E_i = S_i - X_i.$$

The subscript i indicates that it is the error of time period i being examined.

One approach that might be used for determining the accuracy of a forecast would be to add up the errors over several periods of time; for example, if we take the forecast prepared by the supermarket manager, we can compute the error as shown in column 4 of Table 2-2.

To evaluate the forecasting method in this situation we would like some indication of the average error that can be expected over time. If we simply add up the values of the error and compute the average, we find that it is close to zero, since many of the positive errors have canceled out the negative errors. To avoid this problem we can compute the absolute error (disregarding the plus or minus sign) and look at what is commonly referred to as the mean absolute deviation. (This is simply the average absolute error over several periods.) From column 5 in Table 2-2 we see that the value of the mean absolute deviation in this example is 2.5. Although the mean absolute deviation is often used as the measurement of error in evaluating a forecast, an alternative criterion is that of mean squared error, obtained by squaring each of the individual errors and computing the mean of those squared values. Column 6 in Table 2-2 indicates that in the super market example

Table 2-2   Weekly Supermarket Sales

1 Week	2 Sales	3 Forecast	4 Error	5 Absolute Error	6 Squared Error
1	9	—			
2	8	9	1	1	1
3	9	8	−1	1	1
4	12	9	−3	3	9
5	9	12	3	3	9
6	12	9	−3	3	9
7	11	12	1	1	1
8	7	11	4	4	16
9	13	7	−6	6	36
10	9	13	4	4	16
11	11	9	−2	2	4
12	10	11	1	1	1
		Sum	−1	29	103
		Mean	−.08	2.5[a]	8.5[b]

[a] Mean absolute deviation (MAD).
[b] Mean squared error.

the mean squared error has a value of 8.5. One of the differences between the mean absolute deviation and the mean squared error is that the latter penalizes a forecast much more for extreme deviations than it does for small ones; for example, in computing the mean absolute deviation, an error of 2 is counted only twice as much as an error of 1. In computing the mean squared error, however, an error of 2 is squared, which means that it counts four times as much as an error of 1. Thus adopting the criterion of minimizing mean squared error implies that we would rather have several small deviations from the forecast value than one large deviation.

In comparing two forecasting methods applied to a specific situation, one question is the time span that should be used in computing the mean absolute deviation or the mean squared error. This problem arises because of the fact that most forecasting methods take a set of data to determine the underlying pattern for that series. If the error is then computed for the same set of data, we would expect that the forecasting method should do quite well, since it was trained on that set of data. However, if we take a subsequent set of data (one that was not used in identifying the basic pattern), it would seem to be a much better test of the technique. Since this problem of the number of data periods to be used in evaluating alternative techniques is artificial in a naïve forecast, we postpone a detailed discussion of it until Chapter 4, where we deal with the technique of adaptive filtering which does encounter this problem.

Whenever a manager evaluates alternative forecasting techniques in terms of their accuracy, it is necessary to go beyond simple mechanical computation of the error, since there are two forms of accuracy with which the manager is very concerned. The first is the accuracy of the technique in predicting the underlying pattern or relationship. In most cases the mean squared error or the mean absolute deviation is a good criterion for evaluating the prediction of a constant pattern. The other situation, however, is one in which the pattern changes. Here the common error calculations are not an appropriate criterion for evaluation. When the basic pattern changes, what the manager is interested in is how fast his forecasting procedure can respond to that basic change. This means that the procedure must identify the change and then alter the forecast accordingly. As we shall see in subsequent chapters, the value of alternative forecasting methods in making such changes varies tremendously.

THE TYPE OF MODEL REPRESENTED BY FORECASTING TECHNIQUES

The notion of a model has long been used by engineers and scientists in the examination of different processes and physical situations; for example, aerospace engineers generally develop a mock-up of any new aircraft in order to use that model to examine certain characteristics of shape or size in various physical environments. The model becomes a way of experimenting with reality without actually having to invest in a full-scale operation.

Another model which deals with a representation of a previously developed *procedure* or *process* consists of an abstraction of the complexities of the procedure itself to a set of higher level steps that can be used as a summary of its details and is often developed in decision-making situations, information flows, and analysis. It is in this descriptive sense that we use the notion of a model of a forecasting technique which consists of the procedures used by that technique in developing a forecast. Clearly there is a wide range of models that could be used, but they generally fall into a number of fairly well defined categories. By understanding the properties of each of these models (or categories of models) the manager can get a better grasp of the assumptions that underly individual forecasting techniques and the pros and cons of using them in specific situations.

Here we identify four model categories for use in distinguishing alternative forecasting techniques. Although many techniques can be classified as more than one type of model, a knowledge of these basic categories and their properties is useful. The first type, and perhaps the most common in the area of quantitative forecasting, is the time-series model. Two variables are assumed in a *time-series model:* the one we want to forecast (such as weekly supermarket sales) and the period of time we are referring to. A time-series model always assumes that some pattern or combination of patterns is recurring *over time.* Thus by identifying the pattern and the starting point for that pattern we can forecast its value in any subsequent time period simply by knowing the number of periods in each cycle of the pattern and the number of periods since the starting point; for example, if we have a forecasting model that has identified a seasonal pattern in which sales have been 20% above average every January, we know that in any forecast of sales for next January they must be 20% above the average level.

In addition to the importance of the sequence of the periods as a variable in a time-series model, this model also assumes explicitly that the under-lying pattern can be identified solely on the basis of historical data from that series, which means that it is not particularly helpful to the manager in predicting the impact of certain decisions he may make. Any forecasting method that uses a time-series model will give the same forecast for the next period, no matter what the manager's actions may be. Thus a time-series model may be appropriate for forecasting environmental factors such as the general economy and level of employment but inappropriate for forecasting weekly sales resulting from changes in pricing and advertising.

One advantage of time-series models is that the basic rules of accounting are oriented toward sequential time periods. This means that in most firms data is readily available on the basis of these time periods and can thus be used in the application of a time-series forecasting technique.

A second type is the *causal model*, the techniques of which assume that the value of a certain variable is a function of several other variables. In a very narrow sense a time-series model could be called a causal model, since the actual values are assumed to be a function of the time period alone. The term "causal model," however, is generally reserved for models with variables other than sequential time periods. An example would be an equation for predicting sales that bases its forecast on the values of price and advertising within the company and the industry; that is, the equation would state that sales are a function of the other variables.

The real strength of a causal model in a forecasting method is that a manager can develop a range of forecasts corresponding to a range of values for the different variables, but the difficulty of these techniques is that they require information on several variables in addition to the single variable that is being forecast. Thus their data requirements are much larger than the data requirements of a time-series model. In addition, since causal models generally relate several factors, they usually take longer to develop and are more sensitive to changes in the underlying relationships than a general time-series model would be.

A third type which can be used to describe many forecasting techniques is the *statistical model*. This type uses the language and procedures of statistical analysis to identify the patterns in the variables being forecast and in making statements about the reliability of these forecasts. Typically, a statistical model can supply information about the confidence that can be placed in its forecasts and the likelihood of their being in error. In this sense a statistical model is often said to give much more precise results than other models. These results, however, and the additional information accompanying them are useful only to the manager who feels comfortable with statistics and knows how to apply them in decision making.

The fact that most statistical models are more sophisticated than other forecasting methods can often be a drawback. If we examine those forecasting applications that have not had a significant impact on actual decision making, it is usually because the techniques were not understood and in most cases tended to be statistical.

The final model that we shall consider is the *nonstatistical*. Since the division between statistical and nonstatistical is dichotomous, all models that do not follow the general rules of statistical analysis and probability theory can be classed as nonstatistical techniques, which are based much more on intuition and what the manager feels should go on in the forecasting process than on fundamental statistics. Because of this basic orientation, they are often easier to understand than statistical models and simpler to apply. Most nonstatistical models, however, are limited by an inherent lack of guidelines on the level of confidence that can be placed in their forecasts. Sometimes such confidence intervals can be computed after the fact, but in general this is difficult to do with accuracy.

One distinction between statistical and nonstatistical models that the manager should be aware of is that virtually all qualitative or technological forecasting methods are nonstatistical in nature. It is only some of the quantitative forecasting methods that are statistical.

Some forecasting techniques can be categorized as more than one of the four types of model described, all of which are identified in subsequent chapters, as individual forecasting methods are analyzed.

THE COSTS OF A FORECASTING TECHNIQUE

The fourth characteristic of forecasting techniques is cost. Three different aspects are involved in determining the cost of applying a specific technique:

development costs, the costs associated with data storage and acquisition, and the actual operating and maintenance costs.

Development costs include the resources required for defining the actual variable to be forecast and any independent variables that may be included in a causal model, gathering the initial data that can be used to identify the pattern needed for forecasting, actually determining the pattern in that data, and finally establishing a procedure that can be used in making repetitive forecasts.

Storage requirement costs are generally affected by the number of observations needed to apply a forecasting technique and the number of variables involved. Generally speaking, a forecasting technique that employs a causal model is much more costly in terms of data storage than a technique that employs a time-series model.

Finally, operating costs depend largely on the amount of computer time required to make the computations for a single forecast and the frequency with which forecasts are made.

One of the major differences in the costs associated with alternative forecasting techniques is whether the costs are associated with the developmental level, the data storage level, or the operating level. Clearly, a naïve forecasting technique such as that used by the supermarket manager for forecasting weekly sales requires some development costs, virtually no storage costs, and little in the way of operating and maintenance costs. On the other hand, causal models, which are often developed in the area of econometrics, may cost tremendous amounts for development and relatively modest amounts for data storage and usage costs.

In most situations the actual computation of the costs associated with a forecasting technique is not unusually difficult. What does create problems, however, is trading off these costs against the various levels of accuracy, the appropriateness of the model, and the other characteristics of forecasting methods.

THE LEAD TIME IN FORECASTING METHODS

The fact that some forecasting techniques are much more appropriate for making short-term forecasts, whereas others can handle long-term forecasts effectively, is due to the characteristic of time horizon, which can be identified for any forecasting method. This characteristic is closely related to the way in which a forecasting technique prepares its forecast and to the amount of data required.

The time horizon is generally divided into four categories, in which immediate term refers to less than one month, short term to one to three months, medium term to less than two years, and long term to more than two years. One reason that many forecasting methods are appropriate only for the intermediate and short term is that they forecast only one period in advance, which means that if the length of each time period is one month, in order to forecast three months into the future, a forecast must first be prepared for the first month. That forecast must then be used as the actual value to forecast the next month, and then both forecasts must be used as actual values to forecast the third month. The inclusion of forecasts as actual values in a kind of bootstrap approach quickly compounds the error in the forecasting and makes it difficult to forecast more than a few periods in advance.

The difficulty of being able to forecast only one or two periods effectively is compounded by the fact that to use many forecasting methods several periods of data are required. This means that if the period is changed from one month to six months, to obtain 12 data values we must go back six years rather than just one. Thus changing the length of the time period simply replaces the problem of time horizon with that of the number of observations available.

Those forecasting techniques that can be used for several periods into the future are generally based on a causal model, so that what is needed is the value of several independent variables to forecast the dependent variable. Even with these models, however, problems exist, because oftentimes the values of those independent variables must be predicted as well, thus compounding the forecasting problem and the possibility for error. (This is discussed further in Chapters 5 and 7.)

One other aspect of the time horizon characteristic is the number of periods which it takes a forecasting method to adapt to changes in the basic pattern of a series. Some methods are able to adapt much more rapidly to certain types of pattern changes than are other methods. Generally, however, this ability to adapt quickly must be traded off against the amount of randomness which appears in the forecast itself. Forecasts that are able to isolate the randomness almost completely are generally slow to adapt to changes in the basic pattern of a series.

APPLICABILITY

The final major characteristic of forecasting methods, which reflects not only their technical suitability because of the nature of management problems but also the behavioral aspect involved, relates to their applicability-in practice. Since adoption of any forecasting method represents a change in procedure from what has already been done, consideration of the ease with which such behavioral changes can be implemented is an essential step in the evaluation of a forecasting method.

One major aspect is the time it takes to develop a working application of a given forecasting technique for a specific situation. If the appropriate data is not readily available, or if a computer system is not easily accessible for certain techniques, the development of the initial application can take several months or even years. When this is the case, the manager is usually well advised initially to adopt a much less sophisticated technique and then follow an evolutionary approach in upgrading his use of forecasting.

A second aspect of applicability is the ease with which the manager can gain an understanding of the fundamental technical properties of the method and an ability to interpret the results. One of the great advantages of the naïve method we have referred to in the supermarket sales example is that the manager can fully understand its assumptions and limitations and interpret its results. As we consider much more advanced and sophisticated techniques, the number of managers who can readily understand them and use them wisely decreases rapidly. Thus for the most advanced techniques few managers would even potentially find them applicable.

The need for considering the manager's understanding and confidence in any forecasting technique he applies cannot be overstressed. In order for forecasting to have value it must have an impact on the manager's method of making decisions. This will happen only when he feels confident that his use of the forecast represents good judgment and is consistent with his other activities as a manager.

SUMMARY

At this point perhaps a word of encouragement to the reader is needed. Although this chapter has sought to indicate the multitude of different characteristics that determine the appropriateness of a forecasting method for a given situation, the reader should not let this lack of a single criterion discourage him from delving into alternative forecasting techniques and their usefulness. Although some people have suggested that the selection of a forecasting method is a relatively straightforward matter, we feel that such a simplistic approach can often be misleading and deterimental to the manager. By presenting a much more complete description of these characteristics it is hoped that the manager will be able to understand better the relative tradeoffs to be made in the selection process and the advantages and disadvantages of various methods.

The next several chapters present the fundamentals of a number of different forecasting techniques and give examples of the situations in which they are most appropriate. Chapters 12 and 13 return to a general consideration of forecasting as a part of the management function and the corporate organization. Included in these two chapters is a summary discussion of each of the various forecasting techniques covered in terms of the six characteristics described in this chapter. At that point the reader should be well prepared to apply these characteristics in selecting forecasting procedures for his own situations.

CHAPTER 3

FORECASTING WITH SMOOTHING TECHNIQUES

One type of problem that business managers frequently face is that of preparing short-term forecasts for a number of different items. A typical example would be the production manager who must schedule production based on some forecast of demand for several hundred different products in a product line. In many of these situations it is clearly not worth the time or the money to develop a specialized forecasting method for each item. Rather what is needed is a technique that can be employed easily for each of several items and will provide reasonably good forecasts over the short-term period in which they are needed. As a result of the nature of these situations, the variable to be forecast can generally be assumed to change only slightly during each subsequent time period. Obviously there can be occasions on which it might change a considerable amount in a single period, but generally speaking many of these items exhibit a fairly stable series of values over a short time horizon.

Some of the situations that meet these characteristics include monthly demands for several hundred or even thousands of products in a product line, prices for finished products in a company's line or for raw materials and parts used by the company, and fluctuations in stock prices on a number of different companies in an industry. In the government sector forecasting situations with these characteristics would include predicting unemployment figures for each of several industries on a short-term basis and perhaps changes in the price index for each of several commodities.

The techniques that are used most often in the above situations are referred to as "smoothing methods." The most common and those that we will discuss first are moving averages and exponential smoothing. These approaches to forecasting are nonstatistical in nature and are based largely on their intuitive appeal. They also apply a time-series model and thus depend on having a series of data available before a forecasting system can be initiated. This historical data is used to obtain a "smoothed" value for the series which becomes the forecast for some future period. Thus in applying a smoothing technique there are two steps to the process. In the first some kind of smoothed value is computed based on historical data, and in the second that value is used as a forecast for some future time.

The basic notion inherent in moving averages, exponential smoothing, and other forms of smoothing techniques is that there is some underlying pattern in the values of the variables to be forecast and that the historical observations of each variable represent the underlying pattern as well as random fluctuations. The goal of these forecasting methods is to distinguish between the random fluctuation and the basic underlying pattern by "smoothing" the historical values. This amounts to eliminating the extreme values found in the historical sequence and basing a forecast on some smoothed intermediate values.

To understand better how these two forecasting techniques can be used in practice let us consider the situation faced by a manufacturer of knives and forks. For several months this company has kept a record of the demand for knives. To help schedule production the production manager would like to use these observations to prepare a forecast of what the demand will be during the coming month. We determine first how such a forecast might be prepared by using moving averages and exponential smoothing and then examine the possibility of using higher forms of smoothing. (The techniques of moving averages and exponential smoothing discussed here are normally referred to as *simple* or *first-order* smoothing techniques.)

SIMPLE MOVING AVERAGES

In Chapter 2 we saw how a manager might select a naïve forecasting approach by simply taking the most recent observation and using it as a forecast for the coming period. Clearly, if a lot of randomness is contained in the series, a naïve approach will produce a forecast that will vary considerably. To eliminate this randomness we might consider the use of some kind of average of recent observed values. The method of moving averages does this by taking a set of observed values, finding their average, and then using that average as a forecast for the coming period. The actual number of observations included in the average is specified by the manager and remains constant. The term "moving average" is used because as each new observation becomes available a new average can be computed and used as a forecast.

For the manufacture of knives and forks Table 3-1 shows how the technique of moving averages can be applied with a three-month and a five-

Table 3-1   Forecasting the Demand for Knives One Month Ahead by Using Moving Averages

1	2	3	4	5
Month	Time Period	Observed Demand	Forecast with a Three-Month Moving Average	Forecast with a Five-Month Moving Average
January 1971	1	2000	. . .	. . .
February 1971	2	1350	. . .	. . .
March 1971	3	1950	. . .	. . .
April 1971	4	1975	1767	. . .
May 1971	5	3100	1758	. . .
June 1971	6	1750	2342	2075
July 1971	7	1550	2275	2025
August 1971	8	1300	2133	2065
September 1971	9	2200	1533	1935
October 1971	10	2770	1683	1980
November 1971	11	2350	2092	1915
December 1971	12	. . .	2440	2034

month average. In this Table column 4 is the three-month moving average forecast based on the values of the three preceding months; for example, the forecast of 1767 for April 1971 is based on the average demand for periods 1, 2, and 3 (January, February, and March 1971). This three-month moving average value then becomes the forecast for the following month, period 4. The last figure in column 4 (2440) is the average for periods 9, 10, and 11 and serves as the forecast for December 1971, period 12.

Similarly, in column 5 the entry of 2075 for June 1971 represents the average of the observed demand in periods 1 through 5 and is used as the forecast for period 6. The last entry in column 5 (2034) is the average for periods 7 through 11 and serves as the forecast for period 12.

It can be seen that the method of moving averages could be used to forecast two or three months as well as one month in advance. In this case, however, the likelihood of error would be much greater because the same three actual values used in a three-month moving average for one month ahead would be used in a three-month moving average for three months ahead. Thus in most cases the method of moving averages is applied for only one period in advance.

The accuracy of this method of forecasting is shown in Figure 3-1. On this graph are plotted the actual values of demand and the forecast values

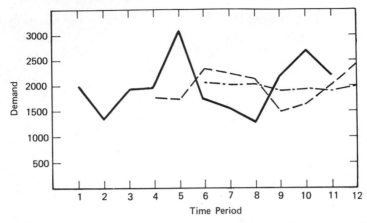

Figure 3-1   Comparison of three-month and five-month moving average.   Forecast for demand for knives (from Table 3-1).   Item 3 ———.   Item 4 – – – – – –.   Item 5 —·—·—·.

for the corresponding period based on a three-month and a five-month moving average. In this graph a couple of characteristics of moving averages are readily apparent. The first is that before any forecast can be prepared the manager must have as many historical observations as are needed for the moving average. Thus it is not until the end of period 3 that a three-month moving average can be prepared to forecast period 4, and it is not until the end of period 5 that a five-month moving average can be computed as a forecast for period 6.

A second characteristic of moving averages is that the more observations included in the moving average, the greater the smoothing effect on the forecast. Looking at the three-month moving average we note that the smallest value is 1533 and the largest is 2440, a range of 907 (2440 − 1533). From the five-month moving average forecasts we can see that the smallest and largest values are 1915 and 2075, respectively. This represents a range of only 160. Thus the impact of increasing the number of periods included in the moving average has a marked effect on the amount of smoothing to be done. If we desire a smoother value, either because we think the historical observations contain a lot of randomness or because we think there is little change in the underlying pattern, a large number of observations (e.g., 36 months) should be used to compute the moving average forecast. On the other hand, if we feel that the underlying pattern in the data is changing (and we want to react to fluctuations more rapidly) or that there is little randomness in the observed values, a much smaller number of observations (e.g., six months) should be used to compute the moving average.

A useful method in this example of determining whether the three-month or five-month moving average is more appropriate for forecasting demand is to compute the error in both forecasts. Table 3-2 not only shows the error for each forecast but it also computes the mean absolute deviation and the mean squared error for comparative purposes. Both forms of error measurement indicate that the five-month moving average gives a better forecast than the three-month moving average. Later on in this chapter we use the same error measurements to compare the accuracy of moving averages with exponential smoothing for this particular example.

Though the five-month moving average may be better than the three-month in terms of its error, the manager must be aware that the data requirements for the five-month average are much greater than for the three-month. When several hundred or even a thousand items are being forecast each month, a 67% increase in the amount of data that must be stored can represent a significant cost differential. Thus it could be, if data storage

TABLE 3-2 Comparison of Forecasting Errors for Moving Averages

Time Period	Observed Demand	Three-Month Moving Average				Five-Month Moving Average			
		Forecast Demand	Error	Absolute Error	Squared Error	Forecast Demand	Error	Absolute Error	Squared Error
1	2000	. . .	. . .	. . .	. . .	. . .	. . .	. . .	. . .
2	1350	. . .	. . .	. . .	. . .	. . .	. . .	. . .	. . .
3	1950	. . .	. . .	. . .	. . .	. . .	. . .	. . .	. . .
4	1975	1767	−208	208	43,200	. . .	. . .	. . .	. . .
5	3100	1758	−1342	1342	1,740,000	. . .	. . .	. . .	. . .
6	1750	2342	592	592	350,000	2075	325	325	105,625
7	1550	2275	725	725	527,000	2025	475	475	225,625
8	1300	2133	833	833	693,000	2065	765	765	585,225
9	2200	1533	−667	667	589,000	1935	−265	265	70,225
10	2770	1683	−1087	1087	1,190,000	1980	−790	790	624,100
11	2350	2092	−262	262	68,500	1915	−436	436	190,096
12	. . .	2440	. . .	. . .	. . .	2034	. . .	. . .	. . .
	Total	−1716	5816	5,200,700		74	3056	1,800,896	
	Mean	−258	727[a]	656,700[b]		12.3	509.3[a]	300,149[b]	

[a] Mean absolute deviation.
[b] Mean squared error.

were extremely costly, that the manager would still choose to use a three-month rather than a five-month moving average forecast. This is a judgmental decision that he must make.

For a better understanding of the assumptions underlying the technique of moving averages and some of its advantages and limitations it is necessary to look briefly at the mathematical representation of this method. In simple terms the technique of forecasting with moving averages can be represented as follows:

$$S_{t+1} = \frac{x_t + x_{t-1} + \cdots + x_{t-N+1}}{N}$$

$$= \frac{1}{N} \sum_{i=t-N+1}^{t} x_i, \tag{3-1}$$

where S_t = the forecast for time t,

x_t = the actual value at time t,

N = the number of values included in the average.

It can readily be seen from (3-1) that in the method of moving averages equal weight (or importance) is given to each of the last N values in the series but no weight is given to values observed before that time. It can also be seen from this equation that to compute the moving average we must have the values of the last N observations. A somewhat shorter form of (3-1) for calculating the moving average can be developed. The moving average for period t is given by

$$S_t = \frac{x_{t-1} + x_{t-2} + \cdots + x_{t-N}}{N}$$

Now it can be seen from (3-1) that S_{t+1} is simply

$$S_{t+1} = \frac{x_t}{N} - \frac{x_{t-N}}{N} + S_t. \tag{3-2}$$

Written in this form it is obvious that each new forecast based on a moving average is an adjustment of the preceding moving average forecast. It is also easy to see why the smoothing effect increases as N becomes larger because a much smaller adjustment is being made between each forecast.

All the manager needs to do to apply moving averages is to obtain historical data and then use either (3-1) or (3-2) to compute the forecast for the coming period. Of course he must also specify the number of periods to be used in the moving averages.

There are limitations to the application of moving averages that should be mentioned at this point. First is the fact that only those situations that have the basic characteristics outlined at the start of this chapter should even be considered. A second major limitation is that when there are changes in the basic pattern of the variable being forecast moving averages may not adapt rapidly to the changes. Two common types of change can help to illustrate this limitation. The first, referred to as a step change, is described graphically in Figure 3-2. The other common type, the ramp change or trend, is shown in Figure 3-3.

These two figures clearly define the limitations of a moving average forecasting method to adapt to patterns in the data that are other than horizontal. This is one reason why moving averages are generally useful in only short-term situations, for in such cases the pattern can be assumed to be horizontal

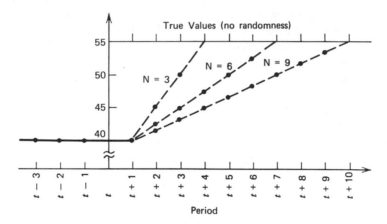

Figure 3-2 Accuracy of moving averages with a step change.

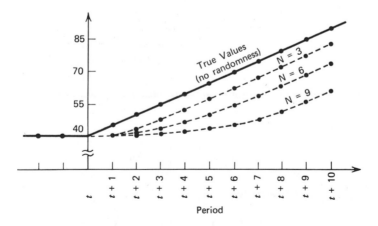

Figure 3-3 Accuracy of moving averages with a ramp change.

without much loss of accuracy. This limitation of simple moving averages to adapt to trend, seasonal and cyclical patterns can be overcome at least in part by using higher order smoothing techniques. In most cases, however, when such complex patterns exist, the manager is well advised to consider a different forecasting technique better suited to these patterns.

EXPONENTIAL SMOOTHING

At least two major limitations to the use of moving averages have prompted many forecasters to apply the method of exponential smoothing in its place. The first is that to compute a moving average forecast it is necessary to store the last N observed values. This takes up considerable space which in many computer systems is costly. A second limitation is that the method of moving averages gives equal weight to each of the last N observations and no weight at all to observations before period $(t - N)$; that is, the weight given to each of the last N observations is $1/N$ and 0 for any previous observations. A strong argument can be made that since the most recent observations contain the most information about what will happen in the future they should be given relatively more weight than the older observations. What we should like is a weighting scheme that would apply the most weight to the most recent observed values and decreasing weights to the older values. Exponential smoothing satisfies this requirement and eliminates the need for storing the historical values of the variable.

In principle exponential smoothing operates in a manner analogous to moving averages by "smoothing" historical observations to eliminate randomness. The mathematical procedure for performing this smoothing, however, is somewhat different from that used in moving averages. The technique of exponential smoothing can be readily developed by using (3-2) for computing the moving average. Suppose we had available only the most recent observed value and the forecast made for that same period. In such a situation (3-2) might be modified so that in place of the observed value in period $(t - N)$ we could employ an approximate value. A reasonable estimate would be the forecast value from the preceding period. Thus (3-2) could be modified to give (3-3):

$$S_{t+1} = \frac{x_t}{N} - \frac{S_t}{N} + S_t. \tag{3-3}$$

This equation can be rewritten as

$$S_{t+1} = \left(\frac{1}{N}\right) x_t + \left(1 - \frac{1}{N}\right) S_t. \tag{3-4}$$

What we now have is a forecast that weights the most recent observation with the weight of value $1/N$ and the most recent forecast with the value of $(1 - 1/N)$. If we substitute a symbol called alpha in place of $1/N$, we have

$$S_{t+1} = \alpha x_t + (1 - \alpha)S_t. \tag{3-5}$$

This equation is the general form used in computing a forecast by the method of exponential smoothing. Note that it immediately eliminates one of the problems associated with moving averages in that all the historical data need no longer be stored. Rather, only the most recent observation, the most recent forecast, and a value for alpha are required to prepare a new forecast. If (3-5) is expanded by substituting in the value for S_t, we have

$$\begin{aligned} S_{t+1} &= \alpha x_t + (1 - \alpha)[\alpha x_{t-1} + (1 - \alpha)S_{t-1}] \\ &= \alpha x_t + \alpha(1 - \alpha)x_{t-1} + (1 - \alpha)^2 S_{t-1}. \end{aligned} \tag{3-6}$$

If this substitution process is carried out even further, we obtain the general relationship

$$S_{t+1} = \alpha x_t + \alpha(1 - \alpha)x_{t-1} + \alpha(1 - \alpha)^2 x_{t-2} + \alpha(1 - \alpha)^3 x_{t-3} + \cdots \tag{3-7}$$

From this equation it can be seen that exponential smoothing also overcomes another limitation of moving averages in that decreasing weights are being given to the older observed values; that is, since alpha is a number between 0 and 1 [thus $(1 - \alpha)$ is also a number between 0 and 1], the weights $[\alpha, \alpha(1 - \alpha), \alpha(1 - \alpha^2),$ etc.] have decreasing magnitude. It is for these reasons that exponential smoothing has gained such wide acceptance as a forecasting method.

An alternative way of writing (3-5) can provide further insight into exponential smoothing. By rearranging terms in (3-5) we can obtain

$$S_{t+1} = S_t + \alpha(x_t - S_t). \tag{3-8}$$

In this form the new forecast prepared by exponential smoothing is simply the old forecast plus α times the error in the old forecast; that is, the term $(x_t - S_t)$ is simply the error in that earlier forecast. In this form it is evident that when α has a value close to 1 the new forecast will include a substantial adjustment for any error that occurred in the preceding forecast. Conversely, when α is close to 0, the new forecast will not show much adjustment for the error from the one before. Thus the effect of a large and small alpha is completely analogous to the effect of including a small number of observations in computing a moving average versus including a large number of observations in a moving average.

By using the example given earlier in this chapter in which the demand for knives was forecast the various aspects of exponential smoothing can be

Table 3-3 Forecasting the Demand for Knives One Month Ahead by Exponential Smoothing

Month	Time Period	Observed Demand	Exponentially Smoothed Values		
			$\alpha = .1$	$\alpha = .5$	$\alpha = .9$
January 1971	1	2000	. . .	. . .	. . .
February 1971	2	1350	2000	2000	2000
March 1971	3	1950	1935	1675	1415
April 1971	4	1975	1937	1813	1897
May 1971	5	3100	1940	1894	1967
June 1971	6	1750	2056	2497	2987
July 1971	7	1550	2026	2123	1874
August 1971	8	1300	1978	1837	1582
September 1971	9	2200	1910	1568	1328
October 1971	10	2775	1939	1884	2113
November 1971	11	2350	2023	2330	2709
December 1971	12	. . .	2056	2340	2386

illustrated. Table 3-3 shows the computed values of the forecast with values for alpha of .1, .5, and .9. The last three columns in this table can be computed with (3-5) or (3-8). The only point that must be remembered is that for the first period no earlier forecast is available and the observed value can best be used. Thus the number 1935 in the $\alpha = .1$ column was obtained by taking 2000 (the preceding forecast) and adding to that (.1) $\times$ (1350-2000). This gives the value of 1935, which can then be used as the forecast for period 3. The effect that the value of alpha has on the amount of smoothing done on previous observed values can be seen in Table 3-3 and in the graph in Figure 3-4. A large value of alpha (.9) gives little smoothing in the forecast, whereas a small value of alpha (.1) gives considerable smoothing.

Although Figure 3-4 indicates that a small value of α tends to produce better forecasts in this example than a large value of α, it is more helpful to consider the mean square error and the mean absolute deviation in comparing these different forecasting procedures. This is done for the three values of α in Table 3-4, from which it can be seen clearly that α of .1 makes much better forecasts than the larger values of α. This is true both for the mean absolute deviation and for the mean squared error. Since we have computed both error measurements for moving averages and exponential smoothing, we can now examine the relative accuracy of the two different methods. Comparing the three-month moving average (which was found to be the better of the two moving averages computed) with the exponential smoothing forecast of $\alpha = .1$ (the best of the three exponential smoothing

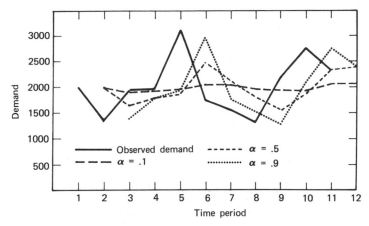

Figure 3-4 Comparison of exponential smoothing forecasts with $\alpha = .1, .5,$ and $.9$.

procedures applied), we can show that exponential smoothing gives only slightly better results than moving averages. When, however, this is considered in light of the reduced data requirement associated with exponential smoothing and the intuitive appeal of weighting most recent observations most heavily, most managers would select exponential smoothing over a moving average approach.

To utilize exponential smoothing a manager need have only the most recent observed value, the most recent forecast, and a value for α. However, just as moving averages have severe limitations when basic changes are made in the underlying pattern of the variable being forecast, exponential smoothing has similar limitations. When the manager expects that a ramp change (see Figure 3-3), a step change (see Figure 3-2), or some other type of complex pattern exists in the data, exponential smoothing will probably be unsatisfactory for meeting his forecasting needs. A final limitation in both exponential smoothing and moving averages in that there is no good rule for determining the appropriate value of the weights. For moving averages the manager must decide what this value is by specifying how many observations to include in the average; in exponential smoothing he must do so by selecting a value of α. Most often this is done experimentally by trying two or three different values to see which is most appropriate.

HIGHER FORMS OF SMOOTHING

In the preceding sections we saw that simple smoothing techniques such as moving averages or exponential smoothing can be used effectively and

TABLE 3-4 Comparison of Forecasting Errors for Exponential Smoothing

Time Period	Observed Demand	Forecast with = .1				Forecast with = .5				Forecast with = .9			
		Forecast Demand	Error	Absolute Error	Square Error	Forecast Demand	Error	Absolute Error	Square Error	Forecast Demand	Error	Absolute Error	Square Error
1	2000	—	—	—	—	—	—	—	—	—	—	—	—
2	1350	2000	650	650	425,000	2000	650	650	425,000	2000	650	650	425,000
3	1950	1935	-15	15	225	1675	-275	275	75,500	1415	-535	535	286,000
4	1975	1937	-38	38	1,440	1813	-162	162	26,300	1897	-78	78	6,000
5	3100	1940	-1160	1160	1,350,000	1894	-1206	1206	1,450,000	1967	-1133	1133	1,290,000
6	1750	2056	356	356	126,000	2497	747	747	560,000	2987	1237	1237	1,540,000
7	1550	2026	476	476	227,000	2123	573	573	330,000	1874	324	324	102,000
8	1300	1978	678	678	460,000	1837	537	537	287,000	1582	282	282	79,000
9	2200	1910	-290	290	84,000	1568	-642	642	412,000	1328	-872	872	760,000
10	2770	1939	-831	831	690,000	1884	-886	886	785,000	2113	-657	657	430,000
11	2350	2023	-273	273	75,000	2330	-20	20	400	2709	359	359	129,000
12	...	2056	...	...	...	2340	...	...	...	2386	...	...	...
Total			-447	4767	3,438,665		-684	5698	4,351,200		423	6127	5,047,000
Mean			-44.7	476.7[a]	343,866[b]		-68.4	569.8[a]	435,120[b]		42.3	612.7[a]	504,700[b]

[a] Mean absolute deviation.
[b] Mean squared error.

inexpensively when the historical pattern of the data can be treated as horizontal. These techniques, however, were not effective in handling trends or other more complex patterns. The higher forms of smoothing (sometimes referred to as linear) can be used in a way that has the same advantages of simple smoothing but can also be applied to trend or even seasonal patterns.

In this section we discuss two forms of linear or second-order smoothing that can be used effectively for data that exhibit a trend pattern. Although these higher forms have the advantage of being cheap to use and can be applied easily to several hundred or even a thousand items, their weakness is that they are still nonstatistical methods and thus hard to evaluate in any kind of exact terms and before they can be adopted it is necessary to identify the basic pattern in the data.

Double Moving Averages

As the name implies, the method of double moving averages starts by computing a set of simple moving averages just as we did at the beginning of this chapter and then computes another moving average based on the first simple moving average values. Table 3-5 indicates how this might be done for a set of data representing demand for a certain product. Column 2 lists the observed values of the data for each of 25 periods. Column 3 then uses those observed values to compute a four-month moving average forecast. In column 4 the values in column 3 are used as the basis of another four-month moving average. If the data in columns 2, 3, and 4 is plotted as in the Figure 3-5, it will show that the simple moving average is always below the actual data, since there is an increasing trend present, and that the double moving average (column 4) is always below the simple moving average. This is as we would have expected, since Figure 3–3 shows that with a ramp change moving averages always lag behind the trend.

An interesting observation to be made about Figure 3-5 is that the double moving average is roughly the same distance below the single moving average as the latter is below the actual data. Thus it is possible to prepare a forecast by taking the difference between the single moving average and the double moving average and adding it back to the single moving average. This is what we do when the technique of double moving averages is applied in forecasting. In perfecting this technique, however, researchers have found that if this adjustment to the single moving average is varied slightly from a simple difference between the single and double averages more accurate results can be obtained. Thus, although the concept underlying this method is as stated above, the actual calculations do require more work.

Table 3-5 contains the results of applying double moving averages to the forecasting of inventory balances in this example. Column 5 gives the results

Table 3-5 Forecasting the Inventory Balance with Double Moving Averages

1	2	3	4	5	6	7
Time Period	Actual Inventory Balance	Four-Month Moving Average of (2)	Four-Month Moving Average of (3)	Value of a	Value of b	Value of $a + bm$ when $m = 1$ (forecast)
1	140					
2	159					
3	136					
4	157					
5	173	148				
6	131	156.25				
7	177	149.25				
8	188	159.5	153.25	165.75	+4.16667	=170
9	154	167.25	158.062	176.437	+6.125	=182.5
10	179	162.5	159.625	165.375	+1.91667	=167
11	180	174.5	165.937	183.062	+5.70833	=189
12	160	175.25	169.875	180.625	+3.58333	=184
13	182	168.25	170.125	166.375	−1.25	=163
14	192	175.25	173.312	177.187	+1.29167	=176
15	224	178.5	174.312	182.687	+2.79167	=180
16	188	189.5	177.875	201.125	+7.75	=209
17	198	196.5	184.937	208.062	+7.70833	=216
18	206	200.5	191.25	209.75	+6.16667	=216
19	203	204	197.625	210.375	+4.25	=219
20	238	198.75	199.937	197.562	− .791667	=197
21	228	211.25	203.625	218.875	+5.08333	=244
22	231	218.75	208.187	229.312	+7.04167	=236
23	221	225	213.437	236.562	+7.70833	=244
24	259	229.5	221.125	237.875	+5.58333	=243
25	273	234.75	227	242.5	+5.16667	=248

when the difference between columns 3 and 4 is added back to column 3; column 6 then computes an adjustment factor that makes the method even more accurate. Finally, in column 7 the actual forecast is presented. This forecast is just the sum of column 5 plus column 6 times the number of periods to be projected. For the manager forecasting one period in advance his forecast is simply the sum of columns 5 and 6. For two periods in advance the forecast would be column 5 plus twice column 6, and so on.

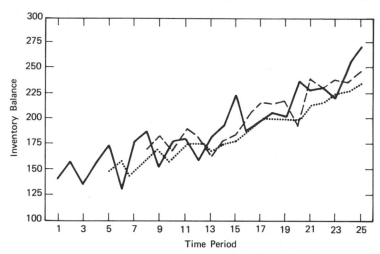

Figure 3-5 Double moving averages—inventory balance. Actual inventory balance = ——. Four-month moving average = ······. Value of a + bm when m = 1 (forecast) — — —.

The graph in Figure 3-5 includes a plot of the forecast made with double moving averages for one period into the future. As the figure shows, this forecast has the advantage of smoothing the random fluctuations in the actual data and can also follow the trend pattern which is clearly evident.

If we let S'_{t+1} be the single moving average, S''_{t+1}, the double moving average, S_{t+m}, the forecast m periods in advance, and b, the adjustment to the forecast, we can summarize in mathematical terms the forecast developed in Table 3-5 as follows:

Column 3 $$S'_{t+1} = \frac{x_t + x_{t-1} + x_{t-2} + \cdots + x_{t-N+1}}{N},$$

Column 4 $$S''_{t+1} = \frac{S'_{t+1} + S'_t + S'_{t-1} + \cdots + S'_{t-N+2}}{N},$$

Column 5 $$a = 2S'_{t+1} - S''_{t+1},$$

Column 6 $$b = \frac{2}{N-1}(S'_{t+1} - S''_{t+1}),$$

Column 7 $$S_{t+m} = a + bm,$$

where $N = 4$ and $m = 1$ in this example.

Using this set of equations to prepare a forecast for period 26, given that we are at period 25, we obtain

$$S_{t+1} = 2(246) - 233.8 + 8.125 = 266.3.$$

If we wanted to forecast period 30, given that $t = 25$, we would have

$$S_{t+5} = 2(246) - 233.8 + 8.125(4) = 270.7.$$

To apply this method of forecasting the manager must have available $2N$ data points, or twice the number required in simple smoothing. Clearly, this need for substantial data storage makes the method of double moving averages less attractive than the method of double exponential smoothing, which is described in the next section.

Double Exponential Smoothing

As is stated early in this chapter, the method of moving averages contains two major limitations. The first is that to compute a forecast the last N data points must be available and stored. The second is that moving averages give equal weight to each of these observations and no weight to earlier observations. The same two limitations apply to the method of double moving averages. Double exponential smoothing, however, can perform the same task as double moving averages but can overcome the two limitations. In fact, in double exponential smoothing only three items of data need to be stored. Thus in the majority of cases this method is preferred to double moving averages.

The basic concept underlying double exponential smoothing is completely analogous to that of double moving averages. Application of single exponential smoothing to a time series with a trend pattern gives results that are consistently below that trend. A subsequent application of exponential smoothing to those smoothed values again produces values lower than the modified trend. Just as in double moving averages, however, we can add to the single exponential smoothed value the difference between itself and the double smoothing and then adjust for the trend.

With the same mathematical notation that we used in discussing double moving averages we can summarize the steps in double exponential smoothing (refer to Table 3-6):

Column 3 $S'_{t+1} = \alpha x_t + (1 - \alpha)S'_t,$

Column 4 $S''_{t+1} = \alpha S'_{t+1} = (1 - \alpha)S''_t,$

Column 5 $a = 2S'_{t+1} - S''_{t+1},$

Column 6
$$b = \frac{\alpha}{1 - \alpha} (S'_{t+1} - S''_{t+1}),$$

Column 7
$$S_{t+m} = a + bm,$$

where α = the exponential smoothing constant,
　　m = the number of periods ahead that we want to forecast.

With the data given in Table 3–6 and a value for α of .2 we can follow these steps in computing a forecast for period 26 (i.e., one period ahead of

Table 3-6　Forecasting the Inventory Balance with Double Exponential Smoothing

1	2	3	4	5	6	7
Period	Inventory Balances for Product E15	Single Exponential Smoothing	Double Exponential Smoothing	Value of a	Value of b	Value of $a + bm$
1	143					
2	152	143	143			
3	161	144.8	143.36	146.24	+ .360001	=146.5
4	139	148.04	144.296	151.784	+ .935997	=153
5	137	146.232	144.683	147.781	+ .387199	=148
6	174	144.386	144.624	144.147	+ .005952	=144
7	142	150.308	145.761	154.856	+1.13696	=156
8	141	148.647	146.338	150.956	+ 57724	=151
9	162	147.117	146.494	147.741	+ .55922	=148
10	180	150.094	147.214	152.974	+ .720039	=154
11	164	156.075	148.986	163.164	+1.77228	=165
12	171	157.66	150.721	164.599	+1.73482	=166
13	206	160.328	152.642	168.014	+1.92145	=170
14	193	169.462	156.006	182.919	+3.36404	=186
15	207	174.17	159.639	188.701	+3.63274	=193
16	218	180.736	163.858	197.613	+4.21938	=202
17	229	188.189	168.724	207.653	+4.86607	=212
18	225	196.351	174.25	218.452	+5.52531	=214
19	204	202.081	179.816	224.346	+5.56621	=230
20	227	202.465	184.346	220.584	+4.52973	=225
21	223	207.372	188.951	225.792	+4.60519	=231
22	242	210.497	193.26	227.735	+4.3093	=232
23	239	216.798	197.968	235.628	+4.70754	=241
24	266	221.238	202.622	239.855	+4.65411	=245

the current period):

$$S_{t+1} = 2(230.19) - 208.136 + \frac{.2}{.8}(230.19 - 208.14)$$

$$= 257.8.$$

If we want to forecast five periods ahead, we would follow the same procedure with $m = 5$ and obtain

$$S_{t+5} = 2(230.19) - 208.136 + \frac{.2}{.8}(230.19 - 208.14)(5)$$

$$= 279.8.$$

The accuracy of using double exponential smoothing in this particular situation can be seen by examining Figure 3-6 which graphs the results. The forecast seems to follow closely the general trend in the series, while smoothing out the fluctuations that seem to occur in some kind of random fashion.

Although we could compute the mean absolute deviation and the mean squared error for both double moving averages and double exponential smoothing, it is not really necessary to choose between the two methods because in virtually all cases double exponential smoothing can achieve results as good as those of double moving averages and do so much more

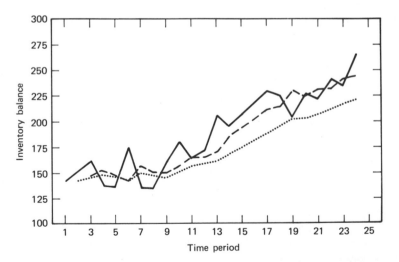

Figure 3-6 Double exponential smoothing for inventory balance. Actual inventory balance = ——. Single exponential smoothing = ·······. Value of a + bm when m = 1 (forecast) = — — —.

easily. We would, however, normally want to calculate these error measures to determine the best value of α for a given series.

The reader will recall that we said earlier that double exponential smoothing is capable of handling a trend pattern. Another advantage of this technique is that it can also handle the horizontal pattern just as well as simple exponential smoothing can. Even when there is a step change in a horizontal problem such as that described in Figure 3–2, double exponential smoothing can adjust rapidly to it. When double exponential smoothing is used in situations in which there is a ramp change or a step change, it exhibits a kind of primitive "learning" ability as it makes that adjustment. This same characteristic will be much more evident when we discuss the technique of adaptive filtering in Chapter 4.

Higher Forms of Smoothing

In a manner completely analogous to that discussed for double moving averages and double exponential smoothing higher forms of smoothing can also be developed and used to forecast patterns of a quadratic or more complex nature. The calculations required for obtaining forecasts in this manner become cumbersome, however, and the need for knowing beforehand the actual pattern of the data makes it difficult to apply these higher forms. Thus, although it is possible to do so, their practical utilization is questionable. In view of this and the fact that several other forecasting methods are available which can handle these more complex patterns readily, smoothing techniques of higher order than double exponential smoothing are seldom applied in practice.

One more complex form of smoothing that deserves at least brief mention was developed by Winters in the early sixties. His model produces results similar to double exponential smoothing as we have discussed it, but it has the extra advantage of incorporating a seasonal coefficient and can therefore be used to predict a data series that combines a trend and a seasonal pattern. The reader desiring more information on this and other smoothing techniques is referred to the suggested readings that follow.

SUGGESTED REFERENCES FOR ADDITIONAL STUDY

Brown, R. G., *Smoothing, Forecasting and Prediction*, Prentice-Hall, Englewood Cliffs, New Jersey, 1963.

Brown, R. G., *Statistical Forecasting for Inventory Control*, McGraw-Hill, New York, 1959.

Winters, P., "Forecasting Sales by Exponentially Weighted Moving Averages," *Management Science*, 324–342 (April 1960).

CHAPTER 4

FORECASTING WITH
ADAPTIVE FILTERING

Chapter 3 described two forecasting methods that can be used in a wide range of short-term forecasting situations for which several forecasts must be prepared. These two techniques, moving averages and exponential smoothing, base their forecasts solely on historical observations. In this chapter we deal with another method called adaptive filtering which also bases its forecasts on historical observations. This method, however, gives much better results than the other two, particularly in situations in which the basic underlying pattern in the data is not simply a constant value. Before describing how the technique of adaptive filtering works and how it can be used, it would be useful to consider the relation between moving averages, exponential smoothing, and the rationale for adaptive filtering.

FORECASTS BASED ON WEIGHTED AVERAGE OF HISTORICAL OBSERVATIONS

A general class of forecasting techniques widely used in practice bases forecasts on some type of weighted average of past observations. The rationale behind this conceptual approach is that these observed values contain information about what will happen in the future and thus can serve for making forecasts. Unfortunately, past observations include random fluctuations (noise) as well as information concerning the underlying pattern of the variable in question. This general class of forecasting techniques attempts to deal with both causes of fluctuations in the past values of the variable by "smoothing" these values. Such an approach inherently assumes that the extreme fluctuations represent the randomness in the historical values. The two specific techniques most often used are moving averages and exponential smoothing.

48

The technique of moving averages (as outlined in Chapter 3) consists of taking the past N values of the variable, finding their average, and then using this average as a forecast for the coming period. Mathematically this computation can be written as

$$S_{t+1} = \frac{1}{N} [x_t + x_{t-1} + \cdots + x_{t-(N-1)}] \qquad (4\text{-}1)$$

where S_{t+1} = the forecast for period $t + 1$,

N = the number of observed values included in the moving average,

x_t = the observed value in period t.

This approach to forecasting is referred to as the method of moving averages because N is held constant for each forecast, t is incremented by 1, and the average is recomputed by dropping the oldest observation and picking up a new one. The value of N determines how much of the fluctuation in observed values is carried into the smoothed forecast S_{t+1}; a larger value of N gives a more smoothed forecast than a smaller value of N.

A major drawback of the technique of moving averages is that it assigns equal weight to each of the past N observations and no weight to observations before that. We could argue that in most situations the recent observations contain more "information" for forecasting purposes than the older ones, which are less important in predicting future values. Following this line of reasoning, many managers utilize the technique of exponential smoothing that gives decreasing importance (weight) to older observations.

Exponential smoothing (as outlined in Chapter 3) can be described mathematically as

$$S_{t+1} = \alpha x_t + (1 - \alpha)S_t, \qquad (4\text{-}2)$$

where S_{t+1} = the forecast for period $t + 1$,

α = the smoothing constant $(0 \leq \alpha \leq 1)$,

x_t = the observed value in period t.

This general equation can be expanded by replacing S_t with its computed value. Carrying out this expansion gives

$$S_{t+1} = \alpha x_t + \alpha(1 - \alpha)x_{t-1} + \alpha(1 - \alpha)^2 x_{t-2} + \alpha(1 - \alpha)^3 x_{t-3} \cdots . \qquad (4\text{-}3)$$

From this expanded form it can be seen that since α is between 0 and 1 decreasing weights are being given to the older observation. The size of α determines the relative values of these weights. A large α (close to 1) will give most of the weight to recent observations, whereas a small value of α (close to 0) will not give much weight to any single observation, thus providing a much more smoothed value for S_{t+1}.

Exponential smoothing has been applied extensively in a number of business situations because it is easy to understand, straightforward to apply, and intuitively appealing to a manager because he has some control over the weights through the assignment of a value for α. A major drawback of exponential smoothing, however, is that there is no easy way to determine an appropriate value of α.

Still another approach to the development of a forecast that is similar in rationale to those described above is the technique of polynomial fitting. Although we will not take the time to go into this approach in detail, we summarize it briefly. Polynomial fitting consists of taking the $N + 1$ most recent observations and then fitting an Nth order polynomial to these observed values. A few examples illustrate this technique. The simplest form employs only a single observation on which to make a forecast. This form is just a constant:

$$S_{t+1} = x_t. \tag{4-4}$$

Taking the case of using two observations amounts to fitting a straight line to these two values:

$$S_{t+1} = x_t + (x_t - x_{t-1})$$

$$= 2x_t - x_{t-1}. \tag{4-5}$$

To fit a polynomial to three observed values the method of first differences can be used to obtain

$$S_{t+1} = 3x_t - 3x_{t-1} + x_{t-2}. \tag{4-6}$$

The use of three points amounts to fitting a parabola to the past data. We can continue on in a similar manner to obtain polynomials of higher order.

The basic shortcoming of the polynomial fitting approach for forecasting is that it takes no account of random fluctuations. Thus it fits a curve exactly to a specified number of past observations, even though those observations may include noise, and then bases a forecast on an extension of that curve.

AN ADAPTIVE PROCESS FOR WEIGHTING PAST OBSERVATIONS

Each of the three forecasting techniques—moving averages, exponential smoothing, and polynomial fitting—described in the preceding section is based on the idea that a forecast can be made by using a weighted sum of past observations. In the most general form this sum can be written as

$$S_{t+1} = \sum_{i=t-N+1}^{t} w_i x_i \tag{4-7}$$

where S_{t+1} = the forecast for period $t + 1$,

      w_i = the weight to be assigned to observation i,

      x_i = the observed value in period i,

      N = the number of observations used in computing S_{t+1} (and thus the number of weights also).

It can readily be seen that each of these three techniques consists simply of a rule or set of rules that describes how the weights w_i should be determined. Obviously, since each approach comes up with a different set of weights, we would expect that different results, in terms of the accuracy of the forecast, will be achieved with each method.

The method of forecasting with adaptive filtering discussed here is simply another approach for determining the appropriate sets of weights. This method, however, seeks to determine the "best" set. As a starting point to an understanding of adaptive filtering consider Figure 4-1.

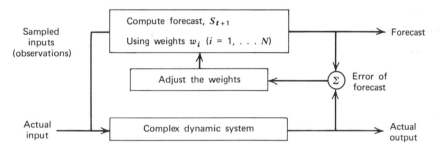

Figure 4-1   A general scheme for determining the weights in a time series forecast.

The bottom line in Figure 4-1 represents what is actually going on; that is, things are developing in the real world which interact in some complex dynamic system and then lead to the actual output for the value of a variable. The boxes and lines above this reality level represent what we would like to do in preparing a forecast. The notion is to take a given set of weights, compute a forecast with them [based on (4-7)], then compute the error of the forecast (the difference between the forecast and the actual value), and finally adjust the weights to reduce that error. If a procedure can be found that will make this adjustment of the weights, the error can be reduced to some minimum level. The method that we will develop for making this adjustment has been referred to as adaptive filtering, a name that originated in telecommunication engineering to describe a process for filtering the noise of transmission out of a message. This is analogous to what we want to do in forecasting, which is to distinguish some basic underlying pattern in the values of a variable from the noise that might be associated with those values.

The theory on which forecasting with adaptive filtering is based is beyond the scope of this book. The essentials of the technique, however, are conceptually fairly simple and the mechanics of using it in practice are also easy to deal with. Before presenting a conceptual explanation of how this technique operates it will be useful to investigate further the concept of adjusting or training the values of the weight. This can be done by referring first to Figure 4-2 in which an example of five weights has been used. It has been assumed also that 20 historical observations are available. The process of adapting or training the weights consists of four steps. First, a forecast can be prepared for period 6 (S_6) by simply weighting the first five observations ($S_6 = w_1x_1 + w_2x_2 + w_3x_3 + w_4x_4 + w_5x_5$). Next the error in this forecast can be computed by taking the difference between the forecast (S_6) and the observed value for period 6 (x_6). On the basis of this error the weights can be adjusted and finally a forecast for period 7 can be prepared with the new set of weights. Just as in moving averages, with adaptive filtering we drop an old observation and pick up a new one, but in the training phase the weights are adjusted when each new forecast is prepared. Once the last five observations have been reached the forecast for period 21 can be prepared, but then the decision maker must wait until an observed value for period 21 is available before readjusting the weights.

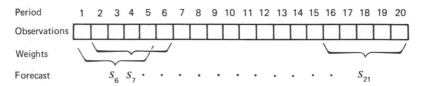

Figure 4-2   Adjusting the weights by adaptive filtering.

The technique of adaptive filtering simply states how the weights should be adjusted after the forecast error has been computed. Conceptually this procedure for adjustment can be developed as follows: to have a good forecast we would like to minimize the average mean squared error over several forecasts; thus the weights should be specified to minimize the mean squared error. In a situation in which only two weights are involved it is easy to visualize this mean squared error as the bowlshaped function represented in Figure 4-3. Essentially what this figure shows is that for any pair of weights the mean squared error over a number of forecasts can be found on the bowl-shaped area. The objective of minimizing this mean square error amounts to finding the bottom of the bowl. Now, in reality the surface of the bowl is not smooth because randomness is included in past observations. Thus we want only to approximate the bottom of the bowl.

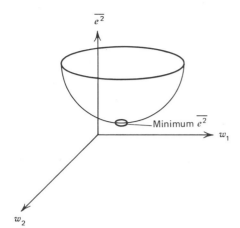

Figure 4-3 The mean square error for forecasts based on two weights.

As described in Figure 4-2, the process of adapting the values of the weights starting from some initial set of weights consists of moving along the surface of this bowl toward the lowest point in it. Mathematically the technique used for doing this is referred to as the method of steepest descent. In terms of the symbols used earlier in connection with the preparation of a forecast, the equation that can be used for adjusting the weights once the error has been computed is

$$W' = W + 2keX \tag{4-8}$$

where W' = the revised set of weights,
$\quad W$ = the old set of weights,
$\quad k$ = a constant term referred to as the learning constant,
$\quad e$ = the error of forecast,
$\quad X$ = the observed values.

This equation states that the revised set of weights should equal the old set of weights plus some adjustment made for the error calculated. The adjustment for each weight is based on the error for that forecast, the observed value and the value of the learning constant k. This learning constant determines how rapidly the weights are adjusted or, in terms of Figure 4-3, how rapidly we approach the bottom of the bowl.

An example will help to illustrate the use of the technique of adaptive filtering. Suppose that we have the 10 observed values shown in Figure 4-4. Now suppose that we wish to use the technique of adaptive filtering to forecast the observed value for period 11 with two weights. What we need to do first is to select an initial value for the weights. Suppose we try $w_1 = .5$ and $w_2 = .5$ (note that the sum of the weights equals 1). The forecast for period 3

Period	1	2	3	4	5	6	7	8	9	10
Observed value	.1	.2	.3	.4	.5	.6	.7	.8	.9	1.0

Figure 4-4 A set of sample values for adaptive filtering.

can now be based on the observed values for periods 1 and 2 and these initial weights. Making the computations gives $S_3 = (.5)(.1) + (.5)(.2) = .15$. From this forecast the error which is $.3 - .15 = .15$ can be computed. If a value for the learning constant is specified (e.g., $k = .9$), then (4-8) can be used to compute a new (adjusted) set of weights:

$$w_1' = w_1 + 2kex_1 = .5 + 2(.9)(.15)(.1) = \quad .517$$
$$w_2' = w_2 + 2kex_2 = .5 + 2(.9)(.15)(.2) = \quad \underline{.554}$$
$$1.081$$

Before these revised weights are used to prepare a forecast for period 4 they must be adjusted so that their sum is 1. This can be done by dividing each of these revised values by the sum of the two, 1.081. The result is a value for w_1 of .487 and for w_2 of .513.

The entire adjustment process can be repeated by forecasting period 4. Using the new weights, we arrive at a forecast value of .2513 [$(.487)(.2) + (.513)(.3)$]. Thus the error in this forecast is .1487 ($.4000 - .2513$). The procedure for adjusting the weights produces the following:

$$w_1' = .487 + 2(.9)(.15)(.2) = 0.541$$
$$w_2' = .513 + 2(.9)(.15)(.3) = \underline{0.594}$$
$$1.135$$

Again these weights can be normalized so that their sum will equal 1 and we have weights of .483 and .517. A continuation of this process will eventually bring us to the point at which observations for periods 9 and 10 are being used to forecast period 11. At this point the manager cannot proceed in adjusting the weights because an observed value for period 11 is not available. The weights that exist at this point, however, can be used as an initial set and the process can be recommenced with the observed values from periods 1 and 2 to forecast the value of period 3. By going through this series of observed values several times a point will eventually be reached at which no change will occur in the weights during the adaptation process because the error will be 0. Although the number of calculations required to reach this point is more than would be practical by hand, it can be done easily with a computer, and the final values of the weights will be $w_1 = -1.0$

and $w_2 = 2.0$. The reader may want to verify from the data given in Figure 4-4 that the forecast error with these weights is indeed zero.

Some important observations can now be made concerning the use of adaptive filtering in forecasting. First and perhaps most important is the fact that it can give accurate forecasts for a much wider range of situations than exponential smoothing or moving averages. Thus in the example above in which the data actually represented a ramp function adaptive filtering was able to achieve a point of having 0 forecast error, whereas it was shown in Chapter 3 that exponential smoothing and moving averages could never achieve this degree of accuracy in this type of function. A second important point is that the manager must specify a value of k, which determines how rapidly the best set of weights can be found. If, however, too large a value is chosen for k, the adjustments in the values of the weights will be too large and the optimal weight values will never be found (this is referred to as divergence in the adaptation process). A third point to note is that the manager must also specify the number of weights to be used. In this situation two weights worked well because the predicted pattern was a straight line and thus two weights could uniquely determine that line. Finally, it should be mentioned that when randomness is present in the observed value a 0 forecast error can never be achieved. Thus the manager must decide when he has performed a sufficient number of adaptation cycles on the weights. This can usually be determined by adapting the weights until a point at which each successive adaptation gives only extremely small changes in the weights is reached. This amounts to accepting a trade-off between the accuracy of the weights and the time (i.e., number of cycles) required to reach that level of accuracy.

USING ADAPTIVE FILTERING IN PRACTICE

The preceding section should make it apparent that for adaptive filtering to be used as a practical forecasting technique it must be implemented on a computer system. In spite of the fact that this may seem like an inconvenience, several features of adaptive filtering make it attractive to the practicing manager. First it uses the "information" contained in past observations to find the best set of weights. Perhaps equally important is the simplicity of the technique. The method for adapting the values of the weights involves only the single equation

$$W' = W + 2keX.$$

This equation is not only easy to use but it also allows the decision maker to adjust the procedure to fit his own situation and data by allowing him to alter the number of observations in setting the weights and to specify the rate at which the weights are adapted.

An illustration of how adaptive filtering can be applied as a forecasting technique in a specific situation should serve to highlight its usefulness. Consider the case of a French wine company which as part of its planning process desires to forecast champagne sales in France on a monthly basis. Actual monthly sales values from January 1962 through September 1970 (105 months) are available from industry sources. These values are shown in Table 4-1.

As pointed out in the preceding section, the use of adaptive filtering in the preparation of a forecast has two distinct phases. The first is the training (or adapting) of a set of weights with historical data and the second is the use of these weights. For purposes of this example all 105 historical observations of monthly champagne sales are used in training the set of weights.

To start the training phase it is necessary first to specify the number of weights N and the learning constant k. Since a brief visual inspection of the historical data in Table 4-1 indicates that champagne sales follow a cyclical pattern 12 months long, the use of 12 weights would seem appropriate. Essentially this says that although the weights will be trained by using several years of data, a forecast for a single month will be based only on the sales for the 12 preceding months. At a starting value for k, we might select a value of $k = .08.$*

With these parameters specified, the set of 12 weights can be trained by using the equations specified in the preceding section and an initial value for each of the 12 weights. (We arbitrarily let each of the weights have an initial value of .085 or $1/N$.) The first training cycle consists of taking the first 12 observations (of the 105 available), computing a forecast for month 13 with

$$S_{13} = \sum_{i=1}^{12} W_i X_i,$$

computing the error of this forecast, $e = (X_{13} - S_{13})$, and then revising the weight vector according to

$$W' = W + 2keX$$

where W' = the new vector of 12 weights,

W = the old (initial) vector of 12 weights,

$k = .08$, a constant,

$e = x_{13} - S_{13}$,

X = the vector of the first 12 observations.

---

* As will be seen in the next few pages and in Table 4-2, this value of k is close to the optimum. Generally speaking, as the amount of randomness in a series increases and as the number of weights increases, the optimal value of k decreases.

Table 4-1 Monthly Champagne Sales (in 1000's of bottles)

Year	Month	Sales	Year	Month	Sales	Year	Month	Sales
1970	September	5.877	1967	December	13.916	1964	December	9.254
	August	1.431		November	10.803		November	7.614
	July	4.298		October	6.873		October	5.211
	June	5.312		September	5.222		September	3.528
	May	4.618		August	1.821		August	1.573
	April	4.788		July	3.523		July	3.260
	March	4.577		June	4.677		June	3.986
	February	3.564		May	4.968		May	3.937
	January	4.348		April	4.276		April	3.523
				March	4.510		March	4.047
1969	December	12.670		February	3.957		February	3.006
	November	9.851		January	4.016		January	3.113
	October	6.981						
	September	5.951	1966	December	11.331	1963	December	8.357
	August	1.659		November	9.858		November	6.838
	July	4.633		October	6.922		October	4.474
	June	4.874		September	5.048		September	3.595
	May	5.010		August	1.723		August	1.759
	April	4.676		July	3.965		July	3.028
	March	4.286		June	4.753		June	3.230
	February	3.162		May	4.647		May	3.776
	January	3.934		April	4.121		April	3.266
				March	4.154		March	3.031
				February	4.292		February	2.475
1968	December	13.076		January	3.633		January	2.541
	November	9.842						
	October	6.424	1965	December	10.651	1962	December	7.132
	September	5.221		November	8.314		November	5.764
	August	1.738		October	5.428		October	4.301
	July	4.217		September	4.739		September	2.922
	June	3.986		August	1.643		August	2.212
	May	2.927		July	3.663		July	2.282
	April	3.740		June	4.539		June	3.036
	March	3.370		May	4.520		May	2.946
	February	2.899		April	4.514		April	2.721
	January	2.639		March	3.718		March	2.755
				February	3.088		February	2.672
				January	5.375		January	2.851

Table 4-2 Training the Weights for Forecasting Champagne Sales

	Weight String Length 12	Forecasting Horizon 1 Period(s)
Series 1	Adaptation Constant .0800	80 Training Iterations

Learning Performance

Iteration	Mean-Square Error	% Error-Mean	% Error-Variance	Error Reduction
1	86.83972	−151.07128	91723.313	.0
11	.84335	−4.65539	6.6.168	.048119
21	.64103	−3.54261	478.208	.015300
31	.59168	−3.08917	440.006	.004372
41	.57770	−2.88744	427.096	.001320
51	.57340	−2.70774	422.836	.000461
61	.57173	−2.75837	420.473	.000195
71	.57094	−2.74221	419.098	.000104
72	.57033	−2.74131	413.992	.000006
73	.57083	−2.74048	418.889	.000002
74	.57078	−2.73970	418.790	.000088
75	.57073	−2.73011	418.604	.000937
76	.57068	−2.73851	418.602	.000082
77	.57004	−2.73796	418.512	.000078
78	.57060	−2.73757	418.428	.000070
79	.57056	−2.73720	418.345	.000071
80	.57052	−2.73086	418.264	.000065

Optimal Weights

Weight No.	Series 1
1	1.018527
2	.071620
3	−.074006
4	.073826
5	−.005556
6	.086222
7	−.093924
8	.034412
9	−.000613
10	.953632
11	−.101788
12	.070522

The forecast for month 14 can then be computed by using the observed values for months 2 to 13 (12 values), after which the process of updating the weights can be repeated. When this process has been followed up by the forecasting of month 105, we can start over again with the first 12 observations and the most recent set of revised weights. Each of these series of revisions of the weights, which is made by going through the entire string of observed data, can be referred to as a *training iteration*. The number of iterations that need to be run depends on the nature of the series under study and the adaption rate k. Table 4-2 shows the results of running 80 such iterations on the 105 months of champagne sales data. Even after this number of iterations it can be seen that the adjusted weights give a forecast value that is quite close to the actual values illustrated by the mean error and the variance for the eightieth iteration.

As we pointed out in the preceding section, a parameter of critical importance in adaptive filtering is k. This constant determines how rapidly the weights are adjusted, and thus the error reduction achieved by each training iteration. As can be seen from Table 4-2, after 60 iterations, with $k = .08$ for our champagne sales data, the error reduction is small and thus there is not much improvement in the mean square error between the sixtieth and eightieth iterations.

A different value of k might give entirely different results, and thus it is instructive to examine the effect of alternative values of k. The results of such an investigation are shown in Table 4-3, from which it can be seen that values of k around .08 and .09 are better in terms of minimizing the mean square error. For 80 iterations values of k above or below this range do not produce good results. For smaller values of k, such as .04, the reason for this poorer performance is simply that a smaller k value gives less error reduction on each iteration and thus more iterations are required to reach a given level of error. For larger values of k, such as .12, the poorer performance results from adapting the weights too rapidly and thus reacting to random fluctuations in the historical observations (for values of k larger than about .25 the adaptive filtering process does not even converge to a set of optimal weights).

It should be clear that the forecasting method of adaptive filtering is much more powerful than smoothing methods but also somewhat more complicated. Adaptive filtering, however, does fill a gap in existing forecasting techniques, since it can effectively handle a wide range of basic patterns in a time series. Because of this effectiveness and its conceptual simplicity and appeal it will undoubtedly gain much wider acceptance in the coming years than it now has. For the interested reader the appendix to this chapter describes some of the current research being conducted on this technique and some additional modifications that can make the approach even more efficient than it is when done exactly as described in this chapter.

Table 4-3 Adaptive Filtering Forecasts for Actual Champagne Sales in France

Computer Run	Number of Weights	Final Weight Values	Value of K	Number of Training Iterations	Mean Square Error on Final Iteration
a	12	.9754 .0991 −.0683 .0787 −.1089 .0885 −.0709 .0433 −.0982 .0630 −.0910 .1053	.04	80	.5971
b	12	1.0185 .0716 −.0741 .0728 −.0956 .0862 −.0939 .0344 −.0906 .0536 −.1018 .0705	.08	80	.5705
c	12	1.0230 .0680 −.0730 .0703 −.0926 .0841 −.0946 .0311 −.0896 .0506 −.1017 .0649	.09	80	.5696

(Continued)

Table 4-3 *(Continued)*

Computer Run	Number of Weights	Final Weight Values	Value of K	Number of Training Iterations	Mean Square Error on Final Iteration
d	12	1.0343	.12	80	.5733
		.0584			
		−.0688			
		.0630			
		−.0841			
		.0779			
		−.0944			
		.0211			
		−.0868			
		.0421			
		−.1006			
		.0496			

SUGGESTED REFERENCES FOR ADDITIONAL STUDY

Unfortunately there is little work of a practical nature that has been done on adaptive filtering. For those interested in the theoretical development, however, there are a couple of good references.

Wheelwright, Steven C. and Spyros Makridakis, "Forecasting with Adaptive Filtering", *Revue Francaise d'Automatique, d'Informatique et de Recherche Operationelle*, Winter, 1973 (Paris).

Wheelwright, Steven C. and Spyros Makridakis, "An Examination of the Use of Adaptive Filtering in Forecasting", *Operational Research Quarterly*, Winter, 1973 (London).

Widrow, Bernard, 1966, *Adaptive Filter I: Fundamentals*, SU-SEL-66-126, Systems Theory Laboratory, Stanford University, Stanford, California, December.

Wilde, D. J., 1964, *Optimum Seeking Method*, Prentice-Hall, Englewood Cliffs, New Jersey.

APPENDIX: ADDITIONAL GUIDELINES TO FORECASTING WITH ADAPT-IVE-FILTERING

As pointed out in this chapter, the adaptive filtering approach is one that has only recently been applied to management forecasting situations. Because of this newness, the details of the actual application are not widely available in the forecasting literature. Therefore this appendix describes some of the our own experiences in using the method. This additional information, along with that provided in the body of the chapter, should supply sufficient information to the forecasting staff member to enable him to adapt it to his own corporate situation.

To use a computerized version of the iterative approach described for training the set of weights for adaptive filtering two things should be done. First the series of historical values should be examined for the presence of any value close to 0. Because of the nature of the weight adjustment procedure, a value of 0 for one of the data points can lead to computational difficulties. If the data series in question does include a value of 0, all that is needed is to add a constant value to each of the data points. Since this does not change the basic pattern but simply shifts it, the adjusted data series will still give the optimal set of weights.

Second, we have found that normalizing the set of data values (so that the maximum value is 1.0) before adjusting the weights makes adaptive filtering more efficient. This causes the training phase to converge more rapidly to the best set of weights.

Another factor that makes the weight training process considerably more efficient is the judicious selection of a set of starting weight values. As already stated, a starting value of $1/N$ will suffice. A much better approach, however, computes the autocorrelations for the time series and uses them as starting weight values. Thus, if five weights are to be used in a given situation, the autocorrelation coefficients for time lags of one, two, three, four, and five periods can be computed as initial values for the weights.

A final area of major importance to the forecaster is a set of rules to guide him in selecting a value for k, the learning constant. We are currently engaged in a research project designed to give information on this problem. Until that work is completed, a couple of rules of thumb should be useful. First, the fewer the number of weights, the larger the value of k can be and still give convergence. Second, the more randomness in the series, the smaller the value of k. Third, if we want to find the k-value that, given a set number of iterations, will give the smallest mean square error (the best forecast), it can be done by trying three different values of k and then plotting them against the mean square error. When a parabola is fitted to these three points, the k-value that gives optimum results (minimum mean square error) can be read from the graph.

One area relating to adaptive filtering not yet fully investigated is the use of statistical measures to determine its accuracy. Clear possibilities for computing statistics surround an adaptive filtering forecast that would enable the manager to develop confidence intervals and significance tests, as now done for regression analysis and the Box-Jenkins Method, and should make the technique of adaptive filtering even more attractive to the practitioner.

CHAPTER 5

SIMPLE REGRESSION
AND CORRELATION

In Chapters 3 and 4 a basic tenet in forecasting techniques has been the notion that a series of historical data values represents a basic underlying pattern combined with some randomness. These forecasting techniques attempt to identify, or at least approximate, that basic underlying pattern. The model used by smoothing techniques and adaptive filtering is a time series one.

In this chapter we consider a somewhat different approach to the forecasting problem which goes beyond trying to approximate the underlying pattern in a time series. Here we assume not only that such a basic pattern exists but also that the form of that basic pattern is linear. This means that if we plotted the data over time it would fall approximately along a straight line. Obviously there are many situations in which this is not a valid assumption; for example, if we were forecasting monthly sales and it was believed that those sales varied according to the seasons of the year, such an approach would be inappropriate. It may be, however, that if we were forecasting the same sales items, but on an annual basis, these sales could be approximated by using a straight line. Figure 5-1 represents the pattern of data points that might exist when we look at annual sales. It can be seen in this figure that a straight line sloping upward (i.e., a trend going upward) as we go from left to right would give a fairly good approximation of future sales. This was the kind of pattern that we saw in Chapter 3 that could be handled with double exponential smoothing and double moving averages. In this chapter, however, we consider a different method of handling the same type of pattern which has several advantages over double smoothing techniques.

Figure 5-1 and those that we have considered in earlier chapters all involve forecasting some quantity in terms of the time period. Thus, if we were to graph each of these situations, we would have the time variable on the

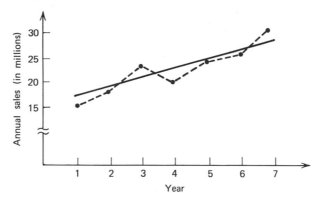

Figure 5-1   Projecting annual sales.

horizontal axis and the variable that we wish to forecast on the vertical axis. Regression analysis is a technique that is not limited to this type of relationship. We can also assume a relationship between any two variables and then base a forecast of one on the values of the other. As an example, consider the situation faced by a large mail-order house. Each day a tremendous amount of mail is received, much of which contains orders that have to be filled. The mailing department has noted over several months that the number of orders to be filled seems to be related to the weight of the mail. They feel that it would be extremely useful to them if they could weigh the mail when it arrives in the morning, use that weight to predict the number of orders that will have to be filled that day, and thus help to schedule the time of the people who will fill those orders. As a first step in determining whether such a relationship exists, they have kept a record over several days of the weight of the mail each day and the corresponding number of orders (see Figure 5-2). These pairs of values can then be plotted on a graph, in which a trend relationship between the weight of the mail and the number of orders is made clear. In this situation the department could approximate this relationship with a straight line. Then, when they receive a certain number of pounds of mail, they could use that straight line to forecast the number of orders. This procedure assumes a *causal* model or relationship between weight and the number of orders. The method we shall examine for obtaining the most appropriate straight line is simple regression.

In the use of simple regression the starting point is the assumption that a basic relationship exists between two variables and can be represented as a straight line. Mathematically, it can be written as

$$Y = f(X),$$

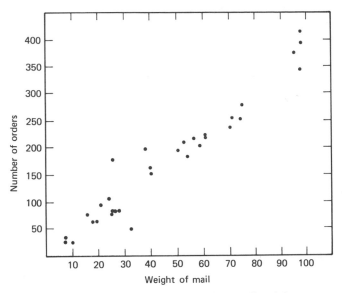

Figure 5-2   Projecting the number of orders based on mail weight.

which simply says that the value of Y is a function of (or depends on) the value of X. In simple regression this is a straight-line relationship, and therefore the mathematical function can be written as

$$Y = a + bX.$$

Since this is the general form of any linear relationship, it is important that the reader understand just what this means. Suppose that the value of X is zero. In such a case Y would have the value a. Thus a is the point at which the straight line intersects the Y axis. If we refer again to Figure 5-2, this would mean that when the weight is 0 pounds the number of orders would have the value of a, which we would reason to be 0, since if no mail is received no orders are received (by mail). The value of b in this equation is called the regression coefficient and indicates how much the value of Y changes when the value of X changes one unit. Thus, if we are comparing the number of orders in 40 and 41 pounds of mail, we would expect an increase of b orders in the 41-pound case. Another term used to refer to this regression coefficient b is that it is the slope of the line. In the next section we discuss exactly how the values of a and b can be determined for a situation like the mail-order example. Before doing so, however, it would be useful to discuss briefly the assumptions associated with a linear relationship between two variables.

In many instances the relation between two variables with which the manager is concerned will appear to be linear. In others it may be that although the relationship does not appear to be linear when plotted directly some transformation of one of the variables will result in that new variable having a linear relationship with the other variable. A few simple cases will help to illustrate this point. Consider first a case in which $W = AB^X$. If A and B are constants and W has an exponential rather than a linear relationship with X, we can transform the function to a linear form by taking the logarithm of both sides. By doing this we obtain $\log W = (\log A) + (\log B) \cdot (X)$. If we then let $Y = \log W$, $a = \log A$, and $b = \log B$, we simply have $Y = a + bX$, which is a linear relationship. Thus regression analysis could be used to determine the values of a and b and this equation could be used to forecast the value of Y.

A second example of a nonlinear function (relationship) which can be transformed to a linear one is $W = e^{a+bX}$. If we take the logarithm of both sides, we get $\log W = a + bX$, and letting $Y = \log W$ simply produces $Y = a + bX$. Again this is the standard linear function that we need to apply regression analysis.

As a final example suppose we had two variables, Y and W, whose relationship can be written as $Y = a + b/W$. If we let $X = 1/W$, this equation can be rewritten as $Y = a + bX$.

Thus there are in fact many situations in which simple regression analysis with its assumptions of a linear relationship can be successfully and appropriately applied. There are really two main strengths to its application in forecasting. First is the one we mentioned earlier, which is that causal models can be represented by regression analysis as well as by time-series models. This means that a much greater range of forecasting situations can be handled with regression analysis than with smoothing techniques. Its second strength is that it uses a statistical model, and thus its accuracy can be closely evaluated in terms of statistical measures. Later on in this chapter we shall see just how this can be done. We shall also find several weaknesses in the method of simple regression analysis, including the fact that it is suitable only for linear relationships, it requires a considerable amount of data to produce statistically significant results, and treats all observations of the data as being equal. (Thus it does not give more weight to recent observations as exponential smoothing techniques do.)

DETERMINING THE PARAMETERS OF A STRAIGHT LINE

In the preceding section the notion of a linear relationship that could be represented mathematically as $Y = a + bX$ was presented. Since it often exists in situations in which the manager would like to forecast or estimate some value of a variable, what is needed is a means of approximating the values of a and b. These values are referred to as the *parameters* in the equation for a straight line. Several methods can be used to approximate these parameters. Perhaps the most straightforward technique is to plot the historical observations, as in Figure 5-2 for the mail-order example, and then visually to draw a line that seems to "fit" these points. In the mail-order case the line would begin at 0.0 and pass approximately midway between the historical points. Once this is done the values of the parameters a and b could be read off the graph. Since a is the point at which the line intersects the Y axis, its value would be 0 in this example, and the value of b would be the increase in Y (the number of orders) for a unit (one pound) increase in X.

Although the graphical method seems to work fairly well in this example, we often have several hundred observations that are widely scattered, and thus it is extremely difficult to draw a straight line that in some sense will give the best approximation of the relationship. What is needed is a technique for determining the values of a and b that can be used consistently and give the "best" result. Regression analysis uses such a method, referred to as the method of least squares. To see just how it fits a straight line to historical observations we consider a simple example that includes only four observations,* the values of which are plotted in Figure 5-3. The dependent variable (the item we want to forecast) is the cost of production per unit and the independent variable (the item that determines the cost of production) is the number of units produced. Thus we would like to determine the relation between the cost and the number of units in such a form that when we specify the number of units to be produced we can forecast (estimate) their cost.

The dashed line in Figure 5-3 approximates the straight line whose equation is $Y = a + bX$ and for which we shall determine the values of a and b. We want to determine these values in such a way that the line represents the "best" line for these four points. This can be done using the method of least squares.

The rationale of the method of least squares is that the distance between the actual observations and corresponding points on the line should be minimized. More precisely, the criterion is that the sum of the squared deviations should be made as small as possible in choosing a and b. To see what this involves we consider Figure 5-4, in which the observed values are labeled Y_1, Y_2, Y_3, and Y_4, the deviations (errors) from the regression are labeled e_1, e_2, e_3, and e_4, and the points estimated by the regression line are labeled Y_{1c}, Y_{2c}, Y_{3c}, and Y_{4c}. The latter points are what we would forecast by using the regression line for X values of X_1, X_2, X_3, and X_4, respectively.

*The reader will note later on that in general regression analysis is applied only when several data points are available. Here we have chosen an example with only four data points to keep the arithmetic at a minimum and to allow focus on the concepts.

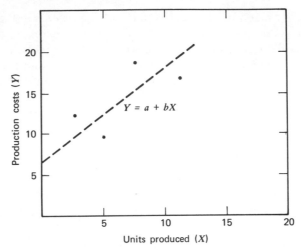

Figure 5-3   Forecasting production costs based on the number of units produced.

In this figure each of the deviations (errors) can be computed as $e_i = Y_i - Y_{ic}$, and each of the values of the regression line can be computed as $Y_{ic} = a + bX_i$. The method of least squares solves for the values of a and b in such a way that the sum of the squared deviations $\Sigma e_i^2 = \Sigma(Y_i - Y_{ic})^2$ is minimized (thus the name least squares) and also such that the summation of the deviations equals 0. The second point simply indicates that the deviations above the line will be exactly offset by the deviations below the line. Using

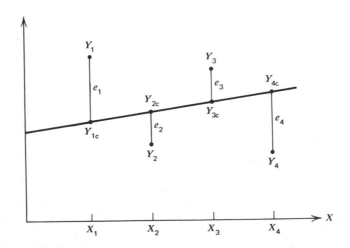

Figure 5-4   Quantities used in the method of least squares.

the requirement that $\Sigma e_i{}^2$ is to be minimized, we can solve for a and b to obtain

$$b = \frac{n\Sigma XY - \Sigma X \Sigma Y}{n\Sigma X^2 - (\Sigma X)^2} \qquad (5\text{-}1)$$

$$a = \frac{\Sigma Y}{n} - \frac{b\Sigma X}{n}, \qquad (5\text{-}2)$$

where n equals the number of observations (data points) to which the line is fitted.

For computational purposes these two equations can be simplified somewhat by using the fact that the mean (average) values of Y and X are, respectively,

$$\bar{Y} = \frac{\Sigma Y}{n}, \qquad \bar{X} = \frac{\Sigma X}{n}.$$

Using these values (5-1) and (5-2) become

$$b = \frac{\Sigma XY - \bar{X}\Sigma Y}{\Sigma X^2 - \bar{X}\Sigma X}, \qquad (5\text{-}3)$$

$$a = \bar{Y} - b\bar{X}. \qquad (5\text{-}4)$$

From (5-3) and (5-4) an additional property of the values of a and b determined by the method of least squares can be seen. This property is that the regression line so determined will pass through the mean value of X and Y (i.e., through the point $\bar{X}, \bar{Y}$). With these properties of the line clearly in mind, the appeal of this technique for determining a and b should be apparent. It ensures that in making a forecast it is equally likely that the actual value will be above the forecast as below it, and most of the actual values will cluster around the line rather than at a considerable distance from it.

To see just how these computations can be made in practice we return to the example given in Figure 5-3. The relevant computations and the resulting equations for the regression line are given below:

Cost Units

Y	X	Y^2	X^2	XY	Y_c	Z	$Y_c - \bar{Y}$
8	3	64	9	24	10.93	−2.93	−1.57
11	2	121	4	22	9.68	1.32	−2.82
16	5	256	25	80	13.04	2.56	.94
15	7	225	49	105	15.05	−.95	3.45
50	17	666	87	231		$\Sigma Z = 0$	$\Sigma(\bar{Y}_c - \bar{Y}) = 0$

$$\overline{Y} = 12.5, \qquad \overline{X} = 4.25,$$

$$b = \frac{n\Sigma XY - \Sigma X \Sigma Y}{n\Sigma X^2 - (\Sigma X)^2} = \frac{4(231) - (50)(17)}{4(87) - (17)^2} = \frac{924 - 850}{348 - 289}$$

$$= \frac{74}{59} = 1.254,$$

$$a = \frac{\Sigma Y}{n} = \frac{b\Sigma X}{n} = 12.5 - 1.254(4.25) = 12.5 - 5.33 = 7.17.$$

Thus $Y_c = 7.17 + 1.254X$.

To illustrate further how the method of least squares can be applied we return to the mail-order example discussed earlier in this chapter. Table 5-1 lists some of the relevant data needed in calculating a and b.

Using (5-3) and (5-4), we obtain

$$b = \frac{\Sigma XY - \overline{X}\Sigma Y}{\Sigma X^2 - \overline{X}\Sigma X} = \frac{338{,}000 - 47.3(5322)}{89{,}593 = 47.3(1420)} = 3.84,$$

$$a = \overline{Y} - b\overline{X} = 177.4 - 3.84(47.3) = -4.36.$$

Thus

$$Y_c = -4.4 + 3.8X.$$

Now, if a manager wants to forecast what the number of orders will be for a given weight of mail, he can do so by using this equation; for example, if the company received 45 pounds of mail, he would estimate that the number of orders Y_c would be

$$Y_c = -4.4 + 3.8(45) = 166.6.$$

The reader will recall that earlier we reasoned that if no mail were received no orders would be received (by mail). If we applied the above equation to the extreme, however, it would say that if no mail were received the company would receive -4.4 orders, which is clearly absurd. This points up the need for applying managerial judgment when using regression analysis results and for identifying a range within which the linear relationship holds but outside of which it has little meaning. In this example the company probably receives several pounds of mail each day unrelated to actual orders, which would explain why on an average more than one pound of mail must be received before any orders are received, as stated by the regression equation.

The versatility and real power of simple regression have been only partly explained so far. Although we have developed the equations necessary to specify the most appropriate straight line, there are two other things with

Table 5-1 Data for Applying the Method of Least Squares in the Mail-Order Example

	1	2	3	4	5
Ob-serva-tion	X Weight of Mail in Pounds	Y Number of Orders	X^2	Y^2	XY
1	70.6591	254.272	4991.3	64654.10	17964.10
2	48.3784	199.311	2340.47	39725.00	9642.35
3	19.8185	64.693	392.77	4185.22	1282.12
4	39.8517	162.644	1588.16	26453.20	6481.65
5	50.127	195.664	2512.71	38284.20	9808.02
6	68.4879	238.021	4690.59	56653.80	16301.50
7	55.7871	219.089	3112.21	48000.00	12222.40
8	96.7574	392.389	9361.99	153969.00	37966.60
9	40.5927	151.125	1647.76	22838.70	6134.55
10	52.7543	210.728	2783.01	44406.30	11116.80
11	7.2491	33.963	52.55	1153.49	246.20
12	73.238	256.993	5363.80	66045.50	18821.70
13	96.3148	347.976	9276.54	121087.00	33515.20
14	18.1598	65.733	329.77	4320.86	1193.70
15	93.50	377.33	8742.26	142378.00	35280.40
16	25.4237	83.491	646.36	6804.89	2097.24
17	24.0767	82.211	579.68	6758.64	1979.37
18	74.6311	281.124	5569.80	79030.70	20980.60
19	53.1468	180.763	2824.58	32675.20	9606.97
20	28.5609	86.153	815.72	7422.41	2460.62
21	10.5201	23.890	110.67	570.74	251.32
22	21.1329	98.291	446.59	9661.13	2077.17
23	58.9518	206.03	3475.31	42448.50	12145.90
24	60.6061	221.245	3673.10	48949.40	13408.80
25	24.4888	105.029	599.70	11031.00	2572.03
26	16.7616	77.943	280.95	6075.26	1306.47
27	7.6762	24.240	58.92	587.62	186.08
28	60.8193	224.298	3698.99	50309.60	13641.70
29	94.3726	369.987	8906.18	136891.00	34916.60
30	26.8395	88.626	720.35	7854.70	2378.70

$\Sigma X = 1419.6$, $\quad \Sigma Y = 5322.0$ $\quad \Sigma X^2 = 89592.9$ $\quad \Sigma Y^2 = 1,281,220$ $\quad \Sigma XY = 337,987$

$$\bar{X} = \frac{1419.6}{30} \qquad \bar{Y} = \frac{5322.0}{30}$$

$$= 47.3. \qquad = 177.4.$$

which we need to be concerned. The first, which is discussed in the next section, is the reliability of the forecasts based on a given regression line; for example, if this forecasting method indicates in the mail-order example that the number of orders will be 166.6, how certain can the manager be that the actual number of orders will not be significantly more or less than that estimate? A second type of situation with which the manager may be concerned is one in which it is not appropriate to say that one of the variables is *dependent* on the other because no causal relationship can be explained. It may be, however, that the movement of one of the two variables is generally accompanied by movement in the other. The calculation of the correlation coefficient which is discussed in a later section can be used to determine the nature of this relationship between the two variables.

THE ACCURACY AND SIGNIFICANCE OF A REGRESSION EQUATION

To determine the accuracy of a regression equation we could treat this forecasting technique as nonstatistical and compute the mean absolute deviation and the mean square error just as we did for the smoothing techniques and adaptive filtering. Doing so, however, would ignore the real power of the method of regression analysis. As stated earlier, regression analysis is a statistical model, and thus it is possible to make statistical statements about the accuracy and significance of regressions. The use of these statistical properties will also allow us to make statements about the likelihood that future values will vary from the forecast by certain amounts, the confidence that we can place in having determined the most appropriate straight line, and the accuracy of the coefficients a and b.

Several questions concerning the significance of an application of regression analysis can be dealt with in statistical terms. We consider three of them at this point:

1. Is the regression coefficient b, significantly different than 0, or did it just occur by chance?

2. What level of confidence can be placed in the regression coefficient b? Within what range around b can the manager be confident that the true value of b is within that range?

3. How confident can the manager be when he makes a forecast of Y that the actual value of Y will lie within a narrow range surrounding that forecast value?

Turning first to the question of the significance of the regression coefficient b, we should like to know whether the true value of b is really different from 0. Since we have estimated the value of b on the basis of a limited number of observations, we might have found a value different from 0 merely by chance. Thus what we should like to do, using statistics, is to say: If we suppose that the true value of b is 0, what is the likelihood (or chance) that we could have had our specific value of b.

The statistic needed in order to determine the significance (or lack of significance) of a regression coefficient is the standard error of that coefficient. This can be computed using (5-5).

$$SE_b = \frac{\sqrt{\Sigma(Y_i - \bar{Y})^2/(n-2)}}{\sqrt{\Sigma(X_i - \bar{X})^2}}.$$ (5-5)

The numerator in this equation is simply the standard deviation of our sample data and the denominator is the square root of the sum of the squared deviations of X from the mean $\bar{X}$. Because there is a lot of arithmetic involved in computing SE_b, the standard error of b, this computation is usually done as an integral part of a computer program. To see how this standard error can be applied in practice, we can compute it for the mail order example:

$$SE_b = \frac{\sqrt{\Sigma(Y_i - \bar{Y})^2/(n-2)}}{\sqrt{\Sigma(X_i - \bar{X})^2}}$$

$$= \frac{14.63}{149.8} = .098$$

Knowing now that the value of one standard error for the regression coefficient b in this example is .098, we can compute the number of standard errors our value of b is from zero. Since $b = 3.84$, we divide 3.84 by .098 and obtain 40. Thus the b value we computed is approximately 40 standard errors from 0. Using a table of normal probability values, we find that the likelihood of computing a regression coefficient in error by 40 standard errors or more is 0. Thus we can conclude with 100% certainty that the regression coefficient is significantly different than 0 in this case.

Generally speaking, we can consider that when the computed regression coefficient in a situation in which at least five observations have been used is three or more standard errors from 0, the regression coefficient is in fact significantly different than 0. Thus in this procedure we first compute the standard error of the regression coefficient [using (5-5)] and then determine how many standard errors the computed regression coefficient is from 0. If it is more than three standard errors from 0 and at least five observations were used in computing the regression coefficient ($n \geq 5$), we can conclude that the regression coefficient is significantly different than 0. If it is not significantly different than 0, we can try to obtain additional data points and recompute the regression analysis or simply conclude that no trend exists and treat it as a horizontal pattern.

A second test of significance determines a confidence interval for the regression coefficient. The 95% confidence interval would be the range within which the manager is 95% certain that the true value of the regression coefficient will be found. Thus in the mail-order example in which we computed the regression coefficient as having a value of 3.84 we should like to know the range around the value wherein we would be 95% certain of finding the true value of the regression coefficient. Although the exact method is beyond the scope of this book, it can be approximated: the true value of the regression coefficient equals $b \pm 2$ times the standard error of estimate (when the sample size—the number of observations—exceeds 15) and the true value of the regression coefficient equals $b \pm 3$ times the standard error of the regression coefficient when the number of observations is between 5 and 15. This merely says that if we take a range of values in which the width of that range is determined by the number of observations and the standard error of the regression coefficient [which can be computed by using (5-5)], we can be 95% certain that the true value of the regression coefficient will fall within that range.

We can apply this procedure to the mail-order example. Above, we found that the standard error of the regression coefficient had a value of .098. Since the number of observations is greater than 15, we can be 95% certain that the true value of the regression coefficient will fall in the range of 3.84 ± 2 (.098). In other words, we can say confidently that the true value of the regression coefficient is between 3.65 and 4.03.

The final point that we deal with here is the significance of an individual forecast. What we would like to know is, once we have found the values of a and b in our regression equation and have substituted a value of X into that equation, how confident can we be that the true value of Y will be close to the value computed with $Y = a + bX$. Again what we would like is a confidence interval around this computed value of Y.

The basis for computing the confidence interval of a specific forecast value is the standard error of forecast (SE_f), which can be computed by using

$$SE_f = \left[\frac{\Sigma(Y_i - \bar{Y})^2}{n - 2} \right]^{1/2} \left[1 + \frac{1}{n} + \frac{(X_i - \bar{X})^2}{\Sigma(X_i - \bar{X})^2} \right]^{1/2}. \qquad (5\text{-}6)$$

As with the standard error of the regression coefficient SE_b, it can be seen that the first term in (5-6) is simply the standard deviation for the sample data. The second term is then an adjustment for how far we are from $\bar{X}$ in making our forecast (i.e., the difference between X_i and $\bar{X}$) and the number of observations n used in determining the regression equation. Note that if X_i is close to the mean $\overline{X}$ and n is large the second term in (5-6) is approximately equal to 1 and the standard error of forecast SE_f is simply the standard deviation of the data. If, however, n is small or if the point being forecast is some distance from $\overline{X}$, the second term in (5-6) will be greater than 1 and the standard error of forecast will be much larger than the standard deviation.

In the forecast we made earlier the value of X was 45 pounds. Thus we can substitute this value for X_i into (5-6) and obtain

$$SE_f = 14.6 \left[1 + .03 + \frac{(45 - 47.3)^2}{22,446} \right]^{1/2}$$

$$= 14.6 \, (1.03) = 14.9.$$

In this example there is little adjustment in the standard deviation value of 14.6 because X is close to the mean value $\overline{X}$. This means that the 95% confidence interval for our estimate of Y [where we had $Y_c = -4.4 + 3.8(45) = 166.6$] will be $166.6 \pm (2) \, (14.9)$. Thus we are 95% certain that the value of Y will be between 136.8 and 196.4 when we receive 45 pounds of mail.

The fact that the confidence interval surrounding a forecast varies according to the distance we are from $\overline{X}$ is shown in Figure 5-5.

From the mail-order example the tremendous amount of information that can be obtained from making these tests of significance should be evident. In

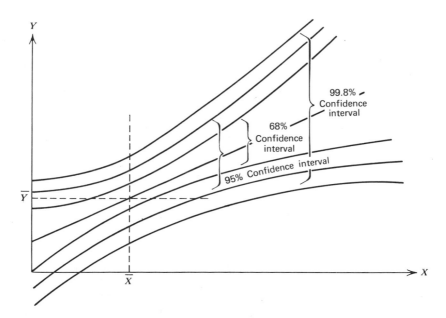

Figure 5-5   Ranges of confidence of individual forecasts.

this instance we found that the regression coefficient was significantly different than 0 and that its true value would lie between 3.65 and 4.03. In addition, we found that in estimating the number of orders included in 45 pounds of mail we could be 95% sure that the orders would be between 136.8 and 196.4. Since this is a wide range, it would reduce the reliance that we would place on the single point forecast of 166.6.

One point that deserves special emphasis in concluding this section on significance is the role that the sample size plays in this area. (The sample size is simply the number of observations used in determining the regression line.) As the sample size becomes larger the range of the confidence interval needed to be 95% sure that the true value lies in that interval becomes much smaller. Thus, if we had 100 observations in the mail-order example, the confidence interval on a specific forecast (e.g., for 45 pounds of mail) would be much narrower than it was when we had only 30 observations. Thus any time the manager can obtain additional observations before computing a regression line he is well advised to do so.

In evaluating the applicability of regression analysis, as opposed to alternative forecasting techniques, this need for a considerable amount of data must be weighted against the benefits of a statistical model. One of the advantages of simple regression analysis is that once the relationship $Y = a + bX$ has been determined it can be used to make any number of forecasts simply by inserting the value of X for which a forecast is desired. The one caution that is necessary is a periodic assessment of the basic relationship. If the manager has some reason to believe that a change may have taken place, it will be necessary to collect a new set of data and recompute the values of a and b.

The majority of the costs associated with simple regression deal with the data collection phase and the computation of a and b. Once that has been done, it is necessary only to store the two values a and b to be able to prepare a forecast on a regular basis.

Because the development costs of regression are substantial, this technique is generally used when only a few items have to be forecast and when the value of that forecast is substantial. Examples are forecasting the corporate growth rate, a company's annual sales, a company's earnings per share, and the index of industrial production. These situations can be contrasted with those most suitable for smoothing techniques that involved forecasts of hundreds or even thousands of items and for which the value of forecasting each item was quite low.

To make the technique of regression analysis truly applicable most companies have found it necessary to have a staff member who is comfortable with statistical methods. It is clear that managers can easily understand the concept of fitting a straight line to past data to obtain either a times series or a causal relationship. They can also work effectively with the concepts of significance, but the actual computation of the standard errors and application of the equations for finding the values of a and b, are tasks that can generally be best performed by a member of the statistical staff.

SIMPLE CORRELATION

The assumption made in the three preceding sections which dealt with simple regression is that one variable is dependent on another. It often occurs that two variables may be related, but it is not appropriate to say that the value of one of the variables depends on or is caused by the value of the other. In such a situation a weaker relationship can be stated, which is that the variables are correlated. The coefficient of correlation r is a relative measure of such a relationship between two variables. This coefficient can vary from 0 (which indicates no correlation) to ± 1 (which indicates perfect correlation). When the correlation coefficient is greater than 0, the two variables are said to be positively correlated; when it is less than 0, they are said to be negatively correlated. The sign of the correlation coefficient is always the same as the sign of the regression coefficient b, assuming that a regression line has been fitted to past observations.

To understand the meaning of the coefficient of correlation we return to Figure 5-4 but we add one element. Figure 5-6 shows this revision. The addition is merely a line representing the mean Y value.

In terms of Figure 5-6 the coefficient of correlation r is simply the square root of the explained variation from $\overline{Y}$ over the total variation. This can be written mathematically as

$$r^2 = \frac{\text{explained variation}}{\text{total variation}} = \frac{\Sigma(Y_c - \overline{Y})^2}{\Sigma(Y - \overline{Y})^2}. \tag{5-7}$$

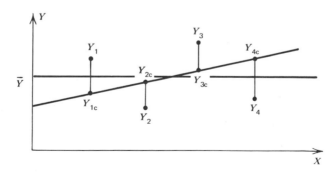

Figure 5-6 The deviations used in computing the coefficient of correlation.

Figure 5-6 shows that the total variation for each observation can be represented as the difference between the mean Y value $\bar{Y}$ and the actual value Y_i. To get the total variation of a sample we simply square these individual variations and add them together. Thus in Figure 5-6 the total variation is $(Y_1 - \bar{Y})^2 + (Y_2 - \bar{Y})^2 + (Y_3 - \bar{Y})^2 + (Y_4 - \bar{Y})^2$.

The explained variation is simply the amount of the total variation explained by the regression line. Thus it is the computed value of Y less the mean value of Y. Again these variations must be squared and summed to get the total explained variation for the sample. In Figure 5-6 the explained variation is $(Y_{1c} - \bar{Y})^2 + (Y_{2c} - \bar{Y})^2 + (Y_{3c} - \bar{Y})^2 + (Y_{4c} - \bar{Y})^2$.

Referring to (5-7) we can see that the correlation coefficient will be 0 only when the computed values of Y are exactly equal to the mean value of Y. This will occur only when the explained variation is 0. Conversely, the coefficient of correlation will be 1 (or -1) only when the explained variation equals the total variation or, in other words, when the computed value of Y equals the actual value of Y for every data point.

We can now return to the simple example given in Figure 5-3 which involves only four points. For this example we can compute the correlation coefficient by using (5-7)

$$r^2 = \frac{\Sigma(Y_{ic} - \bar{Y})^2}{\Sigma(Y_i - \bar{Y})^2}$$

$$= .566$$

and

$$r = .753.$$

In using the concept of the correlation coefficient, the manager should be aware of two major pitfalls. The first can be easily demonstrated by the example in which there are four observations and in which the coefficient of correlation had a value of .753. Oftentimes this could be misinterpreted to mean that the variable X and Y are highly correlated. Such a statement is not really warranted in this instance because only four observations were included in the sample. If a much greater number of observations such as 25 or 50 had been involved and if the correlation coefficient had had the same value, it would have been much more meaningful (significant). This idea of significance is discussed further below. A second point that should be kept in mind is that it is the square of the coefficient of correlation that is the ratio of the explained variation to the total variation. Thus in this example the value of $r^2 = .566$ indicates that 56.6% of the total variation is explained by a straight line fitted to the four observations. Note that this is much less explaining than would be imagined if they had misinterpreted the results from calculating the correlation coefficient. The term generally used in referring to the square of the coefficient of correlation is the *coefficient of determination*.

Let us now compute the coefficient of correlation and the coefficient of determination for the mail-order example in the preceding sections. Again this can be done with (5-7):

$$r^2 = \frac{\Sigma(Y_{ic} - \bar{Y})^2}{\Sigma(Y_i - \bar{Y})^2}$$

and

$$r^2 = .98$$

The appropriate interpretation here is that for the 30 sample observations that were used in fitting the regression line to these observations 98% of the variation from the mean value of Y was explained by that regression line. Now in order to generalize and say how significant that is it is necessary to develop an appropriate test of significance. The one most generally used compares the explained *variance* and the unexplained *variance*. (Note that this is not variation but variance.) The ratio of these two variances is what is called the F-statistic and can be expressed mathematically by

$$F = \frac{\Sigma(Y_c - \bar{Y})^2/(k - 1)}{\Sigma(Y - Y_c)^2/(n - k)}, \tag{5-8}$$

where n = the sample size (number of observations),
k = the number of variables (k is 2 for simple correlation).

It should be readily apparent from (5-8) that the value of the F-statistic is largely dependent on the value of n, the sample size. As n gets larger, the number in the denominator in the F-statistic gets smaller and thus the F-statistic increases in value.

We can now compute the F-test for the mail-order example:

$$F = \frac{\Sigma(Y_c - \bar{Y})^2/(k - 1)}{\Sigma(Y - Y_c)^2/(n - k)} = \frac{808/1}{14.63/28}$$

$$= 1540.$$

This value of F must be compared with the appropriate entry in a table of values of the F-test to determine whether it is significant at the 95% level. Since a complete explanation of this procedure is beyond the scope of this book, it can be approximated by saying that when the number of observations (sample size) is between 6 and 10 the value of F must be greater than 6 in order to be significant at the 95% level, and if the number of observations is greater than 10 the value of F must be greater than 5 to be significant at this 95% level. In our case, since the value of F is greater than 5 (we have 30 observations), we can be more than 95% certain that there is a positive correlation between the weight of the mail and the number of orders and that the coefficient of determination of .98 did not occur by chance.

Let us now determine the significance of the correlation we computed for the simple example of four data points. The reader will recall that we found that $r^2 = .566$, or 56.6% of the variation was explained. Using (5-8) we can compute the F statistic for this example as

$$F = \frac{23.2/1}{17.8/2} = 2.61.$$

To determine whether the correlation of .566 is significantly different than zero we have to compare this F-value of 2.61 with the rule outlined above. The rule was that if we had fewer than five observations the F-statistic had to be greater than 10 to be significant at the 95% level. Thus in this example, even though $r^2 = .566$, we *cannot* say with any confidence that it is significantly different than 0.

The importance of computing the significance of the coefficient of correlation and coefficient of determination in a given situation cannot be over-emphasized. It is only when the manager can say that it is significant that it makes sense to extrapolate the results to a forecast; that is, if the sample size is so small or the relationship so weak that it is not significant, even though the coefficient of determination may be close to 1, the manager should not base his forecast on that data and on the corresponding regression line.

THE REGRESSION EQUATION AS A MODEL

The regression equation $Y = a + bX$, like any other form of equation, can be thought of as an abstract model that represents some aspect of reality. When, for example, we say that Y represents the sales and X represents time, what we are actually doing is making an abstract model. We try to simplify reality and represent it in terms of the interaction of two factors only. As managers are well aware, however, this is a gross simplification, since reality is much more complex. Sales are not influenced only by time but by myriad other factors such as GNP, prices, competitors' actions, transportation costs, production costs, advertising, government policies, or even the illness of a salesman. Then how can we ignore them?

In any modeling effort there is a choice. We can either construct a simple model which may not completely duplicate reality or we can build a highly sophisticated and complex model which can be accurate but which also requires a large amount of effort and resources to be developed and manipulated. Even if the most sophisticated model could be developed, there would still be some part of reality that could not be explained by the model. The number of factors in real-life phenomena is infinite.

To consider the fact that a part of the real process cannot and will not be explained by a regression model we can use the term u which denotes the variations unexplained by the model. This term is often called the disturbance term, white-noise, or residual, and it plays an important role in most forecasting methods.

Actually our simple regression equation is not $Y = a + bX$, but $Y = a + bX + u$, even though the term u is seldom needed for calculation or any other practical purpose. Its theoretical meaning is that the forecast can vary from the mean value of $Y = a + bX$ by an amount u, which we can estimate in probabilistic terms as we learned in the preceding sections of this chapter. It becomes obvious, however, that the magnitude of u will vary from model to model. In general, the more variables we introduce, the smaller the range of values taken on by u. (Multiple regression is in general more accurate than simple regression because it can handle more than one independent variable.) There is a limit, however, to the number of variables we can employ, since they introduce more complexity and higher cost. Thus we have to try to introduce the smallest number of variables (the principle of parsimony) and at the same time achieve a range of values for u as small as possible.

For the regression equation $Y = a + bX + u$ to be statistically correct u must have the following properties:

1. The mean value of u must be equal to zero. This is derived from the fact that a great number of factors influence Y but are not included in the regression equation, whose influence is of opposite directions; they also tend to offset one another on the average.

2. The error term u must be a random variable. At every time period some of the factors not included in the equation will influence Y more than others. This may result in a positive or negative u. However, as long as the individual values of u at each time period are random (not the result of any systematic pattern), their effect on the mean value of Y can be estimated probabilistically.

3. The disturbance term u must be normally distributed. This is a consequence of the large number of factors that influence Y and are not included in the regression equation. As in many other cases, it will be more probable that extreme variations will cancel themselves out and thus be observed only infrequently, whereas in the majority of cases the deviations will be around the mean value. Such a pattern results on a normal distribution.

4. The variance of u must be constant. This means that the error term must neither increase nor decrease within the entire range of observations.

Violations in these properties of u can result in serious trouble, since the complete regression model,

$$Y = a + bX + u$$

will no longer be correct. As we shall see in Chapter 7, however, there are ways of making sure that none of these properties is violated in a specific application.

From now on, as we have done before, we imply $Y = a + bX + u$ when we write a regression equation even though u will not be included. The same is true for multiple regression in which

$$Y = a + b_1X_1 + b_2X_2 + b_3X_3 + \cdots + b_nX_n$$

will also imply inclusion of the error term u.

SUGGESTED REFERENCES FOR ADDITIONAL STUDY

Johnson, J., *Econometric Methods*, 1966, Prentice-Hall, Englewood Cliffs, New Jersey.

Klein, L. R., 1968. *An Introduction to Econometrics*, Prentice-Hall, Englewood Cliffs, New Jersey.

Spurr, W. A., and C. P. Bonini, 1967. *Statistical Analysis for Business Decisions*, Irwin, Homewood, Illinois.

CHAPTER 6

THE CLASSICAL DECOMPOSITION METHOD OF TIME SERIES FORECASTING

Each of the forecasting methods outlined in the preceding chapters is based on the notion that historical values of a time series represent some basic underlying pattern and random fluctuations. These forecasting techniques attempt to distinguish the underlying pattern from the randomness so that the pattern can be projected into the future and used as the basis of a forecast. For the methods discussed so far—moving averages, exponential smoothing, adaptive filtering, and simple linear regression—no attempt has been made to distinguish subparts of that basic underlying pattern. In many instances, however, the pattern could be broken down (decomposed) into two or more factors.

A situation in which this "decomposition" is particularly attractive to the manager occurs when some type of seasonal pattern exists in his data; for example, a retail clothing manufacturer may find that his sales exhibit a strong upsurge toward the end of each calendar year and also in the early spring. These increases may be in addition to any regular growth in the annual level of sales. Many other time series also exhibit seasonal patterns either because of their dependence on the weather or the school cycle or for some other reason.

In many of these situations it would be helpful for the manager to know just what portion of his sales for a given month (or any other time period) reflect an overall increase or decrease in demand and what portion simply represents a seasonal fluctuation.

As we examine these factors in more detail, the usefulness of making such a decomposition of the basic underlying pattern will become more apparent.

Historically, the decomposition method of time-series forecasting has tried to identify three separate portions of the basic underlying pattern: the *trend factor*, a *cyclical factor* and a *seasonal factor*. The trend simply amounts to the long-run linear projection for the series. This long-run projection is usually assumed to be a straight line that eliminates all random fluctuations due to seasonal and cyclical factors.

The cyclical factor in a series is one that might commonly be found in the demand for agricultural products, new housing starts, and even for things such as changes in the prime interest rate. This cyclical factor generally follows the pattern of a wave, passing from a high to a low value and back to a high value.

Finally, the seasonal factor relates to the annual fluctuation (or a fluctuation over some other set time period) in the basic underlying pattern. This third component, the seasonal factor, is one that repeats every 12 months or perhaps every seven days, whereas the cyclical factor is one that repeats over some longer period of time—perhaps three to five years. Depending on the actual data and the variable being forecast, the decision maker may have no reason to believe that a cyclical pattern exists and thus may wish to use only a basic trend and a seasonal factor.

Whether the manager chooses to decompose the basic pattern into two or three separate factors, it must always be remembered that some element of randomness u will always be present. When a pattern is decomposed into three factors, the mathematical form used to represent this decomposition is

$$S = T \times C \times I + u,$$

where T equals the trend factor, C equals the cyclical factor, I equals the seasonal index, u equals the randomness, and S is the forecast. When no cyclical factor is included, the general form is

$$S = T \times I + u.$$

IDENTIFYING THE DIFFERENT FACTORS IN THE PATTERN

To see just how the decomposition method of forecasting can be developed and used it would be helpful to examine a specific example in detail. Consider the situation in which unemployment insurance claims within a county are to be forecast. This problem is of particular interest to state budgeters because they are concerned with both the total amount of funds required for unemployment insurance and the pattern in the claims being made. An understanding of these patterns would be of interest not only in forecasting future claims but also in identifying changes in the basic pattern that may call for legislative or administrative action. The basic data used in this example is that presented in Table 6-1.

In the first step in an analysis of this historical data we determine the factors that should be included in the decomposition. A look at Table 6-1 suggests that a seasonal factor is present which reaches a peak in December or January and has a low point in August or September. Thus the decision maker would want to compute at least a seasonal factor. In addition, it also appears that an increasing trend is present, since the 1971 values seem to be substantially higher than the 1967 values. In relation to a cyclical factor it is hard to tell whether or not one is present, but let us assume that the individual making the forecast feels that one could be present and thus would like to compute it anyway. (If it turns out that the cyclical factor is negligible, it can be dropped before making the forecasts.)

In the procedure for applying the decomposition technique of time-series forecasting we first determine the seasonal factor present. This can be done by computing a 12-month *moving average* for the historical data for each month and then taking the ratio of the actual monthly value to the moving average value and finally the average of these ratios to obtain a seasonal index for each of the 12 months. The rationale behind this set of computations can best be explained once they have been made. Table 6-2 shows the computations of the 12-month moving average and the ratios formed. It should be noted in this table that the moving average has been placed opposite the seventh month in the average; that is, the average of 217 shown for July

Table 6-1   Unemployment Insurance Claims on State Programs (1967-1971)

	Weekly Average Number of Claims (in 000's)				
	1967	1968	1969	1970	1971
January	236	416	356	307	340
February	184	335	257	250	251
March	179	303	216	213	214
April	190	328	238	234	250
May	186	292	205	216	218
June	182	289	202	205	220
July	213	303	228	254	276
August	189	263	189	182	191
September	186	255	163	190	246
October	209	262	278	181	259
November	296	271	211	221	320
December	351	315	270	293	445

Table 6-2 Moving Averages and Ratios for Unemployment Insurance Claims

Year and Month		Number of Claims (Figure 6-1)[a]	Twelve-Month Moving Average	Ratio of Actual to Moving Average
1967	January	236		
	February	184		
	March	179		
	April	190		
	May	186		
	June	182		
	July	213	217	98.2
	August	189	232	81.5
	September	186	244	76.2
	October	209	251	83.2
	November	296	266	111.3
	December	351	275	127.6
1968	January	416	284	146.7
	February	335	291	115.1
	March	303	298	111.7
	April	328	303	108.3
	May	292	313	93.3
	June	289	306	94.9
	July	303	303	100.0
	August	283	298	88.3
	September	255	291	87.6
	October	262	284	92.3
	November	271	276	98.2
	December	315	269	113.4
1969	January	356	262	135.9
	February	257	256	100.0
	March	216	250	86.4
	April	238	242	98.3
	May	205	236	98.7
	June	202	231	87.4
	July	228	227	100.0
	August	189	223	84.8
	September	163	222	73.4
	October	187	222	84.2
	November	211	222	95.0
	December	270	223	121.1

(*Continued*)

Table 6-2 (Continued)

Year and Month		Number of Claims (Figure 6-1)[a]	Twelve-Month Moving Average	Ratio of Actual to Moving Average
1970	January	307	223	137.7
	February	250	225	111.1
	March	213	224	95.1
	April	234	227	103.1
	May	216	226	95.6
	June	205	227	90.3
	July	254	229	110.9
	August	182	231	87.8
	September	190	232	81.9
	October	181	232	78.0
	November	221	233	94.8
	December	293	233	125.7
1971	January	340	235	144.7
	February	251	236	106.4
	March	214	237	90.3
	April	250	242	103.3
	May	218	248	87.9
	June	220	257	85.6
	July	276	269	102.6
	August	191		
	September	246		
	October	259		
	November	320		
	December	445		

[a] In thousands.

1967 (where July is the Seventh month) is based on the 12 monthly values for 1967. The next moving average for August 1967 is based on the values from February 1967 through January 1968, where August is the seventh month in this series of 12 values. Similarly, the rest of the moving averages are centered for the 12 months used in their computations.

Once the moving averages have been computed, the appropriate ratios can be determined. As shown in column 3 of Figure 6-2, these ratios are simply the actual value (column 1) divided by the moving average (column 2).

The ratios in Table 6-2 can now be interpreted. Since a 12-month period was used to compute the moving average, each moving average represents what would happen (on the average) for any one-year period. Thus any deviation that an individual month has from that average represents how much above or below the average the value is for that month. (The ratios can be interpreted as how much above or below the average annual value the individual monthly values are.) Therefore 98.2 for July 1967 indicates that the monthly value was 1.8% below the annual average value. Similarly, for August 1967 the ratio value of 81.5 indicates that the monthly value was 18.5% below the average annual value.

In order to have a seasonal index we should like to know how much above or below the *annual average value* each monthly value will be. Thus, although 98.2 was the ratio for July 1967, in July of 1968 the ratio was 100.0. In July 1969 it was 100.0, in July 1970 it was 110.9, and in July 1971 it was 102.6. This ratio for July varies because of the randomness included in the historical values.

To get an estimate of the monthly index that is somewhat free of these random fluctuations we can average all the July ratios and call that figure our typical ratio for July. This average ratio is commonly referred to as the seasonal index. Table 6-3 shows the computations of these seasonal indices for each month. Note that the average computed is a medial average. This means that the highest and lowest values in the columns have been excluded in computing the average. This is done so that years or months that are extremely unusual will have no overly strong effect on the seasonal index. Thus for the month of July the two extreme values of 98.2 and 110.9 were excluded and the average of the three remaining values (100.0 + 100.0 + 102.6)/3 = 100.9 is used as the unadjusted seasonal index.

The final line in Table 6-3 gives the adjusted seasonal index which represents merely an adjustment of the medial average. This adjustment is simply a division of each medial average by the sum of these averages and is done so that the average seasonal index for the year will be exactly equal to 100.

A full interpretation of the seasonal index can now be given. The index value for each month shows how that monthly value relates to the average annual value. Thus the index for January in Table 6-3 of 137.6 indicates that on the average the January value will be 37.6% higher than the average annual value. Similarly, the September seasonal index of 84.6 indicates that the value for September will generally be 15.4% lower than the average annual value. Clearly, having such a seasonal index is helpful to the manager for purposes of control, since it tells him what fluctuations to expect simply because of seasonal causes; that is if January unemployment insurance claims are 30% above the average annual rate in this example, the manager rather than being irate because of a substantial increase, can tell instead that claims are down about 7.6%, since January claims are normally 37.6% above the annual average.

Table 6-3 Seasonal Index Factors for Unemployment Insurance Claims

Year	January	February	March	April	May	June	July	August	September	October	November	December	Total
1967							98.2	81.5	76.2	83.2	111.3	127.6	
1968	146.7	115.1	111.7	108.3	93.3	94.9	100.0	88.3	87.6	92.3	98.2	113.4	
1969	135.9	100.0	86.4	98.3	87.7	87.4	100.0	84.8	73.4	84.2	95.0	121.1	
1970	137.7	111.1	95.1	103.1	95.6	90.3	110.9	78.8	81.9	78.0	94.8	125.7	
1971	144.7	106.4	90.3	103.3	87.9	85.6	102.6						
Medial average[a]	136.8	108.8	92.7	103.2	90.6	88.9	100.9	83.2	84.1	83.7	96.6	123.4	1192.9
Seasonal index[b]	137.6	109.5	93.3	103.8	91.1	89.4	101.5	83.7	84.6	34.2	97.6	124.1	1200.0

[a] The column average excluding the highest and lowest value.

[b] Adjustment factor $= \dfrac{1200}{1192.9} = 1.0059$.

The second step in the decomposition method of forecasting is to determine the straight line that represents the trend in the data. In one simple way we plot the actual values and then by eye fit a straight line to them. In an easier method we plot a sample of the moving average values and then by visual inspection fit the straight line. This is done in Figure 6–1.

In this particular example it appears that the trend line is a constant horizontal value of approximately 250. This means that there is neither consistent growth nor consistent decline in the historical values.

Although the visual method of approximating a trend line may be satisfactory in many instances, it is often worthwhile to be more accurate and to use a method such as simple linear regression to determine what the trend line is. (This method was explained in detail in Chapter 5.)

At this point the manager could terminate his analysis of the historical data if he did not feel that any cyclical pattern was present. Thus he could base his forecast on

$$\text{forecast} = \text{trend factor} \times \text{seasonal index.}$$

Figure 6-1, however, which plots the moving averages, suggests that there may be some cyclical pattern in addition to the trend and seasonal factors. This can be seen from the fact that the points in Figure 6-1 which represent average values (and thus the seasonal factor is eliminated) seem to follow some pattern over time. If this pattern were a straight line, the trend would seem to explain it all. Similarly, if there were no pattern but the points were scattered randomly around the trend line, again there would seem to be no cyclical pattern. In this case, however, a pattern does seem to be present.

The identification of the cyclical factor is a rather straightforward matter. Starting with the moving average, it will be recalled that since it is a 12-

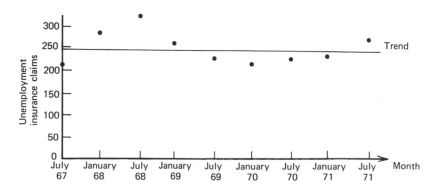

Figure 6-1   Estimating the trend by using moving average values.

month average the seasonal fluctuations have been eliminated. Therefore what we have represented by the moving average is

$$\text{moving average} = \text{cyclical} \times \text{trend}.$$

If the moving average is divided by the trend, what will be left will be the cyclical factor; that is,

$$\frac{\text{moving average}}{\text{trend}} = \frac{\text{cyclical} \times \text{trend}}{\text{trend}}$$

and

$$\text{cyclical} = \frac{\text{moving average}}{\text{trend}}$$

In the example that has been used as an illustration so far in this chapter the computation of the cyclical factor is particularly straightforward, since the trend is constant.* Table 6-4 shows the computed values of the cyclical factors for the historical data.

From Table 6-4 it can be seen that there does appear to be a substantial cyclical factor present in this series of data. It can be seen even more clearly when the cyclical factors are plotted graphically (see Figure 6-2). Although the manager may have trouble giving a clear interpretation of the causes of this cyclical factor, the fact that it does exist may be sufficient motivation for him to include it in his forecasting system. With the analysis of the historical data now complete we can turn to the preparation of a forecast.

PREPARING A FORECAST BASED ON THE DECOMPOSITION METHOD FOR TIME SERIES ANALYSIS

Continuing with the example used in the preceding section, we find that it is now possible to prepare a forecast based on the seasonal index, the trend, and the cyclical factor that have been identified. To illustrate how this is done we can consider the preparation of a forecast for January 1972. Recall first of all that the basic relationship assumed was that

$$S = T \times C \times I + u.$$

Now in preparing a forecast the last term, the randomness, cannot be projected and therefore the relationship for forecasting is simply

$$S = T \times C \times I.$$

---

*If the trend had not been a constant value, it would have been necessary to compute the trend value for each actual value. This could be done by substituting the actual value x_i into the trend line equation $Y_i = a + bx_i$.

Table 6-4 Moving Averages and Cyclical Factors (1967-1971)

Year and Month		Number of Claims[a]	Twelve-Month Moving Average	Cyclical Factor (moving average/ trend) × 100
1967	January	236		
	February	184		
	March	179		
	April	190		
	May	186		
	June	182		
	July	213	217	87
	August	189	232	93
	September	186	244	97
	October	209	251	100
	November	296	266	107
	December	351	275	110
1968	January	416	284	114
	February	335	291	116
	March	303	298	118
	April	328	303	121
	May	292	313	125
	June	289	206	122
	July	303	303	121
	August	263	298	118
	September	255	291	116
	October	262	284	114
	November	271	276	110
	December	315	269	108
1969	January	356	262	105
	February	257	256	103
	March	216	250	100
	April	238	242	97
	May	205	236	95
	June	202	231	93
	July	228	227	91
	August	189	223	89
	September	163	222	89
	October	287	222	89
	November	211	222	89
	December	270	223	89

(Conttnued)

Table 6-4 *(Continued)*

Year and Month		Number of Claims[a]	Twelve-Month Moving Average	Cyclical Factor (moving average/ trend) × 100
1970	January	307	223	89
	February	250	225	90
	March	213	224	90
	April	234	228	91
	May	216	226	91
	June	205	227	91
	July	254	229	92
	August	182	231	92
	September	190	232	93
	October	181	232	93
	November	221	233	93
	December	293	233	93
1971	January	340	235	94
	February	251	236	94
	March	214	237	95
	April	250	242	97
	May	218	248	99
	June	220	257	103
	July	276	269	108
	August	191		
	September	246		
	October	259		
	November	320		
	December	445		

[a] In thousands.

For January 1972 the trend that the manager can expect is 250, since it was found to be constant, and the value of the seasonal index for January from Table 6-3 is 1.376. The value of the cyclical factor for January 1972 is not clearly specified. What the manager must do is estimate what this factor will be. Since this cyclical pattern is fairly smooth (i.e., it does not change radically in a short period of time), the manager's best estimate should not be substantially different from the cyclical factor computed for July 1971 (the most recent one). Looking at the pattern of cyclical factors as well as its most recent value for July 1971, the manager might forecast

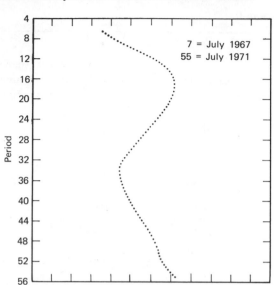

Figure 6-2   Cyclical factors for unemployment insurance claims.

the cyclical factor for January 1972 as 1.10. By using these values of the three factors the forecast for January 1972 would be

$$S = 250 \times 1.10 \times 1.376 = 378$$

We can now summarize the steps that must be followed in applying the decomposition method of forecasting in a management situation. The first three steps involve identification of the seasonal factor, the trend factor, and the cyclical factor. In the final step we apply these three factors in forecasting.

1. Determine the seasonal factor. Start by computing the 12-month moving average for each value and the ratio of that value to the average. Then compute the medial average for each month and adjust it to get the seasonal index for each month.

2. Determine the trend factor. This requires fitting a straight line to the series of moving average values by using either a graphical approach or simple regression. The end product should be values of a and b for the trend equation $Y = a + bx$.

3. Determine the cyclical factor. Since the moving averages have eliminated the seasonal factor, the cyclical factor can be determined for each observed value by dividing the moving average value by the trend value.

4. Forecast for the desired time period. Starting with the time period to be forecast, the seasonal factor for that period can be identified from the adjusted seasonal index, the trend factor can be determined by putting the time period in for x_i in the trend equation, and the cyclical factor can be estimated from the recent pattern in this factor. The forecast is then simply S = seasonal $\times$ trend $\times$ cyclical.

Using these steps, we can prepare a forecast for any month in the future. Again it it should be mentioned that the cyclical factor is the most difficult aspect of this forecasting method with which to work. Perhaps the secret, if there is one, is to have a sufficient amount of historical data so that the manager can see where the cyclical pattern begins to repeat itself. He can then use it as a guide in projecting what it will be for any future time period. Adjustments will undoubtedly still be necessary, however, in order to reflect how the manager thinks the cyclical pattern might change in the future.

To determine the level of accuracy of this forecasting technique we can compute the mean absolute deviation in the forecasts and/or the mean square error. We could do so by using the five years of data that we had in identifying the three basic factors. This would, obviously bias the results, since we would be employing the same data to train the forecasting technique as to evaluate it. It would be much better to use only the first four years of data in determining the seasonal, trend, and cyclical factors and then the fifth year's data to test the accuracy of the forecasts. This has been done in Table 6-5 in relation to the unemployment insurance claims example. This table gives the mean square error for forecasts based on all three factors but also on seasonal and trend factors alone. It can be seen that when the cyclical factor is included much better results can be obtained.

AN EVALUATION OF DECOMPOSITION FORECASTING

The technique of decomposition forecasting that we have been describing in this chapter has found wide acceptance in business because of its intuitive appeal and because it is relatively straightforward to apply. In addition, the notion that the basic pattern of a data series can be decomposed into subparts introduces a degree of sophistication that goes beyond what has been discussed in relation to the forecasting methods presented in Chapters 3, 4, and 5.

Intuitively, this type of breakdown appeals to the manager because it helps to explain why the historical data varies and because it allows him to predict changes in each subpattern separately. These individual subpatterns

Table 6-5 Forecast Errors Applying Decomposition to Unemployment Insurance Claims

	Forecast Obtained with Classical Decomposition Method						
Actual Value (1971)	When Cyclical, Seasonal, and Trend Factors Were Isolated				When Only Seasonal and Trend Factors Were Used		
	Forecast	Error^2	Cyclical	Seasonal	Forecast	Error^2	Seasonal
January $=340$	223	13689	94	141.5	306	1156	131.3
February $=251$	257	36	94	109.0	239	144	103.1
March $=214$	222	64	95	929	214	0	92.2
April $=250$	252	4	97	103.4	231	361	100
May $=218$	225	49	99	90.8	212	36	91.7
June $=220$	230	100	103	89.1	207	169	89.8
July $=276$	274	4	108	101.1	235	1681	102.2
August $=191$	226	1225	108	83.4	199	64	86.8
September $=246$	233	169	110	84.3	199	2209	82.5
October $=259$	233	676	119	83.9	200	3481	87.5
November $=320$	273	2209	112	96.8	239	6561	104.8
December $=445$	354	8281	114	123.7	291	23716	128.1

Sum of squared errors 26,506
Mean square error (MSE)
$\text{MSE} = \Sigma e_i^2/12 = 2208.83$

Sum of squared errors 39,578
$\text{MSE} = \Sigma e_i^2/12 = 3298.16$

are used not only for purposes of forecasting but for management control also.

Unfortunately a number of limitations and disadvantages are associated with the decomposition method of forecasting and are due in part to the type of model encompassed in this technique. First, this method assumes a time-series pattern which means that the only two variables considered are the one being forecast and the independent variable time. This limits the technique because causal relationships cannot be represented.

Perhaps an even greater limitation is that this method is nonstatistical in nature, which means that accuracy can be approximated only by examining forecast errors, as in Table 6-5, rather than by facilitating the development of confidence limits and tests of significance as is possible in statistical methods such as regression analysis. Part of this weakness, however, has been overcome by the development of empirical results based on actual corporate applications rather than theoretical arguments.

In terms of costs most of the expenses associated with decomposition fore-casting are incurred at the development stage rather than in data storage requirements and in actual forecast preparation. Once the seasonal, trend, and cyclical factors have been computed, the preparation of a forecast is a simple and inexpensive matter as long as there is no change in the time-series pattern. But in recomputing the factors following a change or in the initial identification of the factors the costs can be substantial. These costs involve gathering data for at least three years to provide a basis for factor identification and carrying out the actual calculations which can be quite extensive.

Because of these substantial development costs, the decomposition method of forecasting is most often used for situations in which the value of a forecast is high. They can involve either a short or medium time horizon or one of longer term. In most long-term forecasting, however, a general forecast without seasonal adjustments is all that is necessary, and thus decomposition is most useful when medium to short-term forecasts that include seasonality are needed.

In spite of the limitations and drawbacks of decomposition forecasting, many managers have found that the intuitive appeal of this approach is sufficient to make it attractive. This is especially true when some of the improved variations of this method, such as Census II and Foran, which are considered in the next section, are applied. As shown in Chapter 7, however, multiple-regression analysis can handle the same sort of breakdown into three factors, can do it more effectively than decomposition, and can supply statis-tical measures at the same tme. Because of these advantages, many com-panies have been applying it in place of the classical decomposition method of forecasting. Recent results indicate that this preference for regression over decomposition is continuing to grow.

IMPROVED METHODS OF DECOMPOSITION FORECASTING

Because of the tremendous appeal of decomposition techniques of forecast-ing, a number of improved methods have been developed. Although they follow the same basic steps outlined in the preceding sections, the improve-ments made in a couple of them do deserve mention. Here we discuss briefly the techniques known as Census II and Foran.

Census II Method

The Census II method, developed by Julius Shiskin of the United States Census Bureau, has been used widely over the last 20 years by the Bureau, several other government agencies, and recently by many business enter-prises. Census II was introduced in the middle fifties. In principle it is similar to the classical decomposition method, but it contains refinements and elaborations that make the results more accurate. Several users argue that Census II is one of the most powerful forecasting techniques for short and medium term predictions. Indeed the results obtained can be very accurate, and under certain circumstances Census II can even predict forthcoming turning points in a time series.

A computer program of the Census II method, accompanied by instruc-tions on how to use it and interpret the print-outs, can be obtained from the Census Bureau at a minimal charge. The procedure in Census II is the following:

1. The correction of the original data for working- or trading-day differ-ences. This has to be done primarily to monthly data, since the number of working days varies from month to month (and year to year), thus influenc-ing sales or any other variable to be forecast. The adjustment can be done by multiplying the raw data by the ratio of working days or trading days to 21 (W-TD/21).

2. A rough calculation of a seasonal factor by obtaining the ratio of the original data to a 12-month moving average.

3. The elimination of extreme values by the use of statistical control theory (values that are above or below a certain range, plus or minus three standard deviations, are modified or dropped) and the recalculation of refined and final seasonal factors which are projected a year in advance.

4. Irregular movements are identified, smoothed, and printed, and sub-sequently used to forecast.

5. The month-to-month cyclical movements are identified by extracting the seasonal and irregular elements.

6. Graphs and summary measures that pinpoint the importance of each of the components of any time series (seasonal, cyclical, trend, and irregular or random) are provided and clues to forthcoming turning points in the series are identified.

From this description it can be seen that Census II has several advantages over the classical decomposition method, even though they use the same concept of decomposition. The process of Census II is much more refined, it uses more statistical based procedures, and does a much better job in adjusting the seasonal and irregular elements and separating them from the cyclical and trend component of a time series. Census II is intuitive and easily understood by the manager. It can also be manipulated to take into con-sideration special events and the "personal" touch of the decision maker in preparing the final forecast. Finally, it has been tested repeatedly on hundreds of thousands of series and its validity and accuracy of results have been proved, not theoretically (as in sophisticated mathematical methods of forecasting), but empirically. For these reasons Census II is appealing to the manager and is gaining acceptance as a good method for short- and medium-run forecasting.

The Foran System

Another method that deals with time-series decomposition is the Foran system. It was first developed by McLaughlin and later modified by several people. The Foran system has certain advantages over Census II. It can deal with any independent variable (not just time) and is oriented more for forecasting in business organizations in contrast to Census II which is suited more to macroeconomic series and government related data.

The Foran system decomposes a time series into seasonal, cyclical, trend, and irregular elements and provides a summary of the important *contributions* of each of them. Instead of one forecast, it provides the user with a number of alternative forecasts as well as a description of their accuracy over the preceding year and then lets the manager decide which of them (or combination of them) to use for his final prediction. The Foran method extends these forecasts one, two, and three months in advance, and since it can employ any variable as the independent one it allows the user to develop either a causal or a time-series model.

SUGGESTED REFERENCES FOR ADDITIONAL STUDY

Bonini, C., and W. Spurr, 1968. *Statistical Analysis for Business Decisions*, Irwin, Homewood, Illinois.

Freund and Williams, 1969. *Modern Business Statistics*, Prentice Hall, Englewood Cliffs, New Jersey.

Gordon, R. A., *Business Fluctuations*, 1961. Harper, New York.

Hadley, G., 1968. *Introduction to Business Statistics*, Holden-Day, San Francisco.

McLaughlin, R. L., and J. J. Boyle, 1968. *Short Term Forecasting*, American Marketing Association Booklet.

Shiskin, J., "Electronic Computers and Business Indicators," *National Bureau of Economic Research*, Occasional Paper 57.

CHAPTER 7

MULTIPLE REGRESSION AND CORRELATION

In Chapter 5 the techniques of simple regression and simple correlation were introduced and discussed. In simple regression the basic assumptions were that the independent variable could be used to predict the value of some dependent variable (the quantity to be forecast) and that the relation between the two variables was a linear one. In a major example given in that chapter the variable to be forecast was the number of orders received daily by a mail-order house. The independent variable on which that forecast was to be based was the weight of the mail for that day. It often occurs in a decision-making situation that more than one variable can be used to predict or forecast a certain dependent variable; for example, in the mail-order situation it could well be that the number of pieces of mail received as well as their weight could be used to predict the number of orders. In situations in which more than a single independent variable will be used in a causal model simple regression is not adequate. The principles of simple regression can be applied, however, in the technique of multiple regression to allow the manager to consider more than one independent variable in preparing his forecast. This chapter examines the extension and application of the basic principles of simple regression and simple correlation to situations in which several independent variables will affect the outcome of some dependent variable.

The specific example that we are using in this chapter to illustrate the principles and concepts of multiple regression and multiple correlation concerns the forecasting of annual sales for a company in the glass business. Table 7-1 lists some of the historical information that this company, California Plate Glass (CPG), has gathered.

This table not only contains data on the variable, company sales ("Net Sales, CPG"), but also on two other variables, annual automobile produc-

Table 7-1   Historical Data Relating to CPG Sales

Year	Net Sales, CPG (millions of dollars)	Automobile Production (millions)	Building Contracts Awarded (millions)
1953	280.0	3.909	9.43
1954	281.5	5.119	10.36
1955	337.4	6.666	14.50
1956	404.2	5.338	15.75
1957	402.1	4.321	16.78
1958	452.0	6.117	17.44
1959	431.7	5.559	19.77
1960	582.3	7.920	23.76
1961	596.6	5.816	31.61
1962	620.8	6.113	32.17
1963	513.6	4.258	35.09
1964	606.9	5.591	36.42
1965	629.0	6.675	36.58
1966	602.7	5.543	37.14
1967	656.7	6.933	41.30
1968	778.5	7.638	45.62
1969	877.6	7.752	47.38
1970 (est)		6.400	48.51
1971 (est)		7.900	51.23
1972 (est)		8.400	57.47
1973 (est)		8.600	61.03
1974 (est)		8.900	66.25

tion and the annual number of building contracts awarded. The management of CPG believes that its net sales are closely tied to these other two industries, since its major customers are automobile producers and building contractors. We assume that as a part of the planning process top management has asked for a forecast of corporate sales on an annual basis for the next five years.

In the preceding chapters we have examined a number of methods that could be used to prepare this forecast. One would be the technique of exponential smoothing, in which the forecast for one year in advance is based on the results of the preceding year and the preceding smoothed forecast. Unfortunately, with exponential smoothing we would be unable to forecast more than one period ahead. Using the technique of adaptive filtering, we could prepare a forecast based on a weighted sum of the historical observed values for each of the next five years. In doing this we would be assuming that the pattern exhibited by the time series in recent years would continue into the future. A third method would be that of simple regression with which we could develop a causal model that would state that annual sales depend on a single independent variable. We might choose as that independent variable either automobile production or building contracts awarded. In either case we could then forecast each of the next five years, assuming that we have values for the independent variable for each of those years. (The latter values would be forecasts themselves.)

Although the results of exponential smoothing, moving averages, or simple regression analysis may be satisfactory for forecasting sales, it is more likely that management would prefer to utilize the information they have on automobile production and building contracts at the same time; that is, since they know that both factors are important and that they move somewhat independently of each other, they would like to be able to forecast net CPG sales as a function of both automobile production and building contracts awarded. Mathematically such a relationship could be written as

Net sales CPG = f (automobile production, building contracts awarded).

This equation simply states that net sales for the company depend on two independent variables, automobile production and building contracts awarded. Although several different forms of the equation could be written to show the relation between these variables, a straightforward one would be the following:

$$Y = a + b_1X_1 + b_2X_2, \tag{7-1}$$

where Y = CPG annual sales,
    X_1 = annual automobile production,
    X_2 = annual building contracts awarded.

From this equation it can readily be seen that if X_1 or X_2 were eliminated we would have the same problem that we handled with simple linear regression. This situation, in which we have more than one independent variable (X_1 and X_2), is known as multiple regression. Note that the dependent variable (the one we wish to forecast) is linearly related to X_1 and to X_2. Just as we used the method of least squares in Chapter 5 to solve for the coefficients a and b in that equation, we can also use this method here to solve for a, b_1, and b_2. In simple linear regression that method amounted to fitting a straight line to the points in a manner that minimized the sum of the squared errors. We represented that graphically by letting one axis represent Y and the other, X. In the case of two independent variables X_1 and X_2 we need a three-dimensional graph. The situation, however is completely analogous to two dimensions in which we now have three axes, Y, X_1, and X_2, and in which we are trying to fit a straight line to the points located in the three dimensions. We do that by minimizing the sum of the squared deviations from the line.

In general we could have several independent variables and we could still apply the method of least squares to solve for the values of a, b_1, b_2, . . ., b_n. Multiple regression, then, is simply a technique that uses the method of least squares to determine these parameters.

When we move beyond the case of simple regression, the computations and mathematics become quite complicated, although they follow the same basic concepts of simple regression. Because of this complexity, we will not go into the details of applying the method of least squares to compute the values of the parameters. We simply assume that the manager has at his disposal a computer program for multiple regression that will handle all of the calculating for him. This is a valid assumption in most cases, since one generally would not even consider the use of multiple regression unless some kind of computing equipment were available.

THE APPLICATION OF MULTIPLE REGRESSION ANALYSIS

To achieve a better understanding of the concept of multiple regression we can use the data given in Table 7-1 and apply the method of least squares to obtain values for a, b_1, and b_2 in (7-1). In the first step we state just what the problem is and how we want to go about solving it. We assume that the task is to forecast the company's sales for the next five years (1970–1974) and that this forecast will be based in part on the estimated values of automobile production and building contract awards for those years. Since we have a number of historical observations in Table 7-1, we would like to determine values for a, b_1, and b_2 based on these historical values and then use (7-1) to forecast the future values of company sales.

Using this historical information and a multiple regression computer program, we obtain the following results:

$$a = 19.1, \qquad b_1 = 35.7, \qquad b_2 = 10.9.$$

Thus our equation for forecasting company sales can be written as

$$Y = 19.1 + 35.7X_1 + 10.9X_2. \tag{7-2}$$

This simply states that on the basis of our historical observations (1953–1969) the best equation in terms of any linear assumptions is the one we have in (7-2). Some comments can now be made about the interpretation of this equation. Note that the historical values we used in developing the equation were in millions of dollars for net sales, in millions of units for automobile production, and in millions of starts for building contracts.

It is important to remember that the actual values of the parameters depend on the units that we used in developing them. Thus it is incorrect to interpret (7-2) as saying that auto production is much more important than building contracts in determining company sales because 35.7 is much larger than 10.9. If we had used different units for automobile production it could well have turned out that our coefficient for X_1 would have been smaller than our coefficient for X_2. The proper interpretation of the values in (7-2) is that when both X_1 and X_2 are 0, company sales (Y) will have a value of 19.1 million and that when automobile production increases by 1 million units company sales will increase by 35.7 million dollars (other things being held constant). When building contracts awarded increase by 1 million, company sales will increase by 10.9 million dollars (again, other things being held constant). Thus the coefficients in our equation simply tell the manager how changes in each of the variables influence the value of the dependent variable Y.

Once the parameters in our equation have been determined, the equation can be used to forecast the value of annual sales for each of the next five years. We do this by substituting the appropriate values for X_1 and X_2 into this equation. These values for 1970, for example, are 6.4 and 48.51, respectively. Thus our estimate of sales for 1970 would be

$$Y = 19.1 + 35.7(6.4) + 10.9(48.51)$$

$$= 776.3 \ (= \$776,300,000).$$

Similarly the computations for 1971 through 1974 can be made by using the appropriate values for automobile production and building contracts awarded. It should be noted that this approach to forecasting requires that we have estimates of the values of the independent variables (in this case X_1 and X_2). Thus in formulating a multiple-regression equation the manager will want to consider which of the independent variables will provide him with good estimates of future values. The two variables used in this case would seem reasonable, since for economic reasons the country involved would most likely prepare long-range forecasts of those variables to help in general economic planning. The manager must keep in mind that the accuracy of his forecast for annual sales depends in large part on the accuracy of the forecast for building contracts awarded and automobile production. When these independent variables are in error, there is clearly going to be a compounding effect in terms of the annual corporate sales forecast.

A final point that should be mentioned in regard to this example is that the forecast for 1970 was made without first checking the significance of the parameters on which that forecast was to be based. This question of significance will be taken up in a later section.

MULTIPLE CORRELATION AND THE COEFFICIENT OF DETERMINATION

It will be recalled that in simple correlation we could compute a factor called the coefficient of determination which was simply the ratio of the explained variation to the total variation. The same ratio can also be computed in multiple regression, in which again it is the explained variation over the total variation. This coefficient of determination, denoted by R^2, can take on values from 0 to 1, the latter representing a situation in which all the variation is explained. The actual formula for calculating the coefficient of determination in this case is exactly the same as that used for simple regression.

$$R^2 = \frac{\Sigma(Y_c - \overline{Y})^2}{\Sigma(Y - \overline{Y})^2}. \tag{7-3}$$

Returning to the example of the annual sales of the CPG Glass Company, we compute the coefficient of determination, using (7-3), as .976. This means that 97.6% of the variation in annual sales can be explained by the combined variation in automobile production and building contracts awarded.

In multiple regression the correlation coefficient can be computed by taking the square root of the coefficient of determination, much as it was in simple regression. In addition, it is possible to compute the individual coefficient of correlation for *each of the pairs of variables*. Thus a simple correlation coefficient could be computed for company sales and annual automobile production. Another simple correlation coefficient could be computed for annual sales and building contracts awarded. Finally, a correlation coefficient could be computed for annual automobile production and annual building contracts awarded. These three different correlation coefficients are usually referred to as the simple correlations, since they involve only two variables. They are most often represented in a correlation matrix like that shown in Table 7-2.

Table 7-2 Simple Correlation Matrix

	CPG Sales	Automobile Production	Building Contracts
CPG sales	1.00	.56	.99
Auto production	.56	1.00	.53
Building contracts	.99	.53	1.00

The simple correlation matrix is of value to the manager who uses multiple regression because it tells him how the different variables are correlated. Thus most computer programs designed to perform multiple-regression analysis include the computation of the simple correlation matrix. (Later on in this chapter some of the uses of the simple correlation matrix are described.)

TESTS OF SIGNIFICANCE

An important question that must be answered before the results of multiple-regression analysis can be used in forecasting future values is that of significance. The computation of the coefficients in the regression equation is based on the use of a number of historical observations. Subsequently the reliability of forecasts based on that regression equation will depend largely on the number of observations that were used in its development. Thus the question of significance is really one that deals with how reliable the forecasts will be that are based on a multiple regression analysis of a given sample of data.

Although there are many tests of significance, three major ones should be mentioned in connection with multiple regression. The same three tests were discussed in Chapter 5 for simple regression. The first involves testing the significance of the individual coefficients in the regression equation. Essentially, the question is whether the value of each coefficient is significantly different than 0 or whether it simply occurred by chance. This test consists of calculating the amount of variance in each of the coefficients and then using that variance to determine whether the value of the coefficient is significantly different than 0. The actual computation of the amount of variance in each coefficient is generally included in the computer program that performs multiple regression. In most cases these results are given in the form of the standard deviation (which is the square root of the variance) and the t-test for each of the coefficients. This t-test can be used directly to determine the significance of each coefficient. The results of the t-test computations for the CPG sales example are given in Table 7-3. As we can see in this table the t-test is simply the value of the coefficient divided by the standard deviation of that coefficient. Thus it indicates the number of standard deviations that the computed value is from 0. Table 7-3 shows that for a, the constant term in the regression equation, the computed value of 19.1 is only .37 standard deviations from 0. For b_1 and b_2 the number of standard deviations from 0 is much greater, being 3.55 and 11.17 respectively.

The rule for determining whether a coefficient is significantly different than zero at the 95% confidence level is that when the sample size is between

Table 7-3 Tests of Significance of Glass Company Equation

Coefficient	Value	Standard Deviation	t-test (value/standard deviation)
a	19.1	51.9	.37
b_1	35.7	10.1	3.55
b_2	10.9	.97	11.17

5 and 15, the value of the t-test must be greater than 3 to have significance, and when the number of observations in the sample is greater than 15 the t-test must have a value greater than 2 in order to be significant. Thus in Table 7-3 it can be seen that the constant term a is *not* significantly different than 0, whereas both of the coefficients b_1 and b_2 are significantly different than 0. The fact that the value of a, the constant term, is not significantly different than 0 means that, based on statistics, the manager has no reason to assume that the value 19.1 is any more accurate than a constant value of 0. Thus he may choose to rewrite his forecasting equation as

$$Y = 35.7X_1 + 10.9X_2$$

The second test of significance that the manager should be concerned with in using multiple regression is a test that indicates the overall significance in the regression equation. Although the t-test indicates the significance (or lack of significance) of each of the coefficients, we can now discuss a test that indicates the significance (or lack of significance) of the entire regression equation. The test used for this is the F-statistic. (This test was also described in Chapter 5 in connection with the significance of simple regression and correlation.)

The value of the F-statistic is simply the ratio of the explained *variance* over the unexplained *variance*. This can be written mathematically in two equivalent forms:

$$F = \frac{\Sigma(Y_c - \bar{Y})^2/(k - 1)}{\Sigma(Y - Y_c)^2/(n - k)}, \tag{7-4}$$

where k = the number of variables,

$$F = \frac{R^2/(k - 1)}{(1 - R^2)/(n - k)}, \tag{7-5}$$

where R^2 is the coefficient of determination.

Although both forms of this equation give the same numerical value for the F-statistic, (7-5) is generally easier to use because the coefficient of determination (R^2) will normally have been calculated. In the example of the CPG Glass Company we have already computed the coefficient of determination as $R^2 = .976$. Because we used 17 observations in determining the values of our parameters a, b_1, and b_2 and because we have three variables in our regression equation, (7-5) yields

$$F = \frac{.976/(3 - 1)}{(1 - .976)/(17 - 3)} = \frac{.976}{.024}\left(\frac{14}{2}\right)$$

$$= 284.9.$$

For the F-statistic the appropriate decision rule concerning significance at the 95% confidence level is as follows: if the sample size (number of observations) is between 6 and 10, the F-statistic must exceed a value of 6 to be significant, and if the sample size exceeds 10 then the F-statistic must have a value of 5 or greater to indicate significance. In the CPG example the value of the F-statistic is 285, which is well above the cutoff level of 5, and we can therefore conclude that the regression equation is significant.

The final test of significance that the manager may wish to undertake entails calculating the standard error of forecast. This allows him to develop a confidence interval around forecasts based on the regression line. Generally a 95% confidence interval is used. The reader will recall that in Chapter 5 we developed the equation used in computing the standard error of forecast for simple regression. This equation represented the standard deviation of the regression line; an adjustment was made for the sample size and the distance of the point was forecast from the mean value of the independent variable. The standard error of forecast for multiple regression is completely analogous to this, but obviously since two or more independent variables are involved it is difficult to visualize it graphically.

Because of the complexity of computing the standard error of forecast, this measure is generally included in a computer program for multiple-regression analysis. Once the standard error of forecast has been obtained, the manager can use it for developing a confidence interval around any forecast. He can be 95% confident that the actual value will lie within ± 2 standard errors of forecast around the forecast value.

For the California Plate Glass example the standard deviation of the regression line has a value of 40.8. This means that if we wanted to prepare a forecast by using the mean value of automobile production and building contracts awarded we could be 95% confident that the actual value would lie within $+81.6$ units of the forecast value (81.6 equals two times the standard error of forecast). Since we are considering forecasts based on values for automobile sales and building contracts awarded that deviate somewhat from the mean values of these two variables, the interval range of 81.6 units will become larger in order to maintain a 95% confidence level. (It should be noted that the value 81.6 is in terms of millions of dollars, since those are the units we are using for Y.)

With each basic test of significance performed the manager will gain a better understanding of the multiple-regression equation and the level of reliability he can place on the forecasts developed from it. It is the use of these tests of significance that makes statistical methods such as multiple-regression analysis more attractive than the nonstatistical methods such as exponential smoothing.

ASSUMPTIONS INHERENT IN MULTIPLE-REGRESSION ANALYSIS

Four basic assumptions are made each time multiple regression is used in practice. An understanding of these assumptions and the conditions necessary to meet them is important in order that regression analysis may be used wisely and accurately. When these assumptions are not met, the results can be misleading and inaccurate. In this section we discuss briefly each of these assumptions, the means of recognizing possible violations, and the methods of correcting them. Much has been written about the technical aspects of these assumptions, but it is generally beyond the scope of this text. The reader desiring additional information on these four points is referred to the references at the end of this chapter.

The first assumption inherent in the application of the method of least squares is that of linearity. This assumption states that the dependent variable is linearly related to each of the independent variables. As shown in Chapter 5, a number of nonlinear relationships can be transformed into linear ones. Thus this restriction is not nearly so binding in practice as it may appear on the surface. It should be made clear, however, that there is no way of accurately applying regression analysis if the relationships cannot be presented in a linear form.

When the assumption of linearity is not met, the results of regression analysis will generally not be significant (when measured by the statistical tests of significance mentioned in the preceding section), and the coefficient of determination R^2 will generally have a value that is close to 0. The only method of correcting nonlinearity is to transform the variable into a new variable that does exhibit a linear relationship with Y. As a practical step, the manager is usually well advised to graph the relationships between the dependent variable Y and each independent variable X_1 to determine whether the linearity assumption has been met. A separate graph for each pair of variables can easily identify any nonlinearities.

The second basic assumption in regression analysis is that of constant variance of the errors. This is often referred to by the technical name, homoscedasticity. The technical term for the lack of constant variance is referred to as heteroscedasticity. This assumption is simply that the variance and the amount of variation do not change over the range of observations. In other words, the variation remains constant over that range. The lack of constant variance can be recognized by a pattern in the residual values; for example, Figure 7-1a describes the kind of pattern that exists when constant variance is present. Figure 7-1b describes a situation in which the variance increases as the value of the independent variable increases, and thus this assumption is not met. Figure 7-1c presents a different kind of pattern in the variance, but again it is one in which it is not constant over the entire range of values. Thus to meet the assumption of constant variance a pattern like that shown in Figure 7-1a must exist.

The lack of constant variance can be recognized by the presence of a pattern in the residual values. These values are computed as the difference between the forecast value using the regression line and the actual value. If these residuals exhibit a definite pattern either in their size (magnitude) or their sign (plus or minus), a lack of constant variance is generally indi-

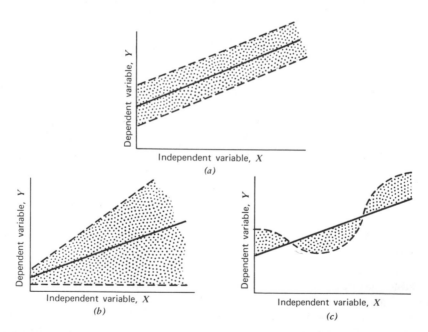

Figure 7-1 Constant variance assumption in regression analysis.

cated. This can be a problem because it leads to regression relationships that are not significant and in which the coefficient of determination R^2 has a value close to zero. In correcting this problem additional variables are introduced or some of the existing variables are transformed. (The lack of constant variance can also be identified by the Durbin-Watson statistic. The test given above, however, will generally suffice in most situations.)

The third basic assumption inherent in regression is that the residuals are independent of one another. This means that each residual value is independent of those values coming before and after it. In technical terms, when this assumption is not met, it is said that serial correlation (or autocorrelation) exists among successive residual values. The means of identifying independence of the residuals include a graphical representation of those values, examining the sign (plus or minus) of the residuals, or computing the Durbin-Watson statistic. Figure 7-1c not only represents the lack of constant variance but it can also be seen that there is a pattern in the residuals in which their signs go from plus to minus and back to plus as the value of the independent variable increases. The Durbin-Watson statistic which can be used to test for the presence of autocorrelation is beyond the scope of this book. In most instances, however, a graphical plotting of the residuals or an examination of their signs can reveal the existence of any pattern in them.

When the residuals are not independent, the implication is that an important independent variable has been omitted in the regression equation. Thus, rather than having the equation explain the basic underlying pattern and letting the residuals represent random errors, those residuals still include part of the basic pattern. Unless that pattern is eliminated from the residuals, the regression equation will not be so accurate as it would otherwise be.

In the procedure for eliminating autocorrelation an additional independent variable is introduced or the functional form of an existing variable is changed. If neither a new variable nor a change of an existing variable can be devised that will eliminate autocorrelation, the method of first differences can be used. Essentially this method finds a new variable that has as its observed value the difference between each subsequent pair of observations originally obtained for that variable. Thus, if a series of observations with values 5, 8, 6, 4, and 7 were observed, the first difference for this set of data would be 3, minus 2, minus 2, and 3. (This is simply the difference between X_i and X_{i+1}.) If the first differences are computed for each of the variables in the regression equation, the regression coefficients can then be recomputed by using those differences as the observed values.

The final basic assumption that the manager needs to consider in applying multiple-regression analysis is that the residuals are normally distributed.

As implied by its name, it assumes that the residual values have a normal distribution. This assumption is generally not restrictive, since the residuals represent the outcome of the larger number of unimportant factors that influence the dependent variable, although each to an insignificant degree. Thus on the average their influence will be canceled out, and it is only in rare instances that they will influence the residuals in the same direction. Thus this randomness creates the exact pattern described by a normal distribution. Generally, if more than 30 observations are used to determine the regression equation, it can be assumed that the residuals have met this assumption.

In the event that this assumption is not met the tests of significance and the confidence intervals developed from them will not apply. Therefore it is of critical importance that the residuals be normally distributed. To determine whether the assumption has been met, we can compare the standard error of regression with the range of values of the residuals divided by six; that is, taking the range of residual values (subtracting the smallest from the largest) and dividing it by six approximates the standard error of estimate. If this approximation is considerably different than the standard error of regression computed (what we have referred to as the standard deviation of the regression line), the residuals may not be normally distributed. The best approach for correcting the violation of this assumption is to increase the number of observations.

One other limitation on the application of multiple regression that should be mentioned is the problem of multicollinearity. Multicollinearity is a computational problem that develops when two or more of the independent variables are highly correlated. Technically the result is a near singular (close to zero) matrix which has the same effect as trying to divide a number by an extremely small number. (You will recall from high school mathematics that dividing a number by zero gives a result of infinity.) Since there is always randomness present, the existence of multicollinearity does not normally result in an answer of infinity but can give a result that is extremely large and cannot be handled by the computer.

The existence of multicollinearity can be recognized by looking at the simple correlation matrix and then choosing only independent variables to be included in the regression equation that are not highly correlated among themselves. Thus the goal is to select independent variables that are highly correlated with Y but are not highly correlated with one another.

In addition to the computational problems presented, multicollinearity also affects the accuracy of the results of regression analysis. One of the problems is that the coefficient of determination (which measures the significance of the regression equation) can be very large, but one or more of the t-tests can be very small, thus indicating that the individual regression coefficients are not significant.

Multicollinearity is a frequent problem in economic and business data because of the high correlation between the different factors, such as population, GNP, personal disposable income, corporate sales, inventory levels, profits, and costs. It is useful to be aware of its existence while actually collecting data so that series that are not highly correlated can be used as independent variables.

USING MULTIPLE REGRESSION ANALYSIS IN PRACTICE

In the preceding sections of this chapter we have talked about the many considerations involved in applying multiple-regression analysis and showed how the technique can be used in a straightforward example. In this section we bring together these different aspects relating to the application of regression analysis by the development of a set of procedures that the manager can use in applying the technique and show how these procedures can be used in a specific situation.

The fact that regression analysis is a forecasting technique based on a causal relationship means that the manager must identify those factors that he thinks influence the variable to be forecast. One of the great advantages of multiple regression over other techniques is that a number of different causal relationships can be hypothesized and tested with little effort when a computer program is available for doing so. Thus the procedure that we outline will really go beyond the formulation of a single regression equation and will describe how in a specific situation a manager might initially hypothesize some causal relationships and by using regression analysis determine the one that will make the best forecast. Seven basic steps are listed and described:

1. Formulation of the Problem. First the manager must state what the problem is and what it is that will be explained or predicted. This formulation should begin with a description of the decision-making situation and an identification of the variable or variables to be forecast rather than with the forecast itself. At the end of the formulation step a number of independent variables should have been identified and the dependent variable to be forecast should have been defined.

2. Choice of Economic and Other Relevant Indicators. Although problem formulation should identify some of the independent variables to be included, it is also necessary to identify further possible causal factors and to determine which of them would be suitable for inclusion in the regression equation. This suitability must be based on the availability of data not only for historical periods but also in the future when the forecast is to be prepared. Some of the factors that are generally relevant include historical data relating to the company's operations and economic series relating to the general economy and the industry.

3. Initial Test Run of Multiple Regression. The initial run should include all the data on the independent and dependent variables. It may also include the testing of a few plausible regression equations in order to observe the results that can be obtained. One of the key outputs of this test run is the simple correlation matrix used in Step 4.

4. Studying the Matrix of Simple Correlation. Economic time series are usually multicollinear; that is, there is a high degree of interdependence among them. Therefore we must make a careful selection of the variables to include in the regression equation. In the majority of cases we cannot use two independent variables whose simple correlation is greater than .7. By studying the simple correlation matrix the manager should try to identify those independent variables that show substantial correlations with the dependent variable, yet show little correlation among themselves. At the end of this phase the manager should have identified three or four regression equations that seem to be promising and can be further tested.

5. Deciding Among Individual Regressions. After obtaining a number of regression equations in phase 4, a computer program should be applied to compute the coefficients of those regression equations based on the data. For each of these regression equations the manager can then consider the significance of the regression coefficients, the entire regression line, and the standard error of forecast. Only equations that are significant for both the regression coefficients and the regression line should be considered beyond this point. Usually the procedure followed is to increase the R^2-value slowly by the introduction of additional independent variables, checking each time to be sure that the tests of significance are still met.

6. Checking the Validity of the Regression Assumptions. Once two or three good equations have been identified, the manager must consider whether they meet the four assumptions outlined in the preceding section. If they are not met, the appropriate steps should be taken to correct them, or additional regression equations must be developed and tested.

7. Preparing a Forecast. Once the manager has found a regression equation that gives a sufficiently high value for R^2 and that meets the assumptions inherent in regression and the tests of significance the manager can use that equation for forecasting. In doing so he should consider the confidence interval for individual forecasts and the accuracy of the values for the independent variable. As we pointed out earlier, most forecasts are based on estimated values of the independent variables rather than actual values. Thus their validity needs to be determined.

As an example of how these steps might be applied to multiple-regression analysis for preparing a forecast, let us consider a company whose marketing manager desires to forecast corporate sales for the coming year. The first step is to determine just why this forecast is needed and how it will be used. We will suppose that the marketing manager wants it for at least three reasons: (a) to supply him with estimates needed as his part in the corporate planning activity; (b) to give him an idea of the kind of staffing requirements he will have in sales and sales service to handle the company's increased sales; and (c) to help in planning budget allocations for advertising, dealer discounts, and so on.

With this initial identification of the problem, the marketing manager might well sit down with the sales manager and others in his marketing organization to determine the factors that might possibly affect the company's sales. Let us suppose that they come up with the following model:

sales $= f$ (personal disposable income, dealers' allowances, prices, research and development expenditures, capital investments, advertising, sales expenses, total industry advertising, random effects).

Clearly, some of these factors will be more important than others in their effect on the company's sales. Since any one of them, however, might have a meaningful impact, it is useful to gather data on all of them at this early stage in the process. Thus the next step is to gather the information on these eight independent variables as well as on the dependent variable, company sales. Table 7-4 presents semiannual data covering the period from 1952 to 1971.

Having collected this data, an initial multiple-regression run can now be made. As a starting point the regression equation

$$Y = a + b_1X_1 + b_2X_2 + \cdots + b_8X_8$$

can be used. This equation contains all eight independent variables, some of which may not be important, but including them all initially gives a good basis for revising multiple-regression equations. The results of applying a computer program by using the above regression equation and the data in Table 7-4 are shown in Table 7-5. The second column in this table lists the value of a, the constant term in the equation, and the coefficient for each of the eight independent variables.

As can be seen in Table 7-5, not all the coefficients in this regression equation are significant. Looking at the t-ratio in the last column, the reader will

Table 7-4 Forecasting Data for 1952-1971 (semiannual)

1	2	3	4	5	6	7	8	9
PDI (personal disposable income, in millions of dollars)	Dealers Allowances (in millions of dollars)	Price (in dollars)	R & D Budget (in thousands of dollars)	Capital Investments (in thousands of dollars)	Advertising (in thousands of dollars)	Sales Expenses (in thousands of dollars)	Total Industry Advertising Budget (in thousands of dollars)	Sales (in thousands of dollars)
398	138	56.2058	12.1124	49.895	76.8621	228.80	98.205	5540.39
369	118	59.0443	9.3304	16.595	88.8056	177.45	224.953	5439.04
268	129	56.7236	28.7481	89.182	51.2972	166.40	263.032	4290.00
484	111	57.8627	12.8916	106.738	39.6473	258.05	320.928	5502.34
394	146	59.1178	13.3815	142.552	51.6517	209.30	406.989	4871.77
332	140	60.1113	11.0859	61.287	20.5476	180.05	246.996	4708.08
336	136	59.8398	24.9579	-30.385	40.1534	213.20	328.436	4627.81
383	104	60.0523	20.8096	-44.586	31.6456	200.85	298.456	4110.24
285	105	63.1415	8.4853	-28.373	12.4570	176.15	218.110	4122.69
277	135	62.3026	10.7301	75.723	68.3076	174.85	410.467	4842.25
456	128	64.9220	21.8743	144.030	52.4536	252.85	93.006	5740.65
355	131	64.8577	23.5062	112.904	76.6778	208.00	307.226	5094.10

364	120	63.5919	13.8940	128.347	96.0677	195.00	106.792	5383.20
320	147	65.6145	14.8659	10.097	47.9795	154.05	304.921	4888.17
311	143	67.0228	22.4940	−24.760	27.2319	180.70	59.612	4033.13
362	145	66.9049	23.3698	116.748	72.6681	219.70	238.986	4941.96
408	131	66.1843	13.0354	120.406	62.3129	234.65	141.074	5312.80
433	124	67.8651	8.0330	121.823	24.7122	258.05	290.832	5139.87
359	106	68.8892	27.0486	71.055	73.9126	196.30	413.636	4397.36
476	138	71.4177	18.2208	4.186	63.2737	278.85	206.454	5149.47
415	148	69.2775	7.7422	46.935	28.6762	207.35	79.566	5150.83
420	136	69.7334	10.1361	7.621	91.3635	213.20	428.982	4989.02
536	111	73.1628	27.3709	127.509	74.0169	296.40	273.072	5926.86
432	152	73.3650	15.5281	−49.574	16.1628	245.05	309.422	4703.88
436	123	73.0500	32.4918	100.098	42.9984	275.60	280.139	5365.59
415	119	74.9102	19.7127	−40.185	41.1346	211.25	314.548	4630.09
462	112	73.2007	14.8358	68.153	92.5180	282.75	212.058	5711.86
429	125	74.1615	11.3694	87.963	83.2870	217.75	118.065	5095.48
517	142	74.2838	26.7510	27.088	74.8921	306.80	344.553	6124.37
328	123	77.1409	19.6038	59.343	87.5103	210.60	140.872	4787.34
418	135	78.5910	34.6881	141.969	74.4712	269.75	82.855	5035.62
515	120	77.0938	23.2020	126.420	21.2711	328.25	398.425	5288.01
412	149	78.2313	35.7396	29.558	26.4941	258.05	124.027	4647.01
455	126	77.9296	21.5891	18.007	94.6311	232.70	117.911	5315.63
554	138	81.0394	19.5692	42.352	92.5448	323.70	161.250	6180.06
441	120	79.8485	15.5037	−21.558	50.0480	267.15	405.088	4800.97
417	120	80.6394	34.9238	148.450	83.1803	257.40	110.740	5512.13
461	132	82.2843	26.5496	−17.584	91.2214	266.50	170.392	5272.21

117

Figure 7-5   Regression Equation for Semiannual Sales

Variable	B	Standard Error	t-Ratio
Constant	2926.09	612.386	4.77817
1 = PDI	3.80918	1.52890	2.49146
2 = Dealer allowances	5.06469	3.13835	1.61381
3 = Price	−17.12610	7.99831	−2.14121
4 = R & D expenditures	−10.25880	6.27417	−1.63509
5 = Capital investments	1.51548	.74654	2.02998
6 = Advertising	8.05355	1.77837	4.52861
7 = Sales expenses	3.86459	2.70223	1.43015
8 = Total industry advertising	−.53940	.37765	−1.42831

$R^2 = 0.912$
Standard deviation of estimate = 243.247
Durbin-Watson statistic = 2.39146
F-Test = 1144.
Degrees of Freedom = 29

recall that this value must be greater than 2 in our size sample in order to indicate significance at the 95% level. It can be seen that independent variables 2, 4, 7, and 8 (dealer allowances, R & D expenditures, sales expenses, and total industry advertising, respectively) are not significantly different than 0 in terms of their impact on sales. This result can be due either to a lack of a significant relationship between variables 2, 4, 7, and 8 and Y or it could be due to multicollinearity between some of the variables, since both R^2 and the F-test are large.

At this point the marketing manager can examine the simple correlation matrix shown in Table 7-6 to determine whether multicollinearity does exist and to see how each independent variable is related to the company's sales. Reading across the bottom line of this table shows the correlation between the company's sales and each of the independent variables. We can see that variables 2, 4, and possibly 8 have a relatively small correlation with company sales. Variable 7, however, whose coefficient was not significant in Table 7-5, seems to have a fairly high correlation with company sales. The problem here is that collinearity does exist between variables 1 and 7. (The coefficient of correlation is .903.) This means that we need to drop either 1 or 7 from our regression equation. If we examine the correlation between sales and variable 1 and sales and variable 7, we see that the correlation is higher with variable 1. Thus we choose to eliminate variable 7 from our regression equation.

Figure 7-6   Simple Correlation Matrix for Semiannual Sales

					Correlation Coefficients				
	1	2	3	4	5	6	7	8	9
Variable	PDI	Dealer Allow- ance	Price	R & D	Capital Expen- ditures	Adver- tising	Sales Ex- pense	Total In- dustry Adver- tising	Com- pany Sales
1	1.000	−.069	.555	.160	.131	.199	.903	−.020	.742
2	−.069	1.000	.028	.005	−.149	−.119	−.051	−.145	.009
3	.555	.028	1.000	.438	−.063	.252	.630	−.182	.285
4	.160	.005	.438	1.000	.217	.102	.361	−.128	.031
5	.131	−.149	−.063	.217	1.000	.277	.228	−.063	.410
6	.199	−.119	.252	.102	.277	1.000	.132	−.197	.526
7	.903	−.051	.630	.361	.228	.132	1.000	−.019	.667
8	−.020	−.145	−.182	−.128	−.063	−.197	−.019	1.000	−.175
9	.742	.009	.285	.031	.410	.526	.667	−.175	1.000

The marketing manager can now test an additional regression equation in which variables 2, 4, 7, and 8 have been eliminated. Thus the equation can be written as

$$Y = a + b_1X_1 + b_3X_3 + b_5X_5 + b_6X_6.$$

The results for this regression analysis are presented in Table 7-7. As can be seen from this new regression equation, the results are good in terms of the R^2 of .781 (corresponding to a coefficient of correlation of .884). All the t-ratios are greater in absolute value than 2, which indicates that the constant term and each of the regression coefficients ($b_1, b_3, b_5,$ and b_6) are significantly different than 0; the F-test's being greater than 5 indicates that the entire regression equation is significant. In practical terms the accuracy of this equation can be seen from the lower portion of Table 7-7, which gives the residuals for the difference between actual values and those predicted by the equation and expresses those residuals as a percent of the actual value. Since the greatest error is only 8.5%, it can be seen that the regression equation is extremely accurate. Further verification of this is the standard error of estimate, which has a value of about 260. This means that we can be 95% confident that our actual value will lie within plus or minus $520,000 of the forecast value in the area of the mean.*

* ±2 standard deviations.

Table 7-7   Regression Results for Semiannual Sales

Regression number 2   Dependent variable is 9

Variable	Value	Standard error	t-ratio
Constant	3276.55	393.68500	8.32276
1	5.69570	.74394	7.65613
3	−15.1783	6.96706	−2.17859
5	1.55114	.70495	2.20033
6	7.57419	1.77507	4.26698

$R^2 = .781$ $R = 0.884$ F-test $= 471.2$

Standard error of Estimate $=$ 259.829   Degrees of freedom $= 33$

Durbin-Watson statistic $= 2.31183$

Actual	Predicted	Residuals	Percentage of Error
5540.39	5349.89	190.501	3.43841E-02
5439.04	5180.44	258.598	4.75449E-02
4290.00	4468.90	−178.895	−4.17005E-02
5502.34	5620.87	−118.530	−2.15417E-02
4871.77	5235.68	−363.912	−7.46982E-02
4708.08	4505.83	202.256	4.29594E-02
4627.81	4539.03	88.783	1.91847E-02
4110.24	4717.04	−606.794	−.14763
4122.69	3991.78	130.914	3.17545E-02
4842.25	4543.44	298.814	6.17097E-02
5740.65	5509.08	231.570	4.03385E-02
5094.10	5069.99	24.105	4.73197E-03
5383.20	5311.28	71.915	1.33593E-02

(*Continued*)

The regression equation determined in Table 7-7 can now be checked for satisfaction of the four basic assumptions inherent in multiple-regression analysis. Since there seems to be no significant pattern in the residuals and since the tests of significance are met and the R^2 is very good, it would appear that the linear equation is, in fact, a good representation of the situation, the residuals seem to be independent of one another, and the deviation or variation of the residuals seems to be fairly constant over the entire range of values. Since we have more than 30 observations in our sample, we can assume that the residuals are in fact normally distributed. Thus all four of the assumptions are met.

This regression equation can now be used in preparing a forecast. The exact form taken from Table 7-7 is

$$Y = 3276.55 + 5.70X_1 - 15.18X_3 + 1.55X_5 + 7.57X_6,$$

Table 7-7 (Continued)

Actual	Predicted	Residuals	Percentage of Error
4888.17	4482.32	405.854	8.30277E-02
4033.13	4198.47	−165.336	−4.09943E-02
4941.96	5054.38	−112.418	−2.27476E-02
5312.80	5254.56	58.234	1.09612E-02
5139.87	5088.84	51.020	9.92636E-03
4397.36	4945.73	−548.365	−.124703
5149.47	5376.45	−226.977	−4.40777E-02
5150.83	4733.14	417.690	8.10918E-02
4989.02	5314.13	−325.107	−6.51645E-02
5926.86	5977.36	−50.498	−8.52030E-03
4703.88	4669.05	34.821	7.40262E-03
5365.59	5132.04	233.550	4.35273E-02
4630.09	4752.48	−122.386	−2.64328E-02
5711.86	5603.36	108.498	1.89951E-02
5095.48	5363.63	−266.150	−5.22326E-02
6124.37	5702.99	421.383	6.88044E-02
4787.34	4728.74	58.606	1.22419E-02
5035.62	5248.74	−213.121	−4.23227E-02
5288.01	5396.88	−108.870	−2.05881E-02
4647.01	4682.28	−35.263	−7.58850E-03
5315.63	5429.94	−114.307	−2.15039E-02
6180.06	5968.57	211.487	3.42208E-02
4800.97	4922.02	−121.043	−2.52122E-02
5512.13	5287.97	224.161	4.06669E-02
5272.21	5316.98	−44.769	−8.49161E-03

where X_1 = personal disposable income,
$\quad X_3$ = price per ton (in dollars),
$\quad X_5$ = capital investments (in thousands of dollars),
$\quad X_6$ = advertising (in thousands of dollars),
$\quad Y$ = semiannual sales (in thousands of dollars).

Since the R^2 value of .781 tells us that the regression equation explains 78.1% of the total variation—that is, that variations in X_1, X_3, X_5, and X_6 explain 78.1% of the variation in the sales—the marketing manager can use this equation with confidence. He must be certain, however, that the values he inserts for the independent variables are accurate to ensure that his forecast of semiannual sales will be as accurate as allowed by this regression equation.

SUMMARY

In the preceding sections we have considered some of the details of applying multiple regression in practice. There are also a number of general considerations that the manager should keep in mind in evaluating the appropriateness of this technique compared with other techniques. The major strength of multiple-regression analysis is that it is a statistical method that includes a number of measures of the accuracy and significance of forecasting equations and actual forecasts. In addition, it can handle virtually any kind of causal relationship or pattern as long as the variables are linearly related to the dependent variable. Because of the power of this technique, it has grown rapidly in its acceptance over the last five years and will continue to do so over the next decade.

There are, of course, some drawbacks to the use of this technique. One is that, since it is statistical, most managers are reluctant to get into its details and to understand fully the power that it can bring to bear on a forecasting problem. Hopefully this chapter will have shown that the method is completely understandable and that by mastering some of the basic principles of its application the manager can use it wisely and in a broad range of situations.

Another potential drawback of multiple-regression analysis is the amount of data it requires and the cost of collecting that data, developing the initial regression equation, and then monitoring its appropriateness over time. This last point is particularly important, for if the causal relationship between the independent variable and the dependent variable changes it becomes necessary to collect an entirely new set of data drawn from the time period when the new relationship existed and to redetermine the most appropriate regression equation. Because of the substantial costs of the initial development of multiple-regression applications, the technique is generally used only for longer term forecasting in which the value of an accurate forecast is substantial. Thus it would be unlikely that multiple regression would be appropriate for forecasting the demand for several hundred or several thousand products. Much more often it would be used for forecasting aggregate variables such as corporate sales, interest rates, or the general level of economic activity.

SUGGESTED REFERENCES FOR ADDITIONAL STUDY

Johnston, J., *Econometric Methods*, 1966. Prentice-Hall, Englewood Cliffs, New Jersey.

Klein, L. R., 1968. *An Introduction to Econometrics*, Prentice-Hall, Englewood Cliffs, New Jersey.

Spurr, W. A., and C. P. Bonini, 1967. *Statistical Analysis for Business Decisions*, Irwin, Homewood, Illinois.

CHAPTER 8

OTHER QUANTITATIVE
METHODS OF FORECASTING

In the preceding chapters we described the quantitative methods of forecasting that are most commonly used in business. These methods represent those that have been found to be most useful and most economical in present corporate situations. There are a number of other quantitative methods of forecasting, however, that for one reason or another are not widely used today but with which the manager should be familiar. The purpose of this chapter is to deal with four of them in order that the manager may have a more complete exposure to those techniques that are likely to be suggested by specialists in forecasting or by others in his company or industry.

The fact that an entire chapter is not being devoted to each of these techniques as in the preceding chapters does not reflect on the value of these techniques in specific situations. All have been found to be extremely powerful in a number of situations. However, they are much more costly than many of the methods we have discussed and the range of situations in which they can be applied is often somewhat limited. The increased costs associated with these methods is due directly to the complexity behind them and thus our discussion of them does not go into the detail of their actual application but deals more with the concepts behind them and the kinds of situations in which they can be useful. As before, the end of this chapter includes a number of suggested references that can be used by the reader who wants more detail on the specific technique.

THE BOX-JENKINS METHOD OF FORECASTING

Perhaps the most common forecasting situation encountered in business is that of a time series in which a number of observations are taken over several periods of time and a forecast of some future time period is desired. As we have discussed in earlier chapters, all forecasting methods designed to handle such situations assume that there is a basic underlying pattern represented by the historical data and that in addition to that pattern some randomness has been exhibited. Thus the focus of the forecasting method is to isolate that basic pattern as well as possible and to use it as the basis for future forecasts. Although a method such as exponential smoothing may be suitable for short-term forecasting of time series in which there is not much fluctuation, we have seen cases in which the real-life situation is much more complicated, and the pattern is made up of combinations of a trend, a seasonal factor, and a cyclical factor as well as the random fluctuations. In these situations a much more complex forecasting method is needed.

The Box-Jenkins method of forecasting is one that is particularly well suited to handling complex time series and other forecasting situations in which the basic pattern is not readily apparent. The real power and attractiveness of this forecasting approach is that it can handle complex patterns with relatively little effort on the part of the manager. However, because it is dealing with much more complicated situations, it is much more difficult to understand the fundamentals of this technique and the limitations of its application. In addition, the cost associated with the Box-Jenkins approach in a given situation is generally much greater than any of the other quantitative methods, but with this greater cost, much greater accuracy can be achieved.

This approach to forecasting is actually quite different from most of the methods that we have discussed (perhaps with the exception of adaptive filtering). The method itself is really a *philosophy* for approaching forecasting situations that has been developed by Professors Box and Jenkins. The reasoning behind the development of this approach is that existing methods of forecasting always assume or are limited to specific kinds of patterns in the data; for example, we have seen that exponential smoothing assumes a horizontal pattern in the data, whereas in regression analysis the user must specify what he imagines the pattern is in order to proceed with the application of that technique. In the Box and Jenkins method there is no need initially to assume a fixed pattern. Rather the approach begins with a tentative pattern that is fitted to the data in accordance with that tentative pattern so that the error will be minimized. Subsequently, the approach provides explicit information to the manager to enable him to judge whether the pattern tentatively assumed is correct for that situation. If it is, the forecast can be developed directly, and if not the Box-Jenkins approach provides further clues for identifying the correct pattern. Thus the manager who uses this approach can tentatively specify a forecasting model that corresponds to an alternative pattern and can isolate the information needed to judge which pattern is closest to the underlying pattern in the data. This iterative procedure allows him to make incremental improvements in his forecasting method and to arrive at a forecasting model that achieves optimization in terms of the basic pattern and minimizes the error of that pattern. When we consider that the user is also supplied with statistical information on the accuracy of the forecasts prepared with this method, it can be seen that it is indeed one of the most powerful available.

In describing their approach to forecasting, Box and Jenkins have developed the schematic diagram shown in Figure 8-1. This approach divides the forecasting problem into four stages. Initially, the person using the Box-Jenkins method postulates a general class of forecasting methods for his particular situation. In stage 1 a specific model that can be tentatively entertained as the forecasting method best suited to that situation is identified. Stage 2 then consists of fitting that model to the available historical data and then running a check to determine whether it is adequate. If it is not, the approach returns to stage 1 and an alternative model is identified. When an

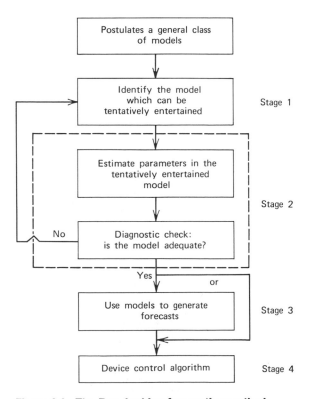

Figure 8-1 The Box-Jenkins forecasting method.

adequate model has been isolated, stage 3 or 4 is pursued, stage 3 being the development of a forecast for some future time period and stage 4, the development of a control algorithm for a situation in which the forecasting method is to be used for control purposes. The remainder of this section describes those elements essential to the application of the Box-Jenkins approach.

Autocorrelation

Since the autocorrelation among successive values of the data is a key tool in arriving at the correct pattern (or rather the model corresponding to it) describing the data, we elaborate its role and importance. As we have seen in Chapters 5 and 7, the concept of correlation between two variables is straightforward. It is the association (mutual correspondence) between two variables and describes what happens to one of the variables if there is a change in the other. The degree of this correlation is measured by the *correlation coefficient* which varies between $+1$ and -1. A value close to $+1$ implies a strong positive relationship between the two variables, which means that when the value of one variable increases the value of the other also increases. Similarly, a correlation coefficient close to -1 indicates the opposite—that increases in one variable will be associated with decreases in the other. A coefficient of 0 implies that no matter what happens to one variable nothing can be said about the value of the other; for example, a correlation coefficient of .80 between a company's sales and GNP would mean that if GNP increased by a certain percentage the sales would also tend to show an increase 80% of the time. In the same way a correlation of $-.80$ between sales and GNP would mean that in 80% of all cases an increase in sales would be accompanied by a decrease in GNP. (Correlation implies nothing about a shift in one variable *causing* a shift in the other.)

An *autocorrelation coefficient* is similar to a correlation coefficient except that it describes the association (mutual dependence) among values of the same variable but at different time periods. To see what is meant by this suppose we construct a number of artificial variables from a single variable by changing the time origin of the data; for example, variable B can be constructed from variable A by simply dropping the first value of A and letting the second value of A be the starting value of B.

In this example variables A and B can be treated as two separate and distinct variables even though they both come from the same data set. In a similar manner we can construct Figure 8-2 in which it can be seen that variable Y_1 is exactly the same as variable Y except that Y_1 begins with the second value (-2) of Y. We can also see that Y_2 is another artificial variable that begins with the third value (5) of Y. Continuing in this way, we can

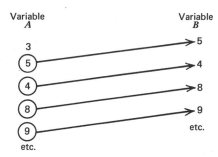

construct Y_3 by starting with the fourth value of Y, and so on. It is obvious that since Y has a finite number of data points and since Y_1 starts with the second value of Y that the last value of Y_1 will be 0, the last two values of Y_2 will be 0, the last three values of Y_3, will be 0, and so on.

We could consider Y and Y_1 as two variables and calculate their correlation coefficients, Y and Y_2 as another two variables, Y and Y_3 as still another two, and so on. For each of these sets of two variables there corresponds a correlation coefficient, the meaning of which is of interest. A coefficient of .80 between Y and Y_1, for example, will imply that successive values of Y with one period (lag) between them (this is how Y_1 was constructed) are positively correlated with each other 80% of the time. Similarly a coefficient

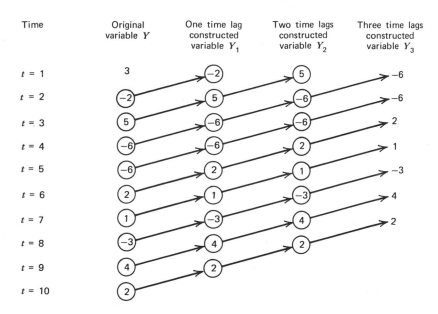

Figure 8-2 Constructing time-lagged variables.

of $-.70$ between Y and Y_2 will tell us that successive values of Y two periods (time lags) apart are negatively correlated 70% of the time, and so on. However, since variables Y_1, Y_2, Y_3, . . ., are actually all derived from the same original variable Y, we call such a dependence auto- (i.e., self-) correlation. Thus autocorrelation is a measure of association among successive values of the same variable.

Autocorrelations provide important information about the structure of a data set and its pattern. In a set of completely random data the autocorrelation among successive values will always be 0, whereas data values of strong seasonal and/or cyclical character will be highly autocorrelated. Figure 8-3, which we examine in the next section, presents the autocorrelations (ρ_k) of different time lags of monthly gasoline consumption in Great Britian. These autocorrelations reveal a strong seasonal pattern, since their highest values (ρ) occur every 12 time periods. The ρ_{12} of .71, for example, implies a positive relation among every 12 successive months about 71% of the time. It is this type of information gained by the calculation of autocorrelations that can

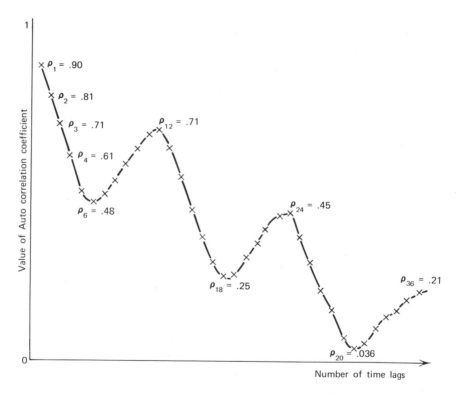

Figure 8-3   Autocorrelation of different time lags for gasoline sales in Great Britain.

be utilized by the Box-Jenkins approach to arrive at the optimal forecasting model. One thing that makes this information particularly useful is that we do not need to know anything about our data or its pattern to obtain its autocorrelation coefficients. These coefficients can then be used to reveal the type of data we are dealing with and its pattern.

Model Types Available

The Box-Jenkins method postulates three general classes of model that can describe any type or pattern of data: (a) AutoRegressive (AR), (b) moving average (MA), and (c) mixed AutoRegressive-Moving Average (ARMA). Identification of the correct model type is made by examining the auto-correlation coefficients.

An AutoRegressive model is of the form

$$Y_t = \phi_1 Y_{t-1} + \phi_2 Y_{t-2} + \phi_3 Y_{t-3} + \cdots + \phi_p Y_{t-p} + e_t, \qquad (8\text{-}1)$$

where Y_t is the dependent variable, say sales, and Y_{t-1}, Y_{t-2}, Y_{t-3}, . . ., Y_{t-p} are the independent variables which in this case are values of sales at some previous time period $(t - 1, t - 2, t - 3, . . ., t - p)$. Finally e_t is the error or residual term that represents random events that cannot be explained by the model.

The model described by (8-1) is called autoregressive because it is like the regression equations $(Y = a + b_1 X_1 + b_2 X_2 + b_3 X_3 + \cdots + b_p X_p + e)$ that we discussed in Chapter 7, except that the independent variables Y_{t-1}, Y_{t-2}, Y_{t-3}, . . ., Y_{t-p} are actually the values of the dependent variable with time lags of 1, 2, 3, . . ., p periods. The relationship described by (8-1) indicates that future values of sales are influenced by those of the past in a specific fashion. Thus, if we could (a) prove that (8-1) is indeed the correct equation to describe our data and (b) estimate ϕ_1, ϕ_2, ϕ_3, . . ., ϕ_p, we could easily arrive at a prediction of sales. If, for example, the sales for the last five periods were as shown in Table 8-1 and the values of ϕ were $\phi_1 = .30$, $\phi_2 = .35$, $\phi_3 = .36$ and $\phi_4 = \phi_5 = \cdots = \phi_p = 0$, the sales for the next period t will be

$$Y_t = \phi_1 Y_{t-1} + \phi_2 Y_{t-2} + \phi_3 Y_{t-3} + e_t$$

$$= .30(115) + .35(110) + .36(130) + e_t$$

$$= 119.8 + e_t,$$

where e_t will be some random quantity. As we show later on, the Box-Jenkins approach also provides statistics on the error of forecast e_t, so that we can determine the range of fluctuations about the forecast value Y_t.

As we can see from this brief example of an autoregressive model, it is similar in form to multiple regression. Unfortunately not all data series can

Table 8-1   Example of Forecasting Sales With an AutoRegressive Model

Time Period	Actual Sales	Forecasted Sales	Residual or Error
t-5	100	98	2
t-4	120	125	-5
t-3	130	131	-1
t-2	110	110	0
t-1	115	112	3
t		119.8	

be handled with such a model. Thus the Box-Jenkins approach also considers two other classes of model. One is the moving average (MA) model, which as we shall see is of the same form as the moving averages that we discussed in Chapter 3. In Box-Jenkins terminology the moving average model is of the form

$$Y_t = e_t - \theta_1 e_{t-1} - \theta_2 e_{t-2} - \cdots - \theta_q e_{t-q}, \qquad (8\text{-}2)$$

where, as before, e_t is the error or residual and $e_{t-1}, e_{t-2}, e_{t-3}, \ldots, e_{t-q}$ are previous values of the error.

Equation 8-2 is similar to (8-1), except that it implies that the dependent variable Y_t depends on previous values of the *error term* $(e_t, e_{t-1}, \ldots, e_{t-p})$ rather than of the variable itself. In the same way we talked about auto-correlation among successive values of Y_t we can talk about the auto-correlation among successive values of the residuals or errors. According to (8-2), the future values of sales could be predicted by utilizing the error of each of several past periods.

Returning to the data given in Table 8-1, if we had computed the values of θ as $\theta_1 = -25$, $\theta_2 = 10.8$, $\theta_3 = -3.2$, $\theta_4 = 9.6$, and $\theta_5 = \theta_6 = \cdots = \theta_q = 0$, then using (8-2) we would obtain as a forecast

$$Y_t = e_t - \theta_1 e_{t-1} - \theta_2 e_{t-2} - \theta_3 e_{t-3} - \theta_4 e_{t-4}$$

$$= e_t - (-25)(3) - (10.8)(0) - (-3.2)(-1) - (9.6)(-5)$$

$$= e_t + 119.8.$$

This corresponds to the same forecast as before, a value of 119.8 plus some quantity e_t that is random but falls within some range that we can estimate. Here, however, we used a moving average model, whereas previously we used an autoregressive model.

The third class of model considered by the Box-Jenkins approach is a mixed model. Oftentimes the pattern of the data may be described best by a mixed process of AR and MA elements. The general form of a mixed model is the following:

$$Y_t = \phi_1 Y_{t-1} + \phi_2 Y_{t-2} + \cdots + \phi_p Y_{t-p} + e_t$$
$$- e_t - \theta_1 e_{t-1} - \theta_2 e_{t-2} - \cdots - \theta_q e_{t-q} \quad (8\text{-}3)$$

As is evident, (8-3) is simply (8-1) and (8-2) combined. It indicates that future values of sales depend on both past values of sales and the errors between the actual and forecast values.

The choice of one of the three models (AR, MA, ARMA) and its degree 1, 2, 3, . . ., $p - q$) can be made by an examination of the autocorrelations and a related measure derived from them, the partial autocorrelation. It is the combination of the two that provides us with hints of the most appropriate model. With experience we can determine a model that best fits the data by observing the autocorrelations and their partial values. An important part of the Box-Jenkins approach is that if a mistake has been made in selecting a model, it can be identified and steps can be taken to correct it. This is done by finding the autocorrelation coefficient of the residuals.

If the correct model is fitted to the data, the residuals must be randomly distributed around the model, and therefore their autocorrelations should be small (close to 0) and exhibit no pattern. If, on the other hand, an incorrect model is fitted, the residuals will be correlated in some manner that can be identified by the Box-Jenkins approach. Subsequently this pattern could be used as a guide to arrive at a new model that would remove the pattern from the residuals. This is illustrated in Figure 8-1 in which stage 3 is not undertaken until the proper model is obtained, that is, until the residuals of the tentative model are randomly distributed. Then the tentative model becomes permanent and can be used for purposes of forecasting and control.

It should be apparent from this brief discussion of the Box-Jenkins approach that although it is versatile and offers a complete system of forecasting, it entails considerable costs in developing the application for a specific situation and is complex in its detail. This last point makes a discussion of how the alternative models are determined and compared beyond the scope of this book. However we will examine a particular application in the next section to illustrate its general usefulness.

An Application of the Box-Jenkins Method

To demonstrate the use of the Box-Jenkins method we apply it to estimating the retail sales of passenger cars in the United States. Table 8-2 lists the historical data for this series. This example was chosen because the data is

Table 8-2   Retail Sales of Passengar Cars (USA) 1965-1971 (in thousands)

Month	1965	1966	1967	1968	1969	1970	1971
January	695	684	564	630	645	539	586
February	684	668	509	624	662	598	637
March	817	854	670	767	722	646	756
April	800	765	710	729	754	691	737
May	773	692	745	811	795	699	748
June	807	751	780	781	798	800	798
July	712	635	627	737	662	641	668
August	610	608	517	635	555	526	566
September	499	501	547	563	709	489	756
October	842	794	665	885	817	630	934
November	801	746	618	785	706	436	848
December	722	678	615	679	639	425	649

erratic and is influenced by strong seasonal and cyclical factors, thus making the job of prediction difficult. We fit the Box-Jenkins model to the first six years (1965–1970) of data and then make predictions for the seventh year (1971), which can then be compared with the actual values for that year.

A tentative model is required to start the Box-Jenkins method (see Figure 8-1). An initial form for this model can be determined by examining the autocorrelation and partial autocorrelation coefficients of the data. We can see in Figure 8-4 that the highest autocorrelation is every 12 months, which suggests a seasonal pattern of 12 months in our data. This is the type of information revealed by the autocorrelations that must be utilized to arrive at the best model. Figure 8-4 also reveals a slight trend in the data, and comparison of this trend with the partial autocorrelation suggests that we should fit an ARMA model to the data. (It should be noted that we are not implying that the process of identifying the data pattern and selecting an appropriate model is an easy one. On the contrary, it requires some knowledge and experience to do so, but this detail is beyond the scope of this book.)

Let us assume that we have chosen the wrong model. We discover this by looking at the autocorrelation coefficients of the residuals. The residuals are found by comparing each forecast with the actual value and computing the error (residual) between them (error = actual − forecast). We then compute the autocorrelations on these errors. As shown in Figure 8-5, the range of autocorrelations for this example increases as the time lag increases, thus suggesting some pattern in the residuals. We can also see that the tenth and twelfth autocorrelations ($\rho_{10} = .32$, $\rho_{12} = -.47$) are large and outside

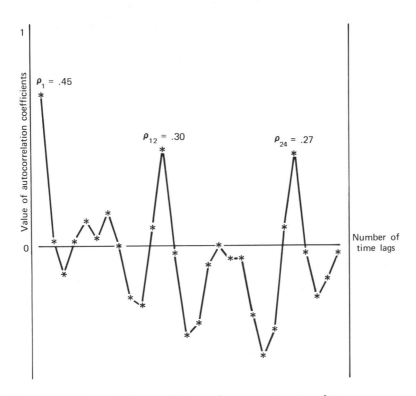

Figure 8-4 Autocorrelation coefficients for passenger-car sales.

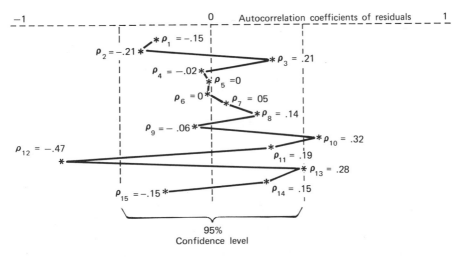

Figure 8-5 Autocorrelation of the residuals of an inadequate model for retail car sales.

the allowable limits (plus or minus two standard errors). This suggests that some of the seasonal influence and some of the pattern occurring every 10 months has not been handled adequately by our initial model.

On the other hand, in Figure 8-6, which is a plot of the autocorrelations for the residuals of the correct model, we can see no pattern in the residuals and no values of the autocorrelations are outside the allowable limits; therefore we can assume that the ARMA model (first degree) used to obtain these improved results is adequate for our forecasting purposes. Indeed, as shown in Figure 8-7, this model does a good job of predicting our rather erratic data for car sales. The average percentage error over the six years of data on which the model was based is 9.1%. For the last year for which the actual data was used only for comparison purposes the average error was a little higher and equal to 12%. In all cases, however, the actual values for the last 12 months fell within the range predicted by the model and shown in Figure 8-7 as the shaded area.

As we have illustrated, the Box-Jenkins approach is the most general of the forecasting techniques. It can deal with any type of pattern of data and can

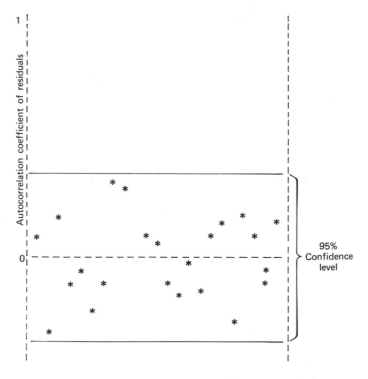

Figure 8-6   Autocorrelation of residuals of an adequate model for retail car sales.

discover an adequate model for it. In this respect it is the only forecasting method that can both optimize the pattern of a set of data and minimize its error. As might be suspected, however, the generality of the approach influences the amount of knowledge required to utilize it. Since it can deal with a wide variety of cases, the complexity is greater than in other forecasting methods. In addition, the Box-Jenkins approach requires a considerable amount of computer time (about 68 seconds of CPU-Central Processing Unit-time on an IBM 370/145 to fit 100 data points in four models during a single computer run) which makes its use expensive. On the other hand, it is one of the most accurate methods available, which poses an interesting dilemma to the practitioner who has to choose between higher accuracy and higher costs.

An advantage of the Box-Jenkins method is that once a correct model has been developed it can be used quite easily and in a routine manner to generate additional forecasts. The computer output is simple and gives the most likely forecasted value, as well as an upper and lower bound (according to some probability range), that the actual values can take. For our example of retail car sales, these limits are shown in Table 8-3. Finally, if for some reason there is a change in the pattern of data, there will be enough signs to indicate the change and initiate the development of a new model to deal with the changed pattern.

In summary, the Box-Jenkins technique is one of the most powerful and accurate forecasting techniques available today, but it is also costly and complex in comparison with other techniques such as multiple regression, decomposition, or adaptive filtering. In the final analysis it is up to the user to decide when the benefits of higher accuracy will compensate for the higher cost associated with the use of this method. The specific situation requiring predictions and personal judgment will be key factors in the final choice.

ECONOMETRIC FORECASTING

An approach to economic forecasting which has recently gained widespread publicity is econometrics. This is the approach used by such organizations as the Wharton School of Business and the Brookings Institute in forecasting the economy of the United States. The basic concept is that a series of equations is developed to represent the major variables in the economy and the relationships among them and then to solve them simultaneously to obtain a forecast for the key variables such as gross national product and consumer spending. Although this approach to forecasting is complex and technical in its detail, we shall examine the rationale behind it and the limitations and advantages that it has in certain situations.

Retail Car
Sales (in 000's)

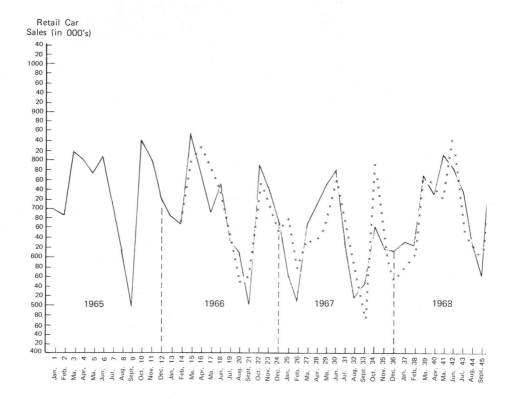

Figure 8-7   Retail car sales in

The best starting point toward an understanding of the basics of econometric forecasting is regression analysis. The reader will recall that in Chapters 5 and 7 in which we examined the technique of regression analysis it was explained that the regression equation was used to forecast a single dependent variable based on the value and the relations between one or more independent variables. Each of these independent variables was assumed to be exogenous or outside the influence of the dependent variable. In many situations this is an appropriate and reasonable assumption; for example, it is not unrealistic to assume that independent variables such as gross national product, consumer spending, and interest rates are uneffected by a dependent variable like company sales. By the use of management judgment independent variables and the dependent variable in a particular situation can be defined to meet the assumptions of regression analysis. We also saw

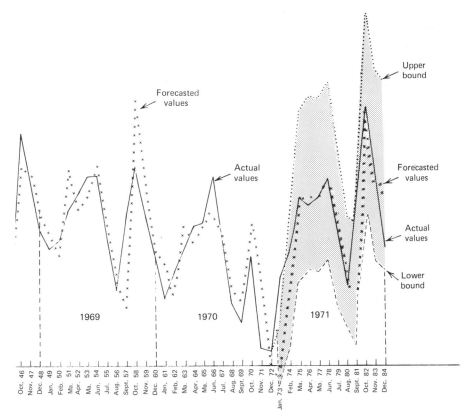

in the USA: 1965-1971.

that the technique itself allows the manager to determine when the assumption of independence among the X's is violated and to take some measures to eliminate that violation.

Unfortunately, in most broad economic situations an assumption that each of the variables, with the exception of a single dependent variable, is independent, is unrealistic. To illustrate this point, assume that sales are a function of GNP, price, and advertising. In regression terms we would assume that all three independent variables are exogenous to the system and thus are not influenced by the level of sales itself or by one another. This is a fair assumption as far as GNP is concerned. If, however, we consider price and advertising, the same assumption may not be valid; for example, if the per-unit cost is of some quadratic form, a different level of sales will result in a different level of cost. Furthermore, advertising expenditures will

Table 8-3   Range of Forecasted Values for Retail Car Sales

	Period	Forecasted Value	Lower Limit[a]	Upper Limit[b]
January 1972	85	693.64	547.88	878.17
	86	707.52	524.03	955.27
	87	832.21	581.34	1191.3
	88	832.84	553.87	1252.3
	89	849.73	540.76	1335.2
	90	897.14	548.50	1467.4
	91	755.53	445.12	1282.4
	92	642.34	365.55	1128.7
	93	680.14	374.64	1234.7
	94	903.89	482.74	1692.5
	95	779.12	404.02	1502.5
	96	685.33	345.50	1359.4
January 1973	97	711.10	342.98	1474.3
	98	729.91	338.94	1571.9
	99	857.40	383.72	1915.8
	100	858.29	370.86	1986.4
	101	875.65	365.80	2096.1
	102	924.51	373.87	2286.2
	103	778.58	305.13	1986.6
	104	661.94	251.67	1741.0
	105	700.89	258.75	1898.5
	106	931.47	334.19	2596.3

[a] −2 standard errors from the forecast
[b] +2 standard errors from the forecast
 (±2 standard errors is the 95% confidence interval)

certainly influence the price of the product, since production and selling costs influence the per-unit price. The price, in turn, is influenced by the magnitude of sales, which can also influence the level of advertising. All of this points to the interdependence of all four of the variables in our equation. When this interdependence is at all strong, regression analysis cannot be used. If we want to be accurate, we must express this sales relationship by developing a system of four simultaneous equations that can deal with the interdependence directly.

Thus, in econometric form we can have

$$sales = f \text{ (GNP, price, advertising)},$$
$$cost = f \text{ (production and inventory levels)},$$
$$\text{selling expenses} = f \text{ (advertising, other selling expenses)},$$
$$price = f \text{ (cost + selling expenses)};$$

that is, instead of one relationship, we now have four. As in regression analysis, we must (a) determine the functional form of each of the equations, (b) estimate in a simultaneous manner the values of their parameters, and (c) test for the statistical significance of the results and the validity of the assumptions. It should be realized that the advantage of econometric forecasting is that it provides the values of several of the independent variables from within the model itself (they are endogenously determined), thus freeing the user from having to estimate them externally.

The estimation of the equation parameters, however, involves problems far more complex than those encountered in regression analysis. It is these problems that make the application of econometric forecasting difficult and expensive for the majority of small or medium-size business firms. Compared with regression analysis, the extra precision gained by the utilization of econometric forecasting rarely compensates for the extra costs incurred by its use. It is only in the largest corporations or in governments that this approach becomes attractive.

A number of mathematical techniques have been developed to help solve econometric models. Some with which managers may be familiar are the method of least squares, the full information-maximum likelihood method of estimation, two-stage least square methods and three-stage least square methods. The details of these techniques are well beyond the scope of this chapter and thus are not discussed further.

An econometric model includes a number of simultaneous equations that can be of different types and functional forms. The translation of econometric theory to the right type and form of equations and their development into a set of functional relationships is referred to as specification. The accurate and most appropriate specification of an econometric model is a key step in the use of this technique of forecasting.

A major part of specification is the identification of the exogenous and endogenous variables. One must arbitrarily decide on the degree of influence of the different factors and choose those that are least determined within the system as exogenous factors. This is similar to the distinction made in regression analysis between the independent variables and the dependent variables. In an econometric model we will want to separate those factors that are most strongly influenced by one another into the endogenous group and those that can be assumed to be determined outside the system of simultaneous equations into the exogenous group.

Once the choice of endogenous and exogenous variables has been made, one equation must be specified for each of the endogenous variables. When the number of the equations specified is equal to the number of exogenous variables, the model is said to be just specified. When the number of endogenous variables is less than the number of equations, the model is under specified and one or more of the variables has to be set arbitrarily to some initial value. These variables then become exogenous factors for that solution to the system of equations. Finally, if the number of endogenous variables is greater than the number of equations, the model is overspecified. It is the overspecified form of econometric models that is most often used for estimating the parameters of a set of simultaneous equations.

Econometric models are used most widely to forecast macroseries of interrelated economic data such as income, consumption, and capital spending and much less for business forecasting. Apart from the econometric models of a few large organizations, mainly in the automobile and steel industries, the majority of models in existence are of the total economy or some specific parts of it. The best known econometric models are at the Brookings Institute and the University of Pennsylvania and in the United Kingdom. The major advantage of these models (consisting of several hundreds of equations) is that they can be used for simulating anticipated or proposed changes in monetary or fiscal policy. The effects of these changes on other economic variables included in the model can be seen and assessed for their desirability. This is achieved by the very nature of the system which in an interdependent manner assesses and points out all the effects of a change in a single factor.

Since the early fifties when the first work on econometrics started, the degree of sophistication and the size of models used have increased tremendously. The second and third generations of computers have made possible the utilization of more advanced methods of estimation and the inclusion of more equations so that today econometric models can represent the workings of a real economy in a fairly accurate manner.

Presently the great advantage of an econometric model is indirect. It can be used to predict the direction and extent of change of the overall economic activity or any of its components. This information can then become the input required to estimate the independent variables of a single equation forecasting model. Since this information can be obtained from outside sources, organizations do not have to develop their own models but can rely on outsiders (consulting groups or nonprofit institutions) to provide them with forecasts when they are needed. Thus individual companies can forego all the high costs associated with developing, maintaining, and running a large-scale econometric model and obtain the information it offers through third parties.

As additional experience is gained in the use of econometric models for forecasting, their application will undoubtedly become more widespread at both government and industry levels. These econometric models of the future should be substantially more accurate than they have been in the past and should provide the manager with additional information he can use in applying other forecasting techniques that are less costly and more suitable for his purposes.

INPUT-OUTPUT TABLES

An input-output table is a technique for determining the transactions taking place within and among different sectors of the economy as well as the magnitude of such transactions. An input-output table summarizes all "taking" and "giving" among and within all industries and between them and the final consumer. In this sense it is an accounting procedure for reporting all transactions. Its main usefulness is for planning purposes at the level of a national economy.

Several countries, mainly European, utilize input-output tables to a great extent for planning purposes. It is obvious that a certain goal, say increasing residential construction to 100,000 units a year by 1975, will require a great number of inputs such as steel, cement, bricks, trucks, cranes, construction machinery, glass, and wood. Thus, if the goal can be achieved, the official planner will first have to assess how much it will cost and then determine what changes or investments in the economy will have to be introduced so that by 1975 enough inputs will be available to build 100,000 housing units. These are not easy questions to answer, since they require a tremendous amount of data. An input-output table is a technique that organizes all these data by dividing the economy into sectors, each sector into industries, etc., and then records all transactions that take place within and among all of the components of the table. If we assume that the basic input-output requirements between each component will be constant for the future, extrapolation can be used to obtain the amount of output that will be required from each component in order to achieve a certain desired goal; for example, if the input-output table indicates that to produce one housing unit requires two tons of steel and 30 tons of cement, we can easily estimate that 100,000 units will require 200,000 tons of steel and 3,000,000 tons of cement. Thus planning can take place by either specifying goals of final consumer expenditure or industry-wide production plans and adapting fiscal or taxing policies to initiate investments in the desired sectors or industry.

It should be realized that the input-output method tends to work better in planned or centralized economies like the USSR or France than in countries like the United States. As one might imagine, input-output tables are expensive to construct and often of doubtful value, since they basically assume a constant technology that is tenuous today when technological breakthroughs and substantial innovations can drastically change the input-output requirement among industries.

To see just how an input-output table can be constructed, we consider the example given in Table 8-4 for a three-sector economy. Each of the rows presents the sales or output of that sector (read across) to the others. Thus agriculture provides 11 units to industry, 9 to services, and 97 to the final

Table 8-4   Input-Output Table for a Three Sector Economy

From Sector	To Sector			Consumers	Total
	Agriculture	Industry	Services		
Agriculture	29	11	9	97	135
Industry	25	56	77	88	265
Services	21	67	94	38	228
Sector income	60	131	48	223	
Total units	135	265	228		628

consumer, whereas it requires 29 units within itself. Each of the columns presents the amount bought or received by each sector. Thus industry receives 11 units from agriculture, 67 for services while there are 56 inter-industry units transacted.

If we divide the units received by a given sector, say services, by the total number of units produced by the sector, in this case 228, the ratio $77/228 = .34$ implies that to increase the output of the service sector by one unit we will have to increase the production of the industrial sector by .34 of a unit. This ratio is known as the technological coefficient which must remain constant if projections are to be accurate.

Conceivably we could construct an input-output for a single business organization. The different divisions, departments, or organizational units can then become the entries of the table among which the transactions can take place and for which forecasts can be made. These forecasts, however, must also be based on future sales projections. Since construction of an input-output table can be expensive and since the technological requirements among departments are not constant, its value in forecasting is rather doubtful. The value of input-output analysis lies more in the planning stages than in forecasting itself, but it is still an expensive planning device for the purposes of individual organizations. With several alternative forecasting methods available, the value of input-output tables for the business forecaster is probably in another direction rather than in the information that can be obtained by the construction of the table. If a government is using input-output analysis for planning purposes, the numbers they list for some future period will become production targets and can thus be an excellent source of indirect forecasts of marcoseries or their individual components. In this direction lies the value of input-output tables to the manager.

INVENTORY-CONTROL THEORY

It is impossible to forecast the quantity of a given item with 100% accuracy. This means that variation due to forecasting error, or unusual events, will occur and will introduce extra factors that will affect planning. In anticipation of fluctuations that cannot be forecast, we must introduce inventories that will compensate for any over-or underestimations in the forecasts. For purposes of inventory planning we have to know when an item (product, material, cash, etc.) should be stocked and how many units should be stored in the inventory. To achieve this forecast an estimation of the mean demand and variance is needed, which in turn is used in the inventory model to minimize the average inventory cost while answering the questions when and how much to store of a given item.

Inventory-control shifts the burden, in particular for the immediate and short run, from forecasting to inventory manipulation, which in many cases is a more practical and cheaper way to deal with the problem of fluctuations in demand.

In this respect the manager has a choice between a more accurate forecast and a smaller average inventory level or a rougher forecast and higher inventories. This trade-off should be made on the basis of the relative value of each product, the pattern of its past behavior, and the cost of inventories as well as the accuracy that a forecasting method can provide. Optimization methods can also be used in conjunction with forecasting techniques and can facilitate the job of the forecaster when he thinks that it is impossible or unprofitabe to provide a more accurate forecast.

As the manager knows, the area of inventory theory is one about which several books have been written. Thus it would not be appropriate to go into it in further detail at this point. The manager who is planning his forecasting system should consider explicitly the relation between forecasting and inventory theory in order to achieve his objectives most economically.

SUGGESTED REFERENCES FOR ADDITIONAL STUDY

Box, G. E., and G. M. Jenkins, 1970. *Time Series Analysis*, Holden-Day, New York.

Christ, C. F., 1966. *Econometric Models and Methods*, Wiley, New York.

Fisher, F. M., 1966. *The Identification Problem in Econometrics*, McGraw-Hill, New York.

Goldberger, A. S., 1964. *Econometric Theory*, Wiley, New York.

Johnston, J., 1972. *Econometric Methods*, McGraw-Hill, New Yor,k.

Klein, L. R., 1965. *An Introduction to Econometrics*, Prentice-Hall, Englewood Cliffs, New Jersey.

Tinter, G., 1952. *Econometrics*, Wiley, New York.

CHAPTER 9

DATA ACQUISITION AND HANDLING IN FORECASTING

Central to any application of a forecasting technique or the development of a forecasting system is the role of data. As pointed out in each of the preceding chapters dealing with quantitative methods of forecasting, each of these techniques requires that considerable amount of data be collected before they can be applied in the preparation of a forecast.

The purpose of this chapter is to examine the characteristics of data that the manager must be aware of in properly applying a forecasting method. A knowledge of these characteristics can help the manager to determine the accuracy of his forecast and the level of confidence that he can place in such forecasts. The first section of this chapter deals with the definition of the variable or variables to be employed in the forecast. This is followed by a discussion of the major aspects of data collection and possible data sources both within and outside the company. Since the problem of accuracy in the data is such an important one, it is addressed in detail in the third section of this chapter. This is followed by a discussion of the development and use of the data base as part of a forecasting system. Although others have discussed the notion of a data base in some detail, it is mentioned here in direct relation to the forecasting function and the application of individual forecasting methods. The final section of this chapter deals with the need for updating historical data and conducting audits of the data used in forecasting.

It is appropriate at this point at least to make a comment about how this chapter on data acquisition and handling relates to Chapters 12 and 13 on the linking of forecasting with planning and controlling and the implementing of forecasting procedures within the firm. In this chapter the focus is at a detailed level of the actual data and the handling of that data in forecasting. Preceding chapters have indicated the nature of some of the data requirements associated with each of the quantitative forecasting methods. Thus, rather than considering the individual requirements, this chapter examines the nature of data acquisition problems and the handling of data in a manner appropriate for forecasting.

Chapter 12 takes a much broader look at the task of forecasting and examines the selection of the appropriate forecasting method for specific applications in a business setting. Thus that chapter seeks to summarize the chapters that have dealt with specific techniques by relating these techniques and their appropriateness to the various requirements for a forecast in a corporation.

Chapter 13, the final chapter in this book, examines the forecasting function in the firm rather than specific applications, as in Chapter 12. Thus Chapter 13 looks at how such a function can be established in the firm, how it should be designed, and how its efforts should be directed and integrated within the total organization.

DEFINITION AND SPECIFICATION OF VARIABLES IN FORECASTING

Most works on forecasting generally assume that the variable to be forecast is known and well defined. Although that is obviously true in situations in which a forecasting method is already being applied, in new situations it is not necessarily the case.

The initial step in most new applications of forecasting is to determine the variable to be forecast that will be most useful to the manager and for which it is feasible to obtain historical information. As a starting point in making this definition, it is necessary to focus on the purpose of the forecast. At the most general level forecasts supply information for planning or control. In terms of data requirements one of the main differences between forecasts for these two purposes is that information for planning generally involves activities and events both internal and external to the firm. Thus a wide range of variables must be forecast to help in this planning.

Information for control, on the other hand, is generally of an internal nature and frequently the data needed is much more readily obtained, since it may well be a part of the existing accounting system or might easily be added to that system.

Beyond this general distinction of the purpose of the forecast it is necessary to define in some detail just how the proposed forecast will help management to define appropriately the variable to be forecast. The actual contribution that the forecast will make to the management function will determine the time span that should be covered by each value of the variable, the level of detail, the frequency with which it is required, the most appropriate units of measurement, and the level of accuracy. Because of the importance of these five aspects of the definition of the variable to be forecast, we discuss each one briefly.

1. The Time Period Covered by Each Data Value. For practical purposes most of the factors in the business situation can be viewed as taking place in a continuous manner; for example, for a large company we can consider that sales take place on a continuous basis rather than at some instant of time each day or each month. For accounting purposes, however, it is necessary to define some period of time and to summarize the value of each variable for that time period. Thus, in talking about the company's sales, we mean sales per week, per month, or per year rather than smaller units. In defining the time period to be covered by each observation of a variable it is necessary to consider the specific application of the forecast. Forecasts that generally contribute to longer range decision making can generally be based on observed data values for fairly long periods of time, such as quarterly or annually. Forecasts aimed at controlling day-to-day operations would need to be based on data values that cover a time period of one day or perhaps even an hour.

2. Level of Detail Required. The time period covered by each value of a variable is one aspect of the level of detail required for specific application of a forecast. Another aspect is the amount of aggregation involved in a variable; for example, for one situation it may be satisfactory to forecast sales units for the company as a whole for a given period of time. In another situation we may wish to forecast sales by product group or even by product group in each geographical region. If time is taken during the definition phase of forecasting to determine just what level of detail is required, it can save substantial cost later on if management decides that its initial forecasts are too aggregated and must go back and collect the data at a more detailed level. As shown in the next section of this chapter, it is always much more efficient to collect data at the most detailed level possible and then to aggregate it rather than collect aggregates and later discover that they must be broken down into finer detail.

3. The Frequency with Which the Data is Required. This characteristic of a variable is generally closely related to the time period covered by each value of the variable. It can differ in some situations, however; for example, a company may wish to forecast monthly sales for the next year but it may do so only on an annual basis. By knowing with what frequency the data will be utilized, it can be collected in the most efficient manner. Thus, if data is used only on an annual basis, there is no need to have it collected within one or two days of its occurrence. If it is to be used for internal control on almost a daily basis, it must be collected much more rapidly.

4. The Unit of Measurement. Historically, accounting systems have been oriented toward reporting in terms of value, such as dollars and cents. Thus data collection in most accounting systems converts whatever units may naturally exist to dollars before actually storing the data. This conversion represents a loss of information in most forecasting situations. An important step in the design and definition of a forecasting application is the determination of the appropriate units to be used. As a rule of thumb, those units that would naturally be associated with the variable should be used and converted only after the raw data has been stored. This allows us to go back to the raw data in its original units and perform various transformations.

5. Required Level of Accuracy. Different applications of forecasting require different levels of accuracy. The factors that determine the most desirable level are the importance of the management situation and the role of the forecast in effecting that situation. It may be that a forecast needed for an important management situation could be peripheral to that situation and thus the level of accuracy required would not be great. On the other hand, a management situation of only medium importance could use as the basis of decision making a forecast of a single variable. In this situation a high degree of accuracy would be desired. Since increased accuracy generally comes only with increased expense, each new forecasting situation requires that appropriate trade-offs be made in selecting the most desirable level of accuracy. (Some of the problems related to maintaining accuracy are discussed later in this chapter.)

In addition to defining the variable to be forecast, the manager is generally well advised also to define several related variables that might serve as surrogates for the variable to be forecast or that might supply additional information for that management situation. Often forecasts of related variables can be prepared without much additional cost and can give considerably more information to the manager.

The final step in the definition and specification of the variable to be forecast is determining the value of the forecast. Clearly, this value is related to the required level of accuracy and the importance of the management situation. At this initial phase of data definition a rough estimate of the value of the forecast is needed so that the cost of alternative data collection procedures may be kept within the upper bound set by the value of the data.

DATA COLLECTION AND DATA SOURCES

There are three sources from which data can be collected: existing accounting records, original data, and published data. We examine each of them and their characteristics in turn.

Existing accounting records are by far the easiest and least costly source of data with which to deal. In addition, with internal accounting records the manager can generally determine their accuracy and thus their appropriateness to his situation. The major drawback of this source of data is that the accounting system may be inflexible, and although it may include data that is similar to that required by the manager for forecasting it may be nearly impossible, either because of cost or resistance to change, actually to get the data that the manager needs. When existing records can be used, however, the only costs are those of accessing the required data.

Often when the existing accounting system does not include the data that management requires, the decision will be made to collect new data. In this collection process it is important to distinguish two types of data. First is the type that relates to a single time period; for example, if we wish to use multiple-regression analysis in forecasting construction costs for a new plant, it may be possible to go out and collect data on similar construction projects recently completed and to use that data as the basis for making the forecast. In this situation the data can be collected in a single detailed survey or study.

The other type of situation for which original data may be needed is a time series in which an initial detailed analysis may be done to collect some of the data and then a new reporting procedure must be established to continue the collection of that data over time. These situations are generally much more costly and more difficult to initiate because they do involve the establishment of an ongoing procedure for data collection rather than a periodic survey or analysis that can be performed by a staff group.

The major advantage of choosing to collect original data is that it can be tailored to the specific needs of the manager and the flexibility that may be desired in the future can be built into the collection procedures. This flexibility and specificity, however, generally incurs considerably greater cost than when existing accounting records are used. These costs will generally be greater than those of using published sources of data as well.

During recent years there has been a tremendous increase in the number of published data sources. Accompanying this increase has been a decrease in the cost of obtaining the data. The most important source of published data is governmental. In the United States the *Survey of Current Business* (SCB), published monthly by the Office of Business Economics, Department of Commerce, is the single most important source of economic data.

The data contained in the SCB that corporations generally find to be most useful are the national income and product accounts, which can be grouped into eight basic components: (a) gross national product and national income; (b) personal income and outlay; (c) government receipts and expenditures; (d) foreign transactions; (e) saving and investment; (f) income and employment by industry; (g) supplementary tables; and (h) implicit price deflators. In many cases the national income series are available on both an annual and quarterly basis. The annual data generally runs from 1929 through the current year, whereas the quarterly series extends from 1946 through the current quarter. Because of the tremendous value of the SCB, we discuss briefly here each of its eight major portions:

Part I of the national income and products accounts includes gross national product and its expenditure components (personal consumption expenditures), gross private domestic investment, net exports of goods and services, inventories, and government purchases of goods and services both in real and current dollars. Consumption investment, net exports, inventories, and government expenditures are further broken down into consumer expenditures on durables, nondurables and services, nonresidential investment in structures, and producers' durable equipment.

Part II, personal income and outlay, supplies data on three time bases: personal income by disposition, monthly; personal consumption expenditures by major type, quarterly, seasonally adjusted, and unadjusted; and type of product consumed, annually.

Part III, government receipts and expenditures, presents a detailed breakdown for federal, state, and local governments' activities. This breakdown is in terms of receipts and expenditures, annually, on a seasonally adjusted quarterly basis, and on an unadjusted quarterly basis.

Part IV, foreign transactions, presents data both annually and quarterly for the various accounts making up these transactions.

Part V, saving and investment, gives the sources and uses of gross savings in the U.S. economy in both real and current dollars and private purchases of producers' durable equipment by type in real and constant dollars. This section also supplies a complete breakdown of annual changes in business inventories and presents an annual comparison of personal savings.

Part VI, income and employment by industry, appears with a FIC, two-digit industry breakdown and includes the following series: annual supplement to wages and salaries by industry division, income of unincorporated enterprises by industry division; noncorporate capital consumption and allowances; net interest by industry division; and both annually and quarterly, before-tax corporate profits and inventory evaluation adjustments by broad industry groups.

Part VII of the national income and product accounts, the supplementary tables, covers annual receipts and expenditures of GNP by major economic groups.

Finally, Part VIII presents implicit price deflators for GNP on both an annual and a quarterly seasonally adjusted basis.

Besides the national income and product accounts there are many other types of economic data that are published at varying intervals by different government agencies. Some of the most important in these series cover financial and industry data. By far the bulk of economic data that is collected is done on a national basis, but some series are also available at regional levels.

One source of data that is particularly helpful to corporations doing long-range planning is the National Bureau of Economic Research. One of the publications put out by the Bureau is a list of business-cycle indicators. These indicators include both leading and lagging series that can be used as the basis for predicting changes in the current business cycle.

A third government source of data that companies have found particularly useful in recent years has been the Census; for example, the 1970 Census supplies detailed information for each geographical unit in the United States. For those companies interested in forecasting a number of different series that depend on demographic characteristics the Census data can be extremely valuable.

There are also numerous industry sources of data. As one would expect, some industries have much more complete published sources than others, but in just about every major industry some published data is available.

A final source of published information is the private firm; for example, the J. Walter Thompson Company maintains a consumer panel of selected families to check the brands of food products being purchased. The A. C. Neilsen company collects detailed information on consumer purchase patterns at regular intervals. These firms and others can often supply needed data either on a one-time or an on-going basis.

PROBLEMS OF ACCURACY IN DATA

In spite of the obvious truth in the statement that a forecast can be no more accurate than the data on which it is based, it is generally the rule rather than the exception that managers fail to check the accuracy of the basic data behind the forecast. This is particularly true in the situations in which published sources are being used. Unfortunately little information is generally supplied concerning the level of accuracy of published data series. At least one author has studied in some detail the importance of accuracy in government data sources. Morgenstern has found that for the national income and product accounts consumption expenditures have a probable error range of ± 10 to $\pm 15\%$. This means that with consumer expenditures currently around \$700 billion this variable could be either over- or understated by as much as 70 billion to 100 billion dollars. Yet in the national income and product accounts consumption is reported to the nearest tenth of 1 billion dollars. Such reporting can obviously be misleading to the manager who does not examine the accuracy of his data sources.

It is imperative that the manager determine the level of accuracy of his data before using it in forecasting. This is necessary because the value of a forecast is directly dependent on the accuracy of the underlying data. Thus, if the manager does not know that level of accuracy, he cannot determine the value of the forecast in his own situation.

There are numerous sources of error that can arise in the collection of data for a forecasting situation. Morgenstern has defined "collection error" as ". . . an expression of imperfection and of incompleteless in description." He has found that these errors originate from seven main sources: (a) sampling methods, (b) measurement errors, (c) hidden information, (d) poorly designed questionnaires, (e) data aggregates, (f) classification and definition, and (g) the time factor. Since these sources of error can arise in original data collection situations as well as published data sources, we discuss each one briefly at this point.

1. Sampling Methods. In many situations data must be estimated from samples. Optimal sampling methods are fairly well developed in statistics, but these methods have not been used extensively in the collection of most data. When these rules of sampling are followed, however, the manager can be sure to minimize the chances of bias and misrepresentation in his samples.

2. Measurement Errors. Measurement errors occur in the actual collection and processing of data. They are usually human errors which range from collecting the wrong information to key punching errors that result in incorrect information being fed into a computer. Generally speaking, the more automated measurements can be made and the fewer transformations involving humans that take place on data, the less likely the chances of measurement error.

3. Hidden Information. Oftentimes information is deliberately hidden or falsified by firms, households, or others reporting in a survey. Managers are well aware that although the accounting profession provides the general guidelines for various accounts within a company there is still tremendous flexibility in terms of the placement of certain items. Thus the manager needs to be sure that the data he has obtained contains exactly what he wants included. With published sources it is particularly difficult to determine just what the data actually represents and the possibilities that might exist for hidden information.

4. Poorly Designed Questionnaires. Much of the data used in forecasting is collected from respondents who fill in questionnaires; for example, McGraw-Hill uses this approach in collecting data on anticipated investments and investment capacity of U.S. corporations. When using such questionnaires, errors can creep into the survey for a variety of reasons which range from the inability of the respondent to understand exactly what is wanted to his desire to avoid the appearance of ignorance by leaving a question blank.

5. Data Aggregates. When aggregated data are collected from large populations, errors will undoubtedly occur as the result of omitting part of the population or double counting elements in the population. Sometimes the time periods used in various published sources will overlap and thus the task of fitting the data together in a meaningful way is difficult. This problem is particularly significant in the area of financial statistics; for example, national financial data are selected by the Federal Reserve System, the FDIC, and the Comptroller of the Currency. Each of these governmental agencies collects data relevant to a somewhat different population than the other two. It is generally impossible for a corporation using these series to sort out the differences in any meaningful way.

6. Classification and Definition. As stated in the initial section of this chapter, proper classification and definition are two of the most important areas in the collection of data. This is especially true in the case of multiproduct firms. Suppose, for example, that a firm produces a number of products made from livestock. Although each of the firm's activities might fall into a different industrial category, it may be difficult for the firm to attribute profits, sales, and costs unambiguously to each product. Since the trend in the United States seems to be toward corporations with more joint production, it is likely that the difficulty of classifying and defining variables to be forecast will become even more important in the future.

7. Time Factors. Since data must be collected at discrete intervals, certain time problems can develop; for example, firms that use cash rather than accrual accounting methods will report financial data for a time period that does not accurately reflect their economic activity during that period. Even with an accrual type of accounting method a problem can be presented when a real transaction is reported in a different time period than the corresponding financial transaction. At the corporate level these time problems can generally be minimized by an effort to make all data series consistent with the accounting system. In the use of external published sources, however, this degree of control may be impossible to maintain.

A final source of error in the use of data for forecasting is that the characteristics of a sample or population may change over time, with the result that different observations will be reported than would be the case without these changes. All the forecasting techniques that we have discussed so far are based on the notion that the historical data used with the method comes from a homogeneous sample. When the relationships and the nature of that sample are changing significantly over time, substantial error may be present in the data. One other area that is related to the accuracy of data and a natural extension of the definition of the variable to be forecast, as discussed at the beginning of this chapter, is identified by Morgenstern as *functionally false data*. A good example of a functionally false series is the construction of price indexes. These indexes are generally based on published prices, which are rarely those at which transactions actually occur because of rebates, discounts on large purchases, and so on. In addition, the weights used to calculate price indexes may sometimes change significantly in a short period of time, which again reflects functionally false data. The solution to this problem is to be sure that the variable for which data is to be collected is appropriately defined initially and that steps are taken to verify that the actual data collected represents that variable.

USE OF A DATA BASE SYSTEM IN FORECASTING

The last couple of years have seen a tremendous increase in the interest in establishing data bases. This interest deserves special consideration in the area of forecasting. The notion of a data base is that data is collected on a number of different variables and then stored on some easily accessed system (such as a computerized data processing system) so that it will be available when needed. Generally three types of data can be included in a data base for forecasting: (a) data needed for existing requirements, (b) data that is currently available but not currently required, and (c) data that may be required in the future but not currently available.

A data base that focuses only on handling existing data requirements is generally the most straightforward and least expensive system to develop. With a small incremental cost such a base can be expanded to include the collection of available data that is not currently required but may be in the future. Finally, with the use of some planning and management judgment the data base can be expanded even further to include data that may be required in the future but is not currently available. The attractiveness of a data base which includes all three types of data is that most forecasting applications require that a history of data be available before the technique can be applied. Thus, if the data base system includes the collection of several different data items, it is likely that when new forecasts are desired the required data will already be available.

Of course, the trade-off involved in the development of such a data base is the cost associated with it. Generally, however, if a flexible data base is developed, the incremental cost of collecting data on an additional variable is quite low. A key aspect in determining the value and flexibility of a proposed data base is the level of detail involved and the structure of the data actually stored there.

In recent years, perhaps fostered by attempts to employ scientific and mathematical methods in business, we hear more and more frequently the opinion: "You can't use accounting information for decision making" or "You can't make inferences from accounting data." Why not? It seems that the major problem—apart from its being historical rather than predictive—is its degree of aggregation, even in a detailed journal of accounts. All transactions are expressed in terms of a single dimension (dollars), and several different kinds of transactions may be summarized under a single account.

But when you aggregate, you lose information: for instance, when the daily sales of a store are aggregated into a total sales figure for the week, you lose information on the daily *pattern* of sales which may be valuable for inventory planning purposes; or if you combine the sales of a product sold at a special low price with its sale at a regular price into a total-sales dollar figure you lose information about the price-quantity *relationship* for that product which might be valuable in product pricing.

Perhaps the basic reason for much of the aggregation is that accounting methods have evolved under a people-orientation; they were designed to be used by people who were processing data collected by people to produce information to be filed by people and reported to people. Thus the convenience of having a single unit of measure, the convenience of having a single system of accounts, and the convenience of summarizing transactions made aggregation both desirable and necessary.

But let us step back and look at accounting methods in light of the computer and information processing capabilities that are currently available. We are no longer talking about *people* doing the gathering, processing, filing, and reporting; we are talking about *machines* doing the bulk of that job. The capabilities and deficiencies of computer systems are different from those of people. Whereas people have difficulty keeping track of and working with large quantities of data, some computer systems can store billions of characters of data "on-line," accessible in a fraction of a second, and can "read" that data at many thousands of characters per second. Whereas people are slow and tend to make mistakes doing the arithmetic to summarize information, some modern computers can accurately perform millions of these operations per second. Whereas people are slow and prone to err in recording and transcribing data, some point-of-origin data recording equipment and data transmission facilities can record and transmit data accurately as fast as it is generated. The point is that if accounting methods had originally been designed for implementation by machines with these capabilities rather than for implementation by people, they would probably be quite a bit different than they are today and would be more appropriate as data bases for forecasting.

Let us suppose that we are all twentieth century Pacioli's and that we are designing an accounting system specifically for implementation on modern computers and use in forecasting. Since computers have the ability to gather, transmit, and store large quantities of data, we might design a system that records data in many dimensions of measurement, rather than just in financial terms, and that retains all the transactions data in their most elementary form rather than aggregating them and posting to accounts. Such a system would, compared with traditional methods, provide a broader more accurate base for management information and would not lose part of that information content in an aggregation process.

The data, however, has little value until it is summarized or otherwise processed for human consumption. How it should be summarized depends on the information needed, and these needs change from situation to situation. Using the high computational speed of the computer, it *might* be possible to summarize the data in *all* conceivable ways and make the results available to the interested parties.

But what a waste! Instead of having our accounting system and data base produce reams of useless information along with what is needed, we could design it to do *no* summarization of the raw data unless or until a particular summary was requested. Rather than posting the transactions to accounts and summarizing them, our system might create a "trail of pointers" to the data, a trail that would provide the computer with the informatiion it needs to find the appropriate data and to construct any kind of summarization that might be requested. Such a system would have the *potential* to construct any information based on the data but would *actually* construct only requested information at the time of the request.

We might call a system of this design a *data base* accounting system. It would exploit some of the capabilities of modern computers to solve two of the difficulties of traditional accounting methods— inflexibility and loss of information through aggregation— in a feasible and usable fashion. Although this system is being suggested merely to illustrate how a data base for forecasting might be made much more attractive than existing data bases resulting from traditional accounting systems, it might be an interesting side tract to pursue it a little further.

Implemented on modern computers, a data base accounting system might work like this. As *relevant events* occur in the enterprise and its environment, data describing them is transmitted directly to the computer from automatic data-gathering devices or by people "phoning in." These relevant events would include what is normally called or makes up accounting transactions but would also include other events that are thought to affect the performance or the activities of the enterprise. As each *event description* enters the computer system, it is automatically assigned an event number and stored in a direct access storage device. These event descriptions, which form the data base for the system, are filed by their event numbers; the computer can, given its event number, directly retrieve any event description from storage.

Perhaps the following example will help to clarify how the data base would be constructed. Suppose there are four kinds of relevant events for a retail enterprise: advertising expenditures, sales, product prices, and product costs. Each would come into the system from its source; the sales events, for example, might come into the system directly from the cash registers, whereas the advertising manager might phone in his media and expenditure decisions. Assume that the sampling interval is one week (events are reported only once a week as totals for the week) and that the system has received the following event descriptions during weeks 13 to 15.

ADVERTISING EXPENDITURES

Event No.	Expenditure	Advertising Media	Week
5	$400	Newspaper	13
12	200	Newspaper	14
13	200	Circular	14
14	400	Newspaper	15

SALES

Event No.	Quantity	Product	Week
1	40	A	13
2	60	B	13
8	50	A	14
9	80	B	14
15	80	A	15
16	60	B	15

PRODUCT PRICES

Event No.	Price	Product	Week
3	$10	A	13
4	5	B	13
10	10	A	14
11	5	B	14
17	8	A	15
18	3	B	15

PRODUCT COSTS

Event No.	Cost	Product	Weeks
6	$4	A	13–15
7	1	B	13–15

Notice three features about the event descriptions:

1. Each consists of one measurable quantity (e.g., quantity sold or price charged) and a series of *tags* or *classifications* to which that quantity is associated (e.g., Product A and week 15).

2. The quantity and tags of an event description are expressed in the terms that illustrate them most naturally.

3. They include controllable events, that is, management decisions, as well as uncontrollable events.

The basis for locating and manipulating the appropriate event description for any requested summarization is a system of *data categories*. These categories, which correspond roughly to the accounts of a traditional accounting system, are *lists of the event numbers* that correspond to the event descriptions containing the data items that pertain to the category. A typical data category might be "Product A"; it would contain the numbers of all the event descriptions pertaining to Product A. Another might be "Quantity Sold"; it would contain the numbers of all event descriptions having to do with sales quantities, regardless of product or time period. In other words, a data category rather than storing the *data* (or aggregated data) that logically belongs in the category is a *list of pointers* that indicates where to get that data when and if it is needed.

The data categories in our example would be the following:

Category	Pointers (event numbers)
Sales	1, 2, 8, 9, 15, 16
Product price	3, 4, 10, 11, 17, 18
Product cost	6, 7,
Advertising	5, 12, 13, 14
Product A	1, 3, 6, 8, 10, 15, 17
Product B	2, 4, 7, 9, 11, 16, 18
Newspaper	5, 12, 14
Circular	13
Week 13	1, 2, 3, 4, 5, 6, 7
Week 14	6, 7, 8, 9, 10, 11, 12, 13
Week 15	6, 7, 14, 15, 16, 17, 18

Notice that the first four categories refer to the *quantities* in the event descriptions, whereas the rest of the categories refer to *tags* that classify the quantities. Of course, once the data categories are updated for a new event description, only the quantity portion of the event description needs to be stored; the information contained in the tags is contained in the data categories themselves.

With the data categories defined, it is possible for the computer to construct any summary of the data by expressing that summary in terms of the data categories; for example, suppose we want to know the total quantity of Product A that was sold during weeks 14 and 15. The computer would scan the list of event numbers in the SALES, PRODUCT A, and WEEK 14 categories and would access from storage all event descriptions whose numbers are in *all three categories.** It would then add the quantities in those event descriptions (in this case there is only one, #8, for which the quantity is 50) and add that sum to the sum of the quantities in the event descriptions listed in the SALES, PRODUCT A, and WEEK 15 categories. Since the only event description listed in all three categories is #15 with a quantity of 80, the desired information for this example would be: "130 units of Product A were sold in weeks 14 and 15."

From this example we can see that it is possible to express any summarization that can be constructed from the data base as a *function of the data categories.* For any commonly used summaries (e.g., total weekly sales and profit) the defining functions are stored in the computer system for immediate use. In a sense, these summarization functions are pointers to data categories which in turn are pointers to the event descriptions. Thus, although the data base remains intact, the system creates a network of pointers that enables the computer to construct desired summaries on request.

In our example the following might be typical summarization functions expressed in an English-like language.

DOLLAR SALES (PRODUCT A, WEEK 13) = SALES (PRODUCT A, WEEK 13) TIMES PRICE (PRODUCT A, WEEK 13)

DOLLAR SALES (PRODUCT B, WEEK 13) = SALES (PRODUCT B, WEEK 13) TIMES PRICE (PRODUCT B, WEEK 13)

TOTAL DOLLAR SALES (WEEK 13) = DOLLAR SALES (PRODUCT A, WEEK 13) PLUS DOLLAR SALES (PRODUCT B, WEEK 13)

PROFIT (WEEK 13) = TOTAL DOLLAR SALES (WEEK 13) MINUS SALES (PRODUCT A, WEEK 13) TIMES COST (PRODUCT A) MINUS SALES (PRODUCT B, WEEK 13) TIMES COST (PRODUCT B) MINUS ADVERTISING (WEEK 13)

---

*Notice that this scanning and matching process could be done relatively efficiently, since the pointers in the data categories are in order of increasing event number.

Notice that the summarization functions can be defined both in terms of data categories and previously defined functions.

To apply the system for information retrieval and analysis the user specifies the summaries he wants [e.g., PROFIT (WEEK 15)]. Using the summarization functions, the computer translates his description into an expression in terms of the data categories and, scanning and matching those lists of pointers, retrieves the necessary event descriptions from the data base. The computer then performs the required computation on the data and displays the results or prints a "hard copy" report for the user.

If the user is requesting a new kind of summary, he can get it by first defining the summarization function for that information in terms of previously defined functions and data categories. In this way the data base accounting system provides the flexibility to get summary information that was not thought of when the system was being designed. Keeping the data in its elemental form with a system of pointers makes this flexibility possible.

Besides enabling the user to get any kind of summary report he wants, a data base accounting system also enables the user to investigate for possible *relationships* between factors in the enterprise or its environment; for example, if the user asks for (or defines if not previously defined) SALES (PRODUCT B, WEEK 13) and PRICE (PRODUCT B, WEEK 13) and also the same information for weeks 14 and 15, the system would produce.

PRODUCT B

Week	Quantity	Price
13	60	$5
14	80	5
15	60	3

The user would observe that the quantity sold increased in week 14, whereas the price stayed constant but decreased to its previous level in week 15 in spite of a 40% price decrease.

Thinking that perhaps the advertising expenditures had something to do with these anomalies, he might ask for ADVERTISING (WEEK 13) ADVERTISING (WEEK 14) and ADVERTISING (WEEK 15), So instructed, the system would produce the following report:

ADVERTISING

Week	Expenditure
13	$400
14	400
15	400

This information does not seem to shed any light on the matter, but the user might guess that aggregating the advertising data by media might have obscured the relationship. If so, he could ask that the following report be constructed from the data base.

ADVERTISING

Week	Expenditure	Media
13	$400	Newspaper
14	200	Newspaper
14	200	Circular
15	400	Newspaper

With this information the user could reach the preliminary conclusion that a *mixture* of newspaper and circular advertising is more effective for Product B than just newspaper ads and the sales of Product B are insensitive to price reductions.

Note: It might be an interesting exercise to record the transactions of this example as they would have been in a traditional system of accounts to see if these conclusions could have been gleaned from the data recorded in that fashion.

Although the preceding pages have suggested but one example of the organization of a data base, the usefulness of such a system in forecasting should be apparent; for example, with the detailed level of data suggested it would be possible to identify sales relationships by using a technique such as multiple regression. In addition, it would be possible to aggregate some of the data to develop desired time-series forecasts of such things as monthly sales and price changes.

UPDATING AND INTERNAL AUDITS

Once the kind of data needed as the basis of a forecast has been identified and the initial collection of that data has been performed it is still necessary to develop and implement a procedure for collecting new data as it is generated and adding it to the existing series of historical observations. As part of such a procedure, we should also include a method of determining when additional detailed analyses are needed to identify possible changes in underlying relationships and other factors that would signal the need for a revision of that data series.

Perhaps equally important as the ongoing procedures for data collection is the development of a system of error checks that can be used to verify the accuracy of the data as it is collected. As stated earlier, there are a number of sources of error in the data collection process, and thus it is necessary to run periodic checks of the data to make sure that such errors are not creeping in systematically and that the data still represents what it is supposed to.

In an earlier section of this chapter the argument was put forward that the person using a forecast must have confidence in it and in the data that lies behind it if it is to have value for him. To ensure that the manager will have the desired level of confidence in the data an auditing function should be initiated for all data series used in forecasting. This auditing function should cover four main areas. First would be a review of the procedure underlying the data collection process to identify possible improvements in that collection. Second would be the detailed observation of actual data collection to ensure that the process outlined is being followed. Verification of this adherence to stated procedures is an important factor in determining the level of confidence that can be placed in the data.

The third auditing function that should be performed is a check of the accuracy of the data and the variable to be forecast for the management situation in question. As management's needs change, the specific forecasting requirements will also change. Thus it is important to review periodically management's tasks to determine whether different variables should be forecast and whether existing forecasting applications are no longer useful.

The final auditing function involves an examination of the costs associated with data collection and determining whether those costs are under control and whether the value of that data still exceeds the costs. Thus to perform this evaluation it is necessary to allocate the costs of data collection at least in some rough form.

SUGGESTED REFERENCES FOR ADDITIONAL STUDY

Butler, William F., and Robert A. Kavesh, 1966. *How Business Economists Forecast*, Prentice-Hall, Englewood Cliffs, New Jersey.

Ijiri, Y., 1967. *The Foundations of Accounting Measurement*, Prentice-Hall, Englewood Cliffs, New Jersey.

McRae, T. W., 1964. *The Impact of Computers on Accounting*, Wiley, London.

Moore, G. H., and J. Shiskin, 1967. *Indicators of Business Expansion and Contraction*, National Bureau of Economic Research, New York.

Morgenstern, Oskar, 1963. *On the Accuracy of Economic Observations*, Princeton University Press, Princeton, New Jersey.

Porter, W. T., Jr., 1966. *Auditing Electronic Systems*, Wadsworth, Belmont, California.

Stekler, H. O., and F. W. Burch, 1968. "Selected Economic Data: Accuracy vs. Reporting Speed," *Journal of American Statistical Association*, 436–444 (June).

Zschau, E. V. W., 1968. "The Impact of Computers and Information Sciences on Accounting." Paper presented at the annual meeting of the American Accounting Association, San Diego, August.

CHAPTER 10

FORECASTS BASED ON SUBJECTIVE ESTIMATES

PROBABILITY AND UNCERTAINTY IN DECISION MAKING

An inherent aspect of any management decision-making situation is the presence of uncertainty concerning one or more of the relevant factors; for example, the entire notion of forecasting the value of some variable in the future is based on the fact that there is uncertainty concerning that variable. What the forecast needs to do is to estimate the most likely value of the variable. In many instances this most likely value or single point estimate is sufficient for the needs of management. In other cases, however, the amount of uncertainty concerning such a likely value may be large, and it may be much more useful to management to have a range of values estimated for that variable.

The idea of estimating the range of values was presented in Chapters 5 and 7 in another format. There the discussion concerned confidence intervals that represent the bounds within which the manager is, say, 95% certain that the true value of the variable will be found. Such a confidence interval simply establishes a range around the most likely value that is being forecast. When a variable such as sales of a new product is uncertain, having a range of values for the possible outcome gives the manager much more information than just simply the expected value. An example of how this information might influence the decision is the following:

Suppose two variables have the same expected value, but one is likely to fluctuate much more than the other. The manager is usually best advised to select the decision that has the least amount of fluctuation if he is risk averse and to select the one with the widest range of outcomes if he is a risk taker.

162

Virtually all the forecasting procedures discussed so far require that the manager have available a series of historical data that can be used directly in preparing a forecast. Unfortunately in many instances such historical data is neither available nor relevant; for example, the manager who is forecasting the cost of a well-established product may have considerable data on past sales of that product, but the introduction of a new competitor's product may make much of this data irrelevant. Another type of situation in which historical data may not even be present is that of developing forecasts for new products. Although the product manager may have had experience with several similar products, he may in fact have no past data that can be used directly with one of the forecasting techniques already described. When a situation develops in which these historical data based methods cannot be used, the manager is still faced with the problem of supplying a forecast that will help him to make his decision. In fact, in such situations the amount of uncertainty involved is generally much greater than it is when relevant historical data is available, and thus it is even more important that the manager have some meaningful forecast for the values of those variables that affect his decision.

The area of forecasting that involves substantial uncertainty is generally tackled with technological or qualitative methods of forecasting. These are discussed in Chapter 11. In between situations suitable for quantitative techniques and those suitable for qualitative techniques are many situations in which a different method involving probability analysis can be utilized. It is on this intermediate area in which existing data series do not apply directly in the preparation of a forecast but in which management has some good ideas about what to expect that we want to focus in this chapter. The technique that we discuss, often subsumed under the title of "decision analysis," is that of using subjective probability estimates as forecasts.

Before we discuss how the manager can handle the particular type of situation just described, it would be helpful to sit back and look first at the general problem of dealing with uncertainty in a decision-making situation. Two approaches can be taken. The first and most widely used is simply to consider it implicitly in the decision-making process. This can be done by obtaining the information concerning uncertainty such as confidence intervals and then simply factoring it into the decision-making process just as information about several other factors is integrated in the manager's mind. Although this is obviously a nonrigorous and unsystematic approach, in many instances it may be the best one available. This implicit approach is the one generally connected with the use of sensitivity analysis; for example, a manager may determine a point forecast (i.e., a single estimate) for next year's sales, but then by examining the sensitivity of those sales to various factors and implicitly considering the likelihood that they will change he can consider the uncertainty that is involved.

The alternative means of dealing with uncertainty in management decision making involves treating it explicitly. This requires that some language be developed that will allow uncertainty to be expressed in a rigorous form. The language that has evolved and been improved over the last few years for handling this uncertainty is that of probability. Probability is simply a means of expressing uncertainty so that it can be dealt with explicitly by managers. The advantage in stating uncertainty explicitly is that the procedures used to deal with it in the decision-making process can also be clearly stated and applied in a consistent manner. In our discussions of probability and uncertainty in this chapter the reader should always remember that our aim is to examine techniques that can help the manager in decision making. Thus probability and the use of decision analysis are simply means to the end of improving decisions. This is completely consistent with the definition we gave of forecasting in Chapter 1.

Most people are familiar with the use of probability in games of chance; for example, it is commonly understood that if we toss a "fair" coin it is equally likely that the outcome will be heads as tails. Thus the probability of achieving an outcome of "heads" is one-half and that of achieving an outcome of "tails" is one-half. Similarly, when we roll a fair die, the probability of realizing each one of the six possible outcomes is one-sixth. We can ask the question: what do such statements about probability really mean? In the two examples just given they can be interpreted in terms of frequency. If we were to toss a coin 1000 times, approximately one-half, or 500, of the tosses would result in an outcome of "heads" and the other 500 would be "tails." Similarly, rolling a die 1000 times would result in a value of 1 for approximately one-sixth of the 1000 rolls, a value of 2 for one-sixth of them and so on. Thus in these particular instances it is possible to run an experiment (tossing a coin or rolling a die) that would develop a frequency pattern corresponding to these probabilities.

It is this type of probability that we are using when we determine the confidence interval on the regression line; for example, if we have determined a 95% confidence interval, it means that if we had several more observations 95% of them would fall within the confidence interval and 5% of them would lie outside that interval. It is important, of course, to realize that such probabilities represent only the long-run average. It could be that if we added 10 more observations to our regression analysis situation two of them (20%) might happen to be outside the 95% confidence interval. Thus we must distinguish between the probability of an event or a value and the actual outcome on a particular example or trial. In each of the examples just mentioned the probability that a certain event will occur (e.g., obtaining a head, obtaining a 1, or observing a value outside the 95% confidence interval) could be based on historical observation. From past data the frequency of these events could be computed, and thus the probabilities could be based on those frequencies. This means that again we have a situation in which past data is required to make estimates. Although it may help the manager somewhat more than simply using the forecasting techniques discussed in earlier chapters, it still does not solve the problem of what he should do when no historical data is available or when the data that is available is not directly relevant. In such situations the manager can still apply the concept of probability, but not based on historical frequencies. In these cases the application is that of subjective probability, which means that the probability is based on some subjective judgments of the decision maker and not on an objective analysis of past information.

A typical example of a subjective probability estimate would be when a manager says something like, "There's only one chance in 10 that if we submit a bid of $100,000 we will obtain the contract." In such a situation, since every contract is different and since the competitors' reactions are uncertain, this probability statement must be based on some kind of subjective judgment of what will happen. If we can make such judgments accurately they will contribute substantial information to decision making. Pursuing this example, suppose that an individual in the company with substantial experience in bidding could tell the manager for each of four different bid prices what the probability would be of winning the contract. This would certainly help the manager in deciding on the price he should submit. (Further on in this chapter we examine some of the ways the manager might use these subjective estimates.)

One point that needs to be made concerning the difference between subjective probability and objective probability is that there is no way to check on a single subjective estimate to determine whether it is correct. In the bidding example one manager might say that for a given bid there is one chance in 10 of winning the contract, whereas in the exact same situation a different manager would estimate that there are two chances in 10 of winning the contract. Who is to say which one of these managers is correct? Even if it turns out that the company wins that particular bid at that price, it does not mean that the probability is .2 rather than .1 or vice versa. Thus we must be sure that managers understand the concepts of subjective probability and that they have a thorough knowledge of the variables being estimated before such subjective estimates are used as the basis of decision making. As we point out in a subsequent section of this chapter, it is possible to take several steps to help train managers in making such subjective probability estimates, and it is also possible for a specific manager to calibrate the accuracy of these forecasts in some situations. This, however, requires checking several forecasts made by that manager over a fairly stable period of time.

There are two important properties of probability that the manager must keep in mind in making subjective probability estimates. The first is that if we consider all possible events (i.e., all possible outcomes) in a given situation, the sum of the probabilities assigned to each of these individual events must be exactly equal to 1; for example, in tossing a coin there are two possible outcomes, a head and a tail. Thus the probability of a head plus the probability of a tail must always equal 1. Similarly, there are six possible outcomes in the roll of a die. The sum of the probability of each of these six outcomes must equal 1. Finally, in the example of bidding on a contract, there would be two possible outcomes, winning the contract and losing the contract. Thus the probability of winning plus the probability of losing must equal 1.

The second important property of probabilities is that the probability assigned to a specific outcome can never be less than 0 nor greater than 1. If an outcome is assigned a probability of 0, it implies that the outcome is impossible; assigning a probability of 1 implies that the outcome is certain to occur no matter what.

USING SUBJECTIVE PROBABILITIES IN DECISION MAKING

In discussing the forecasting techniques in each of the preceding chapters the focus has been on how the manager can obtain a point estimate or forecast for the value of some specific variable. As also discussed earlier, however, having a forecast of a distribution of possible outcomes for a variable would come much closer to representing reality in a situation and explicitly including uncertainty. In our discussion of subjective probabilities in this chapter we examine the likelihood or probability of observing a range of possible outcomes in a situation. Rather than relating how this can be done and then applying it to forecasting and decision making, it would be much more useful to focus on the decision-making process with this as a means of improving that process.

In the preceding chapters it has been assumed implicitly that once the manager had a forecast, even if only a point forecast, he would be able to use it as one input for decision making. We have not really raised any questions about how it can be done; for example, if we give the production manager an estimate of sales for the coming month, we have simply assumed that he will know how to use that estimate best to improve decision making rather than examining the actual process he might follow. In dealing with subjective probability estimates, and for that matter with any kind of probability estimate, it is much more useful to look at the entire decision-making process than at the value of one of the variables in that process. In this section we discuss the methodology referred to as decision analysis, which can be used by the manager as a means of making his decision in a way that explicitly considers the uncertainties involved. The example we use is that of a company which must submit a bid on a proposed contract. To make it simple, we suppose it is a cement company bidding on a single contract that calls for the delivery of 100,000 barrels of cement over a period of two months. Let us also suppose that the management of the company has decided it is necessary to consider only three possible bid prices: $2.90 a barrel, $2.50 a barrel, and $2.10 a barrel.

As a starting point in handling this bidding situation, we can first diagram the situation that the company faces; that is, we can determine what the possible actions are and then relate them graphically by drawing a tree structure. This is referred to as drawing a decision tree. For the cement company the alternative actions are to bid $2.90, bid $2.50, or bid $2.10. Depending on the bid that the company submits, there will be certain probabilities of winning or losing the contract. The relation between winning or losing the contract and the bid price is shown in the decision tree in Figure 10-1.

Note that a square has been used to represent a decision point and a circle, to represent an uncertain event. The distinction between decisions and uncertain events is important and necessary in this type of analysis. Note also in this decision tree that not only have the possible outcomes of the events been enumerated but also that the possible decisions have been explicitly

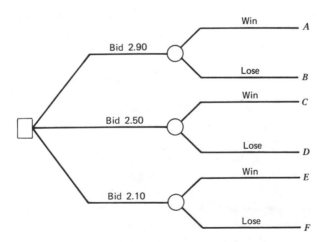

Figure 10-1 Decision tree for cement contract bidding.

identified. Once a decision tree has been drawn the management of the company must evaluate the three alternative actions (bid $2.90, bid $2.50/ and bid $2.10) to determine which of them is the most appropriate to take.

The next step that must be taken in analyzing these alternative actions is to specify the criterion to be used in making a decision; for example, the company may take the action that is likely to lead to the highest profit after tax on this contract. An alternative criterion would be that they might want to obtain the largest contribution possible to their fixed expenses; that is, they might want to take the action that would maximize their expected contribution from the contract. It is this second criterion that we will use to evaluate this situation. One of the characteristics of decision analysis is that a single objective criterion must be specified. In most situations there are usually several objectives that the company wishes to consider. Although advanced techniques of preference and utility theory have been developed to allow decision analysis to handle these situations involving multiple objectives, they are generally complex and difficult to apply. Thus we limit our discussion to consideration of a single objective.

The next step in evaluation is to determine the value of each of the possible paths in this decision tree. These paths have been indicated on the right-hand side of Figure 10-1 by a letter. Three of these paths (B, D, and F) represent losing the contract and the other three represent winning the contract, although with different bid prices. To evaluate each path we can start with path A and ask, "What will be the contribution the company will receive if they bid $2.90 per barrel *and* win the contract?" Since the contract is for a fixed number of barrels (100,000), the company must determine the contribution on each of these barrels when the price is $2.90 and multiply that contribution by the 100,000 barrels. Suppose the company finds that the direct cost associated with this contract is $1.50 per barrel. This means that their contribution per barrel with a price of $2.90 would be $1.40. Thus the value of path A is $1.40 times 100,000 barrels, or $140,000. Next we examine path B, which is a bid of $2.90 and loss of the contract. Since the company will receive no revenue if they lose, we can assign a value of 0 to this path. Similarly we can compute the contributions to paths C, D, E, and F as $100,000, $0, $60,000 and $0, respectively.

At this point it becomes necessary to assign some kind of probability to the uncertain events in the decision diagram. These events are those represented by a circle in Figure 10-1. Although the company may have some historical information that relates directly to similar contracts, it is most likely that this particular bidding situation will be somewhat different than previous situations, either in terms of competition or the details of the contract. Thus the probabilities must be based on management judgment and not merely on historical observations. Let us suppose that the manager has considered the likelihood of winning and losing the bid with each of the three prices and has come up with the following estimates: there is 1 chance in 10 of winning and 9 chances in 10 of losing if the bid is $2.90. If the bid is $2.50, it appears equally likely that they will win or lose, and if the bid is $2.10 the chances are 9 out of 10 of winning and 1 out of 10 of losing the contract. It should be emphasized that these are subjective probability estimates and thus there is no way to verify their correctness.

Most likely these probability estimates were made by an expert in the firm who has worked closely with other bidding problems and knows the market and the competition. The means by which the manager will actually make these subjective estimates is generally left to him. As we show later in this chapter, however, steps which can be taken to help ensure that he will make every effort possible to develop accurate estimates.

What now remains in analyzing this decision situation is the development of some means of working backward from the values A through F at the end points, getting values for the intermediate events, and finally finding the decision with the highest value. This process is referred to as "folding back." To see how this works, let us look at the bid $2.90 option. If the company bids $2.90, there is a 10% chance of winning and a 90% chance of losing; that is, if this situation were to arise several different times, 10% of the time when they bid $2.90 they would win a contract valued at $140,000 and 90% of the time they would lose the contract with a value of 0. Thus the average of several such occasions would give an average value of .10 $\times$ 140,000 + .9 $\times$ 0 = $14,000 in contribution. This value is called *the expected value*. It is computed by multiplying the probability of an outcome by the value of that outcome, and after doing that for all possible outcomes adding the products together.

Another way to look at this computation of expected value is that the value of winning is weighted by the chances of winning—one-tenth in this case— and the value of losing is weighted by the chances of losing—nine-tenths in this case. We can now do the same thing for "bid $2.50" and "bid $2.10," obtaining the expected values of $50,000 and $54,000, respectively. To see just where we are at this point, let us redraw the decision tree and add the computations that we have made. This is done in Figure 10–2.

Let us review the meaning of this decision diagram. It says that if the company makes a bid of $2.90 per barrel the expected payoff from that decision is $14,000. Similarly, a bid of $2.50 has an expected payoff of $50,000 and a bid of $2.10 has an expected payoff of $54,000. Thus this analysis would indicate that the company would be best off—that is, they would maximize their contribution—if they submitted a bid of $2.10. Note

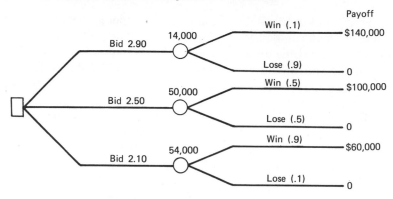

Figure 10-2   Decision tree with computations for cement contract bidding.

that this will maximize their expected payoff, but since the actual payoff depends on winning or losing the bid—uncertain events— the company is still not certain whether they will win or lose whatever bid they submit.

It may be that in such a situation other considerations will influence the final decision taken; for example, the manager might be concerned about starting a price war if he submits a price of $2.10. Thus, since the expected payoff of a bid price of $2.50 is not much lower, he might choose to submit a bid of $2.50 rather than $2.10. Alternatively, it may be that the company is operating close to capacity and thus wants the business only if the profit margin is extremely high. This would argue for submitting a bid of $2.90 and simply taking their chances of winning or losing. Thus the manager who uses subjective probability in this approach to decision analysis should still consider outside factors before making his final decision.

We can now summarize the steps that must be taken in using this approach of decision analysis:

1. Draw the Decision Tree.   This involves identifying the relevant decisions and events and putting them in their proper sequence.

2. Determine the Values of Each Possible Path.   This consists of specifying what the decision criterion will be (e.g., maximize cash flow or net profit or minimize costs) and then evaluating each of the possible paths in the decision tree.

3. Assign Probabilities to the Uncertain Events.   In most instances these probabilities will be based on subjective estimates made by managers involved in the situation. The rules for dealing with probability must be adherred to in doing this.

4. Fold Back the Values to Determine the Best Decisions. This involves working from the end of the tree backward by computing the expected values at each *event point* and then at each *action point* selecting the action branch with the highest expected value.

5. Take the Best Actions that Have Been Identified. Obviously the example that has been used to demonstrate this approach to decision making was a simple one, although probably a common one as well, since it described a typical bidding situation. In many cases the decision tree will be much more elaborate in that several sequential decisions will be required and many event points will occur. Even in these more complicated situations, however, the procedure to be followed is exactly that summarized above. Some of the areas in which forecasts based on subjective estimates have been effectively applied with decision analysis include market test planning, new product introduction, and research and development planning.

OBTAINING SUBJECTIVE PROBABILITIES

A critical point in the use of decision analysis outlined in the preceding section is that the results of the analysis are only as reliable as the probabilities assigned to the various events. The notion of preparing subjective probability is a new one for many managers. It is not enough in such situations to ask them for the required probabilities; they must be trained and guided in developing the ability to make such assessments.

The reader will undoubtedly be familiar with certain individuals who always seem to overestimate the favorable outcome in a situation and, likewise, other individuals who always seem to underestimate the likelihood of a favorable outcome. The former are generally referred to as optimists, the latter as pessimists. If a decision maker is to use subjective probability estimates developed by himself or others in the firm (or outside it), he will want to determine whether these individuals are generally optimistic or pessimistic in their assessment of probabilities. This can be done by comparing the outcomes of events for which they have prepared estimates with their estimated values. It must be stressed that this cannot be done for one or two events and their assessments and results. Rather what we must do is obtain several estimates for different events and then determine the results of those events and see if they generally occur in the same likelihood as the estimator had predicted or if there is some pattern of bias. This evaluation procedure is often called calibrating a forecaster.

To see just how this calibration can be carried out in practice let us consider a specific example. Most forest-product firms are faced with the task of estimating the amount of timber that can be cut from specific parcels of land. Suppose that one such company follows the procedure of sending an estimator out to examine each new parcel and then having him prepare an estimate of the yield per acre in thousands of board feet. Of course once the parcel is actually harvested, the company will know the yield exactly. On the last 10 parcels the estimator's record has been as follows:

Forecast (Estimate)	Actual	Actual/Forecast
170	175	1.03
190	178	.93
165	175	1.06
203	200	.98
169	170	1.01
183	190	1.04
190	180	.95
200	205	1.02
206	200	.97
185	160	.86

The third column computes A/F for each parcel, the ratio of the actual value to the forecast value. This ratio can be used to determine both the extent of bias in the estimator's forecasts and their dispersion.

In this example the average A/F value can be computed as .98, which suggests that the estimator may be slightly biased on the side of overestimating the yield of a given parcel. If this pattern were observed consistently, the manager might want to revise the estimator's forecasts downward by 2% each time to compensate for this. The dispersion in this estimate can be approached in two different ways. First we compute the standard deviation by using

$$SD = \left(\frac{\Sigma(X_i - \bar{X})^2}{n}\right)^{1/2},$$

which produces SD = .06 and suggests that the estimator is quite precise. (Recall from Chapter 5 that the values will be within ±3 SD 99% of the time, which says that the timber yield estimaor will be within = 18% of the actual value virtually all of the time.)

An alternative means of viewing the dispersion in the estimates is to draw a cumulative probability graph of A/F. This can be done by ranking the A/F values and then plotting them in the manner shown in Figure 10-3. This approach has the advantage of being able to determine a distribution for any new estimate; for example, suppose the estimator forecasts a value of 180 for a new parcel of timber. The second axis in Figure 10-3 shows the

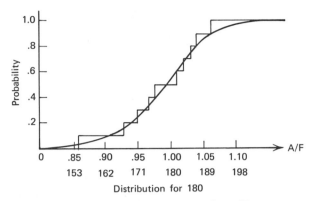

Figure 10-3   Calibrating a forecaster with A/F.

range of possible outcomes for the actual value based on the estimator's record. As we can see, there is only a 20% chance in this situation of the actual value's being outside the range, 162–193. Other probability ranges could also be estimated in the same fashion. Thus the calibration of a forecaster is a practical method of assessing the bias and dispersion that can be expected in a subjective estimating situation that is repeated over time.

This means of checking the reliability of subjective probability estimates is limited, but unfortunately it is one of the few available. A somewhat related approach would be to have those engaged in making such estimates practice on situations in which the results can be obtained immediately; for example, a manager might be shown a transparent jar filled with blue and white marbles and asked to estimate the proportion of each color. This can be approximated by asking what the probability is that a white marble will be drawn if a single sample is taken from the jar. After the estimate has been made, the person can then be told what the true proportion is and a somewhat different jar can be presented and the process repeated. In this way the individual learns how to modify his estimates so that they will come closer to reality. A drawback of this approach is that estimating sales of a product is not the same thing as estimating marbles of a certain color. It does, however, serve to make the manager familiar with probabilities and some of the rules that must be used in developing them.

One of the major faults in the application of subjective estimates and decision analysis in business is that oftentimes the decision maker will need information on the value of a certain variable and will ask the appropriate individual in his firm for a range of values and their probability. If the individual doing the estimating is not familiar with probability assessments, he could give erroneous results. It is always much better to have someone sit down and ask him about these estimates and then discuss them to make sure that they represent what he intended; for example, during the discussion the estimator could be asked to supply the likelihood that, say, certain levels of sales will be achieved for a new product. The questions might consist of, "What is the likelihood that sales will be 2 million units of more?" and "What is the likelihood that sales will be 1 million units or more?" A slightly different approach is to ask the individual what level of sales represents the most likely result, what level of sales there is only a 10% chance of exceeding, and what level of sales there is a 99% chance of exceeding.

From the range of questions that can be asked and the importance of having reliable probability estimates, it can be seen that the value of spending some time interviewing the estimator certainly exceeds the cost of such interviewing time. As companies develop the ability to work with subjective probability, much of this interviewing can be eliminated.

LIMITATIONS AND EXTENSIONS

Forecasts based on subjective probability estimates require the use of a statistical model. Generally this model is referred to as Bayesian statistics or Bayesian analysis. As pointed out for the techniques of simple and multiple regression, a statistical model allows us to establish certain confidence intervals and statistics that can be used to check the validity of the model. This is what we were actually doing in developing the calibration of a forecaster in the preceding section. The drawback of a statistical model, however, is that it requires a better understanding on the part of a manager of statistics and mathematics that do most nonstatistical models.

It should be clear from the previous discussion that any pattern of data can be represented by subjective probability estimates. In fact, since these estimates are made for only a single point in time, it is not really necessary to assume explicitly any pattern at all. Rather it is necessary to estimate that single point. This means that the method of decision analysis can be applied to a wide range of problems.

In terms of the data requirements of this technique, it can be based on information that already exists within the firm or of which the manager doing the estimating is aware. Thus on the preparation side the data requirements are not really substantial, except that the mere fact that all possible decisions must be enumerated and all possible outcomes of uncertain events specified means that in making the decision analysis complete the manager will generally have to consider much more information than he normally would in his own decision-making approach. This can often be a problem, since it involves getting estimates from other people in the firm who are often located in other organizational units. As managers know, working across such organizational lines is not always a trouble-free prospect.

One area in which this technique has substantial data requirements is on the output side. Since the manager is supplied with an entire range of possible values, he can sometimes feel overloaded with information and not be adequately prepared to cope with it. It can happen that the manager will simply ignore all this data and make the decision the way he always has. Thus in implementing this technique it is important that it be done in a stepwise fashion so that the manager can learn to cope with the new data that is supplied in a small way and then expand his understanding and his application of the technique as he learns more about it.

The costs associated with decision analysis and subjective forecasts are generally different in nature from those associated with other forecasting techniques. Here the costs are related to management time rather than to actual expenditure on staff support, data storage, and computation. They are, however, still just as real and must be computed before making major commitments to implement a forecasting procedure based on this technique.

One of the things that make the technique of decision analysis so powerful is that other forecasting methods can actually be used with it in place of subjective probability estimates; for example, we saw in Chapters 5 and Chapter 7 that regression analysis is a statistical method that can supply estimates of the standard error of regression. Thus it is possible to use the point forecast prepared with the regression equation and then the standard error of forecast to determine a distribution on that forecast. This probability distribution then becomes the basis for identifying the likelihood of various outcomes in a decision-tree analysis. Thus the possible outcomes and their likelihood need not always be estimates based on subjective forecasts but may be estimates based on some other statistical forecasting technique.

Although the use of probability estimates is appealing intuitively, there are many situations in which this type of analysis involving a decision tree is not really appropriate. Therefore some other method of handling the probabilities must be found. In such instances the approach most often taken is that of Monte Carlo simulation. Although simulation is beyond the scope of this book, it does deserve a brief mention and description.

The simulation of decision problems involving uncertainty requires first the development of a decision tree. Then, rather than folding back to obtain expected values, it becomes necessary to run experiments to estimate the results of taking alternative decisions; for example, suppose that the bidding situation represented in Figures 10-1 and 10-2 is thought of as a game in which a marble can be rolled down each of the possible paths. Suppose a marble is rolled down the bid $2.90 path. When it reaches the "win or lose" event, the game is set up so that 90% of the time it will roll down the "lose" path and 10% down the "win" path. Thus, if the game were run several hundred times, 90% of the marbles started down the bid $2.90 path would end up in the "lose" portion of the event branch and 10% would end up in the "win" portion. By taking the average value of each of the end points (i.e., the proportion of the marbles multiplied by the value of that end point) we can summarize the results of the entire game.

In many instances the number of branches and the number of events and actions are so large that it is not feasible to solve the problem by the method we described in the preceding section. However, by using a computer and random numbers, we can set up a type of game (a simulation) such that a situation analogous to playing the marble game can be tested. Essentially the computer will run the game several thousand times after which the averages can be computed to determine the overall outcome of the game. If a sufficient number of plays are executed, that average will approximate the results that can be expected in the real situation. In this way the various paths and branches in the tree will have been evaluated and the best decisions will have been identified.

Clearly this chapter has been limited in its discussion of the topic of decision analysis and subjective probability forecasts. It is hoped, however, that the reader will have gained an appreciation of the power of the technique and the range of situations in which it can be applied. For further information the reader is referred to the following books which deal with this topic.

SUGGESTED REFERENCES FOR ADDITIONAL STUDY

Raiffa, Howard, 1968. *Decision Analysis: Introductory Lectures on Choices Under Uncertainty*, Addison-Wesley, Reading, Massachusetts.

Schlaifer, Robert, 1959. *Probability and Statistics for Business Decision*, McGraw-Hill, New York.

Hillier, P. S., and G. J. Lieberman, 1967. *Introduction to Operations Research*, Holden-Day, San Francisco.

Barton, Richard F., 1970. *A Primer on Simulation and Gaming*, Prentice-Hall, Englewood Cliffs, New Jersey.

CHAPTER 11

QUALITATIVE APPROACHES
TO FORECASTING

Each of the forecasting techniques we have discussed is based on the assumption that a number of historical observations are available and that these historical observations represent some underlying pattern as well as randomness. In this chapter we consider a number of forecasting methods that can be used when no set of historical data is available. These forecasting methods are used primarily in two types of situation. First is to forecast *when* a given new process or product becomes widely adopted; for example, a government organization may be aware of a number of scientific discoveries that have not yet been applied, and they may wish to predict the point in time at which their application will become widespread. Similarly, a company may be concerned about the time horizon for the adoption of a new development or process. As an example, we can consider the development of laser technology and the problem of forecasting the point at which that technology will gain widespread industrial application. This would be of interest to companies who feel that there is a tremendous market for that technology and who have the ability to exploit it, but are concerned with timing their own products and marketing efforts to coincide with the demand for that kind of product.

The second situation that might require a qualitative approach to forecasting would be one aimed at predicting *what* new developments and discoveries will be made in a specific area; for example, at the government level certain agencies might be concerned with the breakthrough of new medical discoveries for various diseases as well as what those discoveries will be. At the corporate level the type of situation that might exist would be one in which the corporation would like to forecast new processes and technologies that will be developed in their industry over the next 15 or 20 years to help

177

them in planning their plant expansion program and their long-range market development.

In both types of situation—predicting the time at which some technology will be adopted and predicting what technology and discoveries will be made—it is impossible to use the quantitative methods developed in the preceding chapters. These quantitative approaches were based on the assumption that historical data was available and that from that historical data a basic pattern could be extracted and used in forecasting events. In the kind of situation we have described, however, such historical data is not available. This gives rise to the need for more qualitative forecasting methods.

The basis of all the qualitative forecasting techniques discussed in this chapter is the employment of experts to help in preparing the forecasts. The various techniques simply present alternative procedures for helping these experts to express their subjective judgments of the future. It is this dependence on the judgments of experts that makes qualitative approaches to forecasting less attractive than quantitative methods when we have a choice between the two. These experts not only vary considerably in their judgments, thus making the forecast dependent on the specific expert concerned, but their employment is generally quite expensive, particularly when the reliability that can be attached to their judgments is considered.

Qualitative methods of forecasting, or *technological methods* as they are often called, do *not* provide a detailed procedure or a single point forecast as do most quantitative forecasting techniques. Rather qualitative methods must be flexible and their use must always be adapted to the situation in question. In these approaches man, rather than a mathematical model, is the primary processor of facts, knowledge, and information. Experts must arrive at the "best" forecast by the application of mental processes rather than by the use of formulas as in quantitative approaches. Clarke in the introduction of his book *Profiles of the Future* describes the task faced in making a qualitative forecast.

(The forecast) does not try to describe the future, but to define the boundaries within which the possible futures must lie. If we regard the ages which stretch ahead of us as an unmapped and unexplored country, what (one) is attempting to do is to survey its frontiers and to get some idea of its extent. The detailed geography of the interior must remain unknown until we reach it.

Work on qualitative forecasting methods was started in the fifties. In its initial phases it was applied mainly to government situations because of the high costs and the level of aggregation to which it is best suited. In recent years, however, a number of corporations have begun to employ these methods with positive results. Although the final section in this chapter cites the findings of a recent survey of the experiences of government and industry with a number of specific techniques, it is useful at this point to refer to the increased interest of corporations in qualitative forecasting methods and to examine the reasons for that interest.

In his recent work Jantsch (1967) estimated that about 500 to 600 medium and large American companies had established a technological forecasting function as a part of their operations. Cetron and Ralph (1971) in a more recent study estimated that 50% of their respondent companies were using some form of qualitative forecasting.

Most recently examinations of the use of these forecasting methods have linked them with corporate long-range planning. In these studies, such as those reported by Gerstenfeld (1971) and Cetron and Ralph the results indicate that more than 70% of the middle and large corporations in the United States are currently using qualitative forecasting and/or long-range planning methods. This link between these forecasting methods and long-range planning is a natural one, and the tremendous interest in long-range planning in the last decade undoubtedly accounts for most of the adoption of these forecasting methods.

Recent studies indicate that the motivation for adopting both long-range planning systems and qualitative methods of forecasting is the increased rate of technological change and the reduced length of time between the discovery of a new technology or process and its commercial application. Jantsch (1967, pp. 41–46) has examined this increasing rate of change and found that before 1900 several decades elapsed between the time an invention was conceived and its practical utilization. In recent years, however, he found that time span to be slashed to about one-tenth of its former length.

These tremendously shorter lead times mean that plant and investment decisions which generally have a physical life of 20 to 30 years must be made without complete knowledge of what the industry will be like even in a decade. It is in such an area that qualitative forecasting methods can aid the company by helping them to identify *what* changes will take place and *when* they are most likely to occur.

Writers who have sought to describe specific methods of qualitative forecasting have generally distinguished two subclasses—exploratory and normative. Exploratory methods start with today's knowledge and its orientation and trends and seek to predict what will happen in the future and when. Normative methods, on the other hand, seek first to asses the organization's goals and objectives and then work backward to identify the new technologies and developments that will be most likely to lead to the achievement of those goals. Thus exploratory methods seek only to describe what may happen, whereas normative methods put the organization in a leadership role in effecting the developments that will occur.

The importance of selecting a forecasting method from the appropriate subclass can easily be seen on the recent example of the supersonic transport plane (SST) in the United States. By application of any form of exploratory forecasting it would have been identified as a forthcoming reality. It now appears, however, than an American SST may never be developed, not because technological problems were insurmountable nor because resources were not available but because the allocation of the country's resources to this development were deemed inappropriate, at least at the present time. Current social trends will undoubtedly have a much greater impact on the development of future technologies than they have had in the past. Thus, although exploratory methods are more widely used today than normative methods, this balance will probably shift in favor of normative approaches to qualitative forecasting.

In the remainder of this chapter we examine five methods of qualitative forecasting. The first two—logistic or S-curves and time independent technological comparisons—are exploratory methods. The next two approaches —morphological research and the Delphi method—can be exploratory or normative because the experts concerned can consider either evolutionary developments or projects aimed at specific goals. The final approach to be examined—the PATTERN type of relevance tree—is normative in nature.

LOGISTIC AND S-CURVE APPROACHES

In the preceding chapters we have described a number of quantitative forecasting methods that were basically curve-fitting approaches. They sought to identify an underlying pattern in the historical data and then fit a curve to that pattern. A similar principle is the basis of a qualitative forecasting method. In the latter approach, however, little historical data is used directly and expert judgment takes its place.

As an example of a qualitative curve-fitting approach, suppose that we are interested in predicting the efficiency of man-made illumination (Cetron, 1969, p. 58) and we have only six data points available, a number not nearly adequate for any form of quantitative prediction. Furthermore, we cannot extrapolate the curve indefinitely because it is not possible to exceed the theoretical efficiency of light. This means that the trend line will have to bend (See Figure 11-1) at the level of theoretical efficiency of white light, a fact that indicates the free interpretation of the results.

One of the most applicable and frequently used curves by technological forecasters is the S-type. An S-curve (see Figure 11-2) implies a slow start, a steep growth, and then a plateau. This curve is a characteristic form of many technological developments and the sales of several products.

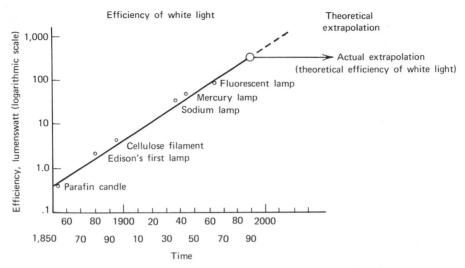

Figure 11-1 Curve-fitting approach to forecasting man-made illumination.

Chambers et al. (1971) report that the sales of black-and-white and color TV have followed an *S*-pattern. Ayres (1969, pp. 94–142) and Jantsch (1967, pp. 143–174) also report a number of different technologies that have followed *S*-type curves.

The use of an *S*-curve in representing growth can be applied not only to a given product but also to a given technology or even more broadly to a given parameter; for example, Ayres (1960) has applied this approach in qualitative forecasting to such things as the maximum speed of transportation.

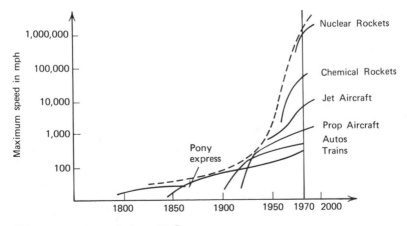

Figure 11-2 Trend fitting with *S*-curves.

Figure 11-2 shows his results for the time period from the pony express to the nuclear rocket.

By connecting the tangents of each of the individual growth curves (Figure 11-2), an envelope S-curve can be developed. In this particular case the upper limit of the curve can be recognized as the absolute or natural limits on transportation speed, such as the velocity of light or the exhaustion of some fixed resource. In most instances, however, predicting the point at which one finds himself on such an envelope S-curve may be extremely difficult. Thus in the business setting the S-curve approach may be of limited usefulness.

Another problem in the use of S-curves is finding the most appropriate type. It depends on the technology or the product we want to forecast. Thus by previous experience we must know the approximate S-type form in order to use this method of forecasting, and here expert judgment must be applied. Other functional forms of curves such as exponential, logorithmic, or double exponential can be used to fit the data, but the problem as always is to know what form or curve to assume is the correct one. This can be as difficult as the prediction itself. It is obvious that the choice of curve will influence the forecast significantly.

To illustrate some of the difficulties of qualitative curve fitting we refer to a comparison of two forecasting attempts in which the envelop S-curve concept was used. Ayres (1969, p. 21) refers to the application of S-curves by two different forecasters who by employing different scales have produced strikingly different results. A similar example is shown in Figures 11-3, 11-4, and 11-5. By using the data of Figure 11-3 one forecaster may assume that an exponential pattern will prevail. This gives the result shown in Figure 11-4. Another forecaster may reason that a saturation is in sight and

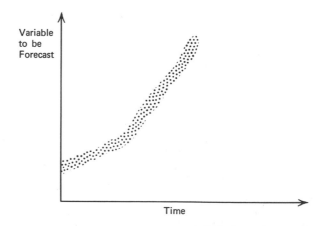

Figure 11-3   Historical data for use in forecasting.

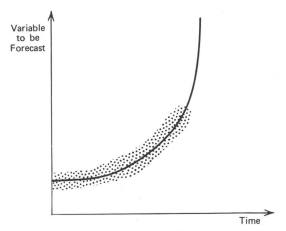

Figure 11-4   Exponential assumption in curve fitting.

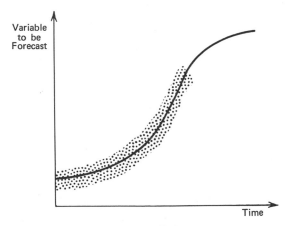

Figure 11-5   Saturation assumption in curve fitting.

by using an *S*-curve approach will obtain the results given in Figure 11-5. The significant differences in these results emphasize the need for management judgment in checking assumptions and the appropriateness of this method of forecasting in a specific situation.

TIME-INDEPENDENT TECHNOLOGICAL COMPARISONS
(Gerstenfeld, 1971)

In many quantitative methods of forecasting it is necessary to identify a trend or pattern and extend it into the future. As pointed out earlier, with many technical or cultural changes such an approach is difficult to apply because of its complex relationships. It is often possible, however, to predict the developments in one area on the basis of developments in another area. (The reader will recall this as one of the basic premises of multiple regression discussed in Chapter 7.) In many areas of interest the forecaster can identify a trend in one part of the area that he thinks will lead to new developments in another. Thus he can forecast the second area and its development by following the trend in the first. The difficulty arises, however, in trying to determine how the two subareas are related. The qualitative approach of time-independent comparisons assigns the responsibility of representing this interrelationship between the two trends to the forecaster.

The essential aspect of this approach is the identification of a primary trend in an area that the forecaster thinks will lead to developments in the subarea which he wishes to forecast. (To this he must add his knowledge of and judgment about what the relationship will be between these two trends.) The forecast can then be completed by plotting the primary trend and projecting the unknown trend on the basis of the relationship between the two.

As a specific example of the use of the time-independent comparison method of forecasting, we can consider the plausible relationship between the maximum speed of military aircraft (the primary trend) and the maximum speed of commercial aircraft (the item to be forecast). Since it is reasonable to assume that the speed of military aircraft would lead developments in the speed of commercial aircraft, a diagram (see Figure 11-6) can be developed to relate these two trends. From this diagram the forecaster can deter-

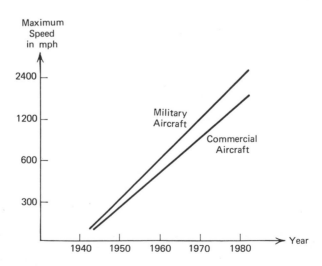

Figure 11-6   Time-independent technological comparison for aircraft speeds.

mine that the rate of increase in speed of military aircraft is such that it will double every 10 years, whereas for commercial aircraft it will double every 12 years. Thus by projecting increases in military aircraft the forecaster can predict what the increases in commercial aircraft will be as well.

There are many difficulties in implementing this time-independent comparison approach, the main ones of which are identifying a reliable primary trend and then deciding just what the relationship is between that trend and the item we wish to forecast.

MORPHOLOGICAL RESEARCH METHOD

The morphological method was developed by the well-known Swiss astronomer Zwicky in his work in the field of jet engines. Zwicky claims more than 30 industrial applications of this approach in addition to a large number of purely theoretical uses in the area of technological possibilities. The General Electric TEMPO Center is using a morphological orientation in its research, and the same is true of several projects being conducted by the Stanford Research Institute in the political and social fields of human endeavor.

Morphological research "concerns itself with the development and the practical application of basic methods which will allow us to discover and analyze the structural or morphological interrelations among objects, phenomena and concepts, and to explore the results gained for the construction of a sound world" (Zwicky, 1967, p. 275). Such a definition of the morphological method goes beyond just another forecasting application to a systematic approach toward thinking and finding ways to solve problems. We shall not discuss the universality of this approach, but we shall describe morphological research as a forecasting method and examine its ability to effectively and accurately predict technological and environmental developments.

Zwicky distinguishes five essential steps that constitute the morphological method.

STEP 1. The problem must be explicitly formulated and defined.

STEP 2. All parameters that may enter into the solution must be identified and characterized.

STEP 3. A multidimensional matrix (the morphological box) containing all parameters identified in Step 2 must be constructed. This matrix will contain all possible solutions.

STEP 4. All solutions of the morphological box should be examined for their feasibility and analyzed and evaluated with respect to the purposes to be achieved.

STEP 5. The best solutions identified in Step 3 should be analyzed, possibly in an additional morphological study, according to their feasibility and the resources and means available.

As an example of this approach Zwicky describes his attempts in the late thirties to identify possible propulsive powerplants that can be activated by chemical energy. He distinguishes six parameters that define all possible jet engines that can be activated by chemical energy.

P_1: The medium through which the jet engine moves. Four components relate to the first parameter.

P_{11},   denoting that the jet engine moves through vacuum,
P_{12},   denoting that the jet engine moves in the atmosphere,
P_{13},   denoting that the jet engine moves in large bodies of water,
P_{14},   denoting that the jet engine moves in the solid surface strata of the earth.

P_2: The type of motion of the propellant in relation to the jet engine, with the following four components:

P_{21},   denoting a propellant at rest,
P_{22},   denoting a translatory motion,
P_{23},   denoting a oscillatory motion,
P_{24},   denoting a rotary motion.

P_3: The physical state of the propellant, with the following three components:

P_{31},   denoting a gaseous physical state,
P_{32},   denoting a liquid physical state,
P_{33},   denoting a solid physical state.

P_4: The type of thrust augmentation, with the following three parameters:

P_{41},   denoting no thrust augmentation,
P_{42},   denoting no internal thrust augmentation,
P_{43},   denoting no external thrust augmentation.

P_5: The type of ignition, with the following two parameters:

P_{51},   denoting a self-igniting engine,
P_{52},   denoting an external ignited engine.

P_6: The sequence of operations, with the following two parameters:

P_{61},   continuous operation,
P_{62},   intermittent operation.

From this morphological box of six parameters we can identify 576 combinations of parameters $(4 \times 4 \times 3 \times 3 \times 2 \times 2 = 576)$ which might represent different jet engines. Each would have to be studied for its feasibility and analyzed and evaluated with respect to its ability to achieve a specific set of objectives. The large number of alternatives makes impossible the examination of all of them (Step 4); therefore Zwicky had to pick some of them at random and start studying them or discover some principle that would relate a number of possible alternatives so that he could study them as a group. Thus the aim is to reduce as far as possible the number of alternatives to be evaluated. Even after that Zwicky was still faced with a large number of engines which had to be carefully studied to determine their characteristics, desirability, feasibility with existing or developing technologies, costs, and the possibility that a certain combination of factors would have a high chance of combining in the near future. If we can solve the problem related to the huge amount of work required, we can then utilize the morphological method successfully. Zwicky, for example, was able with the above analysis, to suggest several radical new inventions that were sound, at least conceptually, and many of which were later developed successfully. He also mentions 16 patents that were granted to him as a result of his study of jet engines, and he claims that they were obtained mainly because of the use of the morphological approach.

An attractive characteristic of morphological research is the assessment of the likelihood that a future technology (or a square in the morphological box) will be realized. This is calculated as a function of what Zwicky calls morphological distance. (It is the number of parameters by which the existing technology differs from a specific one inside the morphological box.) The greater the distance, the smaller the chance of that technology being realized. In a similar fashion technological opportunities can be evaluated as a function of the number of combinations existing in the neighborhood of that technology that would depend on it. The greater the number, the higher the chance that the technology will materialize either by accident or because it will be needed before some future developments can occur.

Morphological research can be viewed as a kind of checklist which in a systematic manner enumerates all combinations of technological possibilities. Its major advantage is that it allows the user to identify "hidden," missed, or rare opportunities of technological factors that can be profitably developed. It is from this checklist, or morphological box, that both the search for new technologies and their chances of being materialized are calculated. Even though morphological research is simple in nature, it can be a powerful tool in the search for a clearer picture of the future.

THE DELPHI METHOD

This approach to forecasting is perhaps the most common of the qualitative methods and has been developed extensively by Olaf Helmer (1966) and others at the RAND Corporation. In this technique the experts doing the forecasting form a panel and then deal with a specific question, such as when will a new process gain widespread acceptance or what new developments will take place in a given field of study. Rather than meeting physically to debate the question however, these experts are kept apart so that their judgments will not be influenced by social pressure or by other aspects of small group behavior. An example of how this approach has been used should demonstrate its procedural characteristics.

PHASE 1.   The experts on the panel (numbering five) were asked in a letter to name inventions and scientific breakthroughs that they thought were both urgently needed and could be achieved in the next 50 years. Each expert was asked to send his list back to the co-ordinator of the panel. From these lists a general list of 50 items were compiled.

PHASE 2.   The experts were then sent the list of 50 items and asked to place each of them in one of the five-year time periods into which the next 50 years had been divided, on the basis of a 50-50 probability that it would take a longer or shorter period of time for the breakthroughs to occur. Again experts were asked to send their responses to the panel coordinator. (Throughout this procedure the experts were kept apart and asked not to approach any other members of the panel.)

PHASE 3.   Letters were again sent to the experts which told them on which items there was a general consensus and asking those who did not agree with the majority to state their reasons. On those items on which there was no general agreement the experts were also asked to state their reasons for their widely divergent estimates. As a result, several of the experts, re-evaluated their time estimates and a narrower range for each breakthrough was determined.

PHASE 4.   To narrow the range of time estimates still further the Phase 3 procedure was repeated. At the end of this phase 31 of the original 49 items on the list could be grouped together as breakthroughs for which a relatively narrow time estimate of their occurrence has been obtained. Thus the government agency which had initiated this forecasting exercise was able to obtain considerable information about the major breakthroughs and, for at least 31 of them, when they were most likely to occur.

The Delphi method, unlike many forecasting methods, does not have to produce a single answer as its output. Instead of reaching a consensus, the Delphi approach can leave a spread of opinions, since there is no particular attempt to get unanimity. The objective is to narrow down the quartile range as much as possible without pressuring the respondent. Thus justified deviant opinion is allowed by this approach. Helmer describes a characteristic of the Delphi technique as follows:

The effect of placing the onus of justifying relatively extreme responses on the respondents had the effect of causing those without strong convictions to move their estimate closer to the median, while those who felt they had a good argument for a deviationist opinion tended to retain their original estimate and defend it (Helmer, 1966).

The Delphi method is by no means without disadvantages. The general complaints against it have been insufficient reliability, oversensitivity of results to ambiguity of questions, difficulty in assessing the degree of expertise, and the impossibility of taking into account the unexpected (Gordon, 1964). These complaints are only relative, and the Delphi method should be judged in terms of the available alternatives. The same objections apply even more critically to the less systematic methods of forecasting.

A variety of situations exist within business or nonprofit institutions in which the Delphi technique can be utilized with only minor modifications. In the corporate setting this technique is generally used by groups of experts both in and outside the company. An important aspect of such a group is that each expert need not be well qualified in exactly the same area. Rather, each can be qualified in only subparts of the area of concern, with at least one expert in every subpart. In this way the entire problem area is covered and information can be processed about several areas of interest.

In the corporate setting the initial questionnarie distributed to the group of experts might seek to establish the general products or production processes for which there will be future demand. The subsequent phases would then give the panel members feedback on the results of the first phase and would attempt to have the panel reach some consensus on the problem. The final phases might seek to detail some of the specific products and processes on which there was a consensus and attempt to discover the best of the available alternatives and the time at which they could be expected to be ready.

PATTERN: A RELEVANCE TREE METHOD

The relevance tree is not a new forecasting concept. Its origin is decision theory and the construction of decision trees to aid the decision maker in selecting the best course of action from a number of alternatives (see Chapter 10). The relevance tree method uses the ideas of decision theory to assess the desirability of future goals and to select those areas of technology whose development is necessary to the achievement of those goals. The technologies can then be singled out for further development by the appropriate allocation of resources.

The initial and best-known application of relevance trees is PATTERN (Planning Assistance Through Technical Evaluation or Relevance Numbers), an approach that has been developed and used by Honeywell Corporation for military, space, medical, and other purposes (Sigford and Parvin, 1965). The aim of the PATTERN approach (as with all variations of the relevance tree method) is to aid planners in identifying the long-run developments that are most important to the accomplishment of specific objectives.

As an example of what the PATTERN approach consists and how it can be implemented, consider the situation faced by a country that has set pre-eminence in the areas of science and the military as its long-range goals. As a starting point in helping the planners to identify the developments necessary to the achievement of this objective, a scenario can be prepared. This scenario will be a brief description of the future and what the situation may be like surrounding military and scientific developments. Such a scenario could be developed by some expert or long-range planner in the government. It will serve mainly as a starting point for a panel of experts and thus need not be extremely accurate in all its details but rather should suggest the types of problem that must be considered when the objective is military and scientific pre-eminence.

Based on this scenario, a panel of experts can develop a relevance tree (see Figure 11-7) to show the relation between the objective and subobjectives and to break down those subobjectives until a level is reached at which specific technological deficiencies, or what might be thought of as areas requiring major breakthroughs, are identified. In the relevance tree shown in Figure 11-7 eight levels have been developed. The elements of the final level represent some of the nation's critical areas in which breakthroughs are required to achieve the long-run objective given on the first level.

By the development of the relevance tree the experts, who have met to develop it, become familiar with the various aspects of achieving that objective. In the next phase relevance numbers are assigned to each element of the tree. This is done by having the experts vote (individually on a secret ballot),

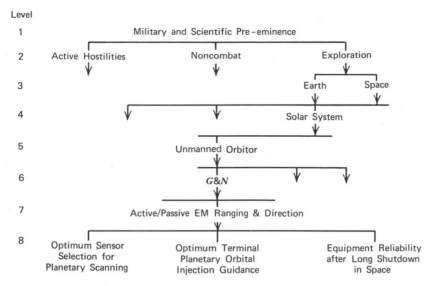

Figure 11-7   A sample relevance tree (PATTERN).

according to their own judgment of the relevance and importance of each element of the tree. Once the voting has been completed, the results can be tallied and an average of some kind can be determined for each of the elements. At this point the experts are allowed to discuss among themselves how they think the relevance numbers should be determined.

Following this phase, a set of computations must be made that will give the total relevance for each element in the tree. To compute the total relevance number the individual relevance number for that element is multiplied by the relevance number of each element in the line above. Thus a high relevance for something like "active hostilities" would be reflected in the total relevance of all elements below it in the tree.

The final result is that the experts have developed a tree that not only indicates the breakthroughs needed to achieve a long-run objective but also tells those who will use the forecast in planning just what the relative importance is of each of these breakthroughs.

The PATTERN method of qualitative forecasting is actually interactive with the planning it will affect. As critical areas are identified, the planner can make modifications in his long-range decisions and have the experts determine the additional breakthroughs that may be needed for the plan to be completed successfully. Thus this procedure helps the planner to carry out his entire function of planning by giving him the advice of experts in a form that relates directly to his planning concerns.

Table 11-1 Questionnaire and Responses of 162 Companies Concerning the Use of Technological Forecasting

1. Does your company use a formal system of long-range planning or technological forecasting?

115	(71%)	Yes
47	(29%)	No
162	(100%)	

2. Have you ever had the occasion to use

23	(11.3%)	Delphi
68	(33.6%)	trend fitting (*S*-curves)
24	(11.8%)	PATTERN
25	(12.3%)	time-independent technological comparisons
39	(19.2%)	PERT (for technological forecasting)
24	(11.8%)	others (please name)
203	(100.0%)	

(Ninety-five of the 162 respondents indicated that they use at least one specific method of technological forecasting. Most of the firms stated that they use more than one method of technological forecasting.)

3. Please circle the average number of years into the future that you perform technological forecasting:

0   1   2   3   4   5   6   7   8   9   10   11   12   13   14   15

Average answer: 7.06 years

(Ninety-three of the 95 firms that indicated a specific technological forecasting method showed the number of years into the future that they perform technological forecasting. The other two firms stated that they used no fixed time periods.)

4. How many people are in your technical forecasting or related group?

Average answer: five

(Ninety of the 95 firms that indicated a specific technological forecasting method showed the number of people in the technological forecasting group. Five firms indicated that they had no formal group and the work was performed by various people as needed.)

RECENT EXPERIENCE IN QUALITATIVE FORECASTING
(Gerstenfeld, 1971)

In a recent study Arthur Gerstenfeld surveyed the use of qualitative forecasting techniques in 162 of the major corporations in the United States. The questionnaire that was sent to these companies asked four questions that dealt with the extent of their use of technological forecasting methods (the term "technological forecasting" was employed throughout the survey) and the specific type of forecasting method that was most common. The questions and their responses obtained by Gerstenfeld are summarized in Table 11.1.

In addition to an analysis of general responses which indicated that a majority of the firms did in fact use some approach to technological forecasting, Gerstenfeld examined his data to see if the use of technological forecasting was affected by the rate of growth in the industry in which the firm competed. In the sample of 162 companies the researcher identified 12 industries, six of which could be classified as high-growth industries and six could be classified as low-growth industries. Responses regarding the use of technological forecasting in these different industries are summarized in Table 11-2. From this table it is apparent that high-growth industries feel the need for qualitative forecasting techniques more than low-growth industries. This is as might be expected for the importance of identifying long-run changes as early as possible in high-growth industries is often critical to the survival of the firm.

Table 11-2 Relationship Between Industry Growth Rate and the Use of Technological Forecasting

	High-Growth Industry	Low-Growth Industry	Total
High use of forecasting	5	1	6
Low use of forecasting	1	5	6
Total	6	6	12

In summary, the survey indicated that in high-growth industries in particular management had found technological forecasting methods to be useful and in fact were applying them on some kind of regular basis. Thus we can expect that in the future these techniques will become more reliable and highly refined and that their application will be even more widespread.

SUGGESTED REFERENCES FOR ADDITIONAL STUDY

Ayres, Robert U., 1960. "A Technological Forecasting Report," HI-484DP, Hudson Institute, Harmon-on-Hudson, New York, January 17.

Ayres, Robert U., 1969. *Technological Forecasting and Long Range Planning*, McGraw-Hill, New York.

Cetron, Marvin J., 1969. *Technological Forecasting*, Gordon and Breech, New York.

Chambers, S. K., et al., 1971. "How to Choose the Right Forecasting Technique," *Harvard Business Review*, 65 (July-August).

Clarke, Arthur C., 1962. *Profiles of the Future*, Harper & Row, New York.

Gerstenfeld, Arthur, 1971. "Technological Forecasting," *Journal of Business*, *44*, No. 1, 10–18 (January).

Gordon, T. J., 1964. *Report on a Long-Range Forecasting Study*. The Rand Corporation, Santa Monica, California, September, p. vi.

Helmer, Olaf, *Social Technology*, 1966. Basic Books, New York, 1966.

Helmer, Olaf, 1966. *The Use of the Delphi Technique—Problems of Educational Innovations*, The RAND Corporation, Santa Monica, California, December, pp. 2–3.

Jantsch, Erich, 1967. *Technological Forecasting in Perspective*, OECD, Paris.

Sigford, J. V., and R. H. Parvin, 1965. "Project PATTERN: A Methodology for Determining Relevance in Complex Decision-Making," *IEEE Transactions on Engineering Management*, *12*, No. 1 9–13 (March).

Zwicky, Fritz, 1962. "Morphology of Propulsive Power," *Monographs on Morphological Research No. 1*, Society for Morphological Research, Pasadena, California.

CHAPTER 12

MATCHING THE FORECASTING METHOD WITH THE SITUATION

The reader will recall that in Chapter 2 we examined six criteria that can be used in selecting a forecasting method for a particular situation. At that point in our discussion we were not yet familiar with the available forecasting techniques and thus our comments were rather general. Following that in several chapters we described specific forecasting methods and the characteristics that make them valuable to the manager. There still remains one task that must be completed before this information can be applied. That is to carry out a detailed comparison of these methods in relation to the six criteria.

The purpose of this chapter is to match a forecasting technique with the characteristics of a particular situation in which a management forecast is needed. We also want to examine the details of what must be done once a method has been selected. We shall do this by actually outlining the procedure that must be followed in adapting a forecasting method to that situation.

For purposes of clarity this chapter is divided into two parts. The first deals with the evaluation of alternative forecasting methods for a specific situation. The second then looks at the step-by-step procedure that a manager might use when faced with a new situation that requires a forecast. Building on this kind of microdiscussion of forecasting and its use, Chapter 13 then examines the forecasting function in the firm and how it can be integrated with other parts of the organization.

APPLYING EVALUATION CRITERIA IN SELECTING A FORECASTING METHOD

It is a common misconception that the overriding criterion in selecting a forecasting method for a particular situation should be the accuracy of the available methods. As we have seen in earlier chapters, this view of forecasting is much too simplistic. We have tried to discuss the various forecasting methods in terms of several criteria that can be used to differentiate them. It is on these criteria that management must apply its judgment in selecting a method that is best suited for its particular situation. The characteristics that we have found to be most helpful in making these judgmental decisions are the following:

1. The lead time for which the method is most appropriate (often referred to as the "time horizon").
2. The pattern of data that can be recognized and handled.
3. The type of model inherent in the method.
4. The cost associated with using that method.
5. The accuracy of the method.
6. The applicability of the method.

The specific forecasting techniques to which we shall apply these criteria are those that have already been covered in some detail. Table 12-1 summarizes this comparison, which we discuss in the next several pages. This table not only includes these detailed forecasting methods but also a few that we have merely mentioned at the conclusion of some chapters. The purpose of this table is to serve as a guide as we make the comparison of the various methods on these six basic criteria and to help the manager in his selection process when he is faced by a particular situation that requires a forecast. A few brief comments should help the reader to understand this table. For the first three criteria an "x" has been used to indicate those techniques that are suitable for that particular criterion; for example, it can be seen that several of the quantitative techniques are adaptable to an immediate time horizon of less than one month, whereas none of the technological or qualitative techniques is applicable. Similarly, looking at criterion 3, the type of model, we see that most of these techniques, both quantitative and qualitative, are suitable for a time-series model but only a few of the quantitative methods involve a statistical model.

For the last three criteria used in evaluating forecasting methods a point scale of 0 to 10 has been used to evaluate the various techniques; for example, a technique that has virtually no cost associated with it would be given a cost rating of 0; a technique like Box and Jenkins, which is expensive to run, would have a cost figure of 10 associated with it. Similarly, for the criterion of accuracy a value of 0 would be associated with low accuracy, whereas a value close to 10 indicates accuracy in a high degree. These value ratings are based on our own experiences and the experiences that have been reported in the literature on the various forecasting techniques. Although these values are certainly not absolute, they do serve a useful purpose in helping the manager to compare various forecasting methods on the basis of these particular criteria.

Rather than spending a considerable amount of time at this point to understand Table 12-1, it is suggested that the remainder of this part of Chapter 12 be read now. The reader can then return to this table with a much better understanding of its usefulness.

The Lead Time for Which a Forecasting Method is Most Appropriate

One of the most useful criteria for matching a specific forecasting situation with the most appropriate technique is the time horizon involved. Different forecasting and planning tasks require different lead times. Although most authors divide these lead times into short, medium, and long term, we identify the immediate term as a fourth time horizon. By immediate term we mean those forecasts that are prepared for one month or less in advance. Short term is used in referring to a one- to three-month time horizon. Medium term refers to three months to two years and long term to a time horizon greater than two years.

Although our definition of the various time horizons gives a specific amount of time for each, it should be remembered that these same four terms are often used in very different ways depending on the company, the industry, and the problem at hand. For a foreman immediate planning or forecasting could be related to the next hour or two, whereas long range in his mind may refer to something one or two months away. For top management, however, planning for the next month or two may be immediate term and long term may involve 20 to 30 years. For companies in different industries this same relative difference is also apparent. In the aerospace industry long term may be anything from 20 to 50 years; for a cosmetic firm three or four years away may be long term.

To see just how each of these time horizons affects the most appropriate forecasting technique for a given situation we shall examine each in turn and give a number of examples. A summary comparison of these four time horizons and the various situations in which they might be applied appears in Table 12-2.

Immediate-Term Forecasting (less than one month). Immediate-term forecasting is generally concerned with activities relating to the operational aspects of a company that are conducted mainly by middle and lower management. These operational tasks are aimed at finding ways to do things better by incremental improvements rather than by trying to change the course of events to come or to make major changes in procedures. Forecasting for the immediate horizon is simpler than for longer term horizons because the predictions involve situations for which there is generally a large

Table 12-1   A Comparison of Forecasting Techniques on Six Basic Criteria

Forecasting

Factors					Quantitative						
				Smoothing					Decomposition		
		Naive	Mean	Simple Moving Average	Simple Exponential Smoothing	Linear Moving Average	Linear Exponential Smoothing	Classical Decomposition	Census II	Foran System
Time horizon	Immediate Less than one month	X	X	X	X	X	X	X	X	X
	Short one to three months	X	X	X	X	X	X	X	X	X
	Medium Less than two years	X								
	Long Two years and more	X								
Pattern (type) of data *Correlated*	Horizontal Auto-	X		X	X			X	X	X
	Horizontal Non		X							
	Trend Auto-	X				X	X	X	X	X
	Trend Non									
	Seasonal Auto-	X						X	X	X
	Seasonal Non									
	Cyclical Auto-	X						X	X	X
	Cyclical Non									
	Minimum Data requirements	5	30	5–10	2	10–20	3	5 seasons	6 seasons	2 seasons
Type of model	Time-series	X	X	X	X	X	X	X	X	X
	Causal	X								X
	Statistical		X							
	Nonstatistical	X		X	X	X	X			
	Mixed								X	X
Costs (scale from 0 to 10, 0 smallest; 10 highest)	Development	0	1	1	.5	1.5	1.	4	6	5
	Storage requirements	3	5	1	0	1.5	1	7	8	8
	Running	NA	1	1	0	1.5	1	4	7	6
Accuracy (scale from 0 to 10, 0 smallest; 10 highest)	Predicting pattern	1	1.5	2	3.5	2	2.5	5	7	7
	Predicting turning points	3	0	0	0	0	0	3	8	7
Applicability (0 smallest, 10 highest)	Time required to obtain forecast	5	2	1	.5	1.5	1.	3	5	5
	Easiness to understand and interpret the results	10	10	10	8	9	7	9	7	8

Techniques

Quantitative											Technological					
Control		Regression			Others						Exploratory				Normative	
Adaptive Filtering	Box-Jenkins	Simple Regression	Multiple Regression	Econometric Models	Surveys	Leading Indic. or Diffusion Indexes	Input-Output Analysis	Life-Cycle Analysis	Inventory Control	Mathematical Programming	Delphi	S-Curves	Historical Analogies	Morphological Research	Relevance Trees	System Analysis
X	X								X	X						
X	X		X	X		X										
X	X	X	X	X												X
		X	X	X			X	X			X	X	X	X	X	X
X	X					X	X	NA								
									X	X						
X	X					X										
		X	X	X			X						NA			
X	X															
									X	X						
X	X															
									X	X						
5 seasons	6 seasons	30	30+4 (Ind)	Few 100's	NA	NA	Few 1000's	15–30	NA	NA						
X	X	X	X			NA		X	X		X	X	X	X	X	X
	X	X	X	X		NA	X			X	X		X	X	X	X
	X	X	X	X					X							
X						X	X	X		X	X	X	X	X	X	X
4	8	3	6	8	NA	0	10	5	5	6	5	5	5	9	8	8
7	7	6	8	9	NA	2	10	4	1	4	NA	NA	NA	NA	NA	NA
7	10	3	6	8	NA	NA	10	2	1	9	NA	NA	NA	NA	NA	NA
7	10	5	8	10	5	4	6	5	NA	NA	5	5	5	5	5	5
6	8	0	4	6	8	5	0	0	0	0	0	0	0	0	0	0
4	7	2.5	6	9	NA	0	10	3	1	5	4	5	5	10	10	10
7	4	9	7	3	10	10	3	8	8	6	8	6	9	7	7	8

Table 12-2 Using the Time Horizon to Match the Situation with the

	Quantitative Forecasting					
	Business					
Time Horizon	Marketing	Production	Inventory	Finance	Purchasing	R & D
Immediate-term (less than one month)	1, 1	1, 2	1, 3	1, 4	1, 5	1, 6
	Sales of each product type. Sales by geographical area. Sales by customer. Competition. Prices. Inventory levels.	Demand of each product. Plant loading.	Demand of each product. Production. Demand for material. Demand for semifinished products. Weather conditions.	Sales revenue. Production costs. Inventory costs. Leading indicators. Cash inflows. Cash outflows.	Production. Cash availability. Purchasing of supplies and material.	
Short-term (One to three months)	2, 1	2, 2	2, 3	2, 4	2, 5	2, 6
	Total sales. Product categories. Major products. Product groups. Prices.	Total demand. Demand of product categories and product groups. Scheduling. Employment level. Costs.	Demand for material. Demand for semifinished products. Demand for products.	Total demand. Inventory levels. Cash flows. Short-term borrowing. Prices.	Demand for products. Demand for material. Lead time for purchasing.	
Medium-term (Three months to less than two years)	3, 1	3, 2	3, 3	3, 4	3, 5	3, 6
	Total sales. Product categories. Prices. General economic conditions.	Costs. Budget allocations. Buying or ordering equipment and machinery. Employment level.		Budget allocations. Cash flows.	Demand for products. Demand for raw and other materials.	New product introduction.
Long-term (Two years or more)	4, 1	4, 2	4, 3	4, 4	4, 5	4, 6
	Total sales. Major product categories. New product introduction. Saturation points.	Costs. Investments selection. Expansion of plant and equipment; ordering of heavy machinery and equipment.	Total sales. Expansion of warehouses.	Total sales. Investment selections. Capital expenditure. allocations of resources. Cash flows.	Contracts for buying raw material.	Total sales. Technological, social, political, and economic conditions of future. New product development.

Appropriate Forecasting Technique

Quantitative Forecasting			Technological Forecasting			
Business			Environment			
Top Management	Economic	Technology	Social	Political	Competition	Natural
1, 7	1, 8	1, 9	1, 10	1, 11	1, 12	1, 13
Competition. Evaluation.	Leading indicators. Coincidental indicators. Diffusion indexes.				Price advertising campaign and selling promotion of competitors.	Weather conditions.
2, 7	2, 8	2, 9	2, 10	2, 11	2, 12	, 13
Total sales. Sales breakdowns. Pricing.	Leading indicators. Coincidental indicators. Interest rates. Availability of money. Level of economic activity.			Availability of money. Interest rates.	Price advertising selections. Selling promotions. New product introduction.	Weather conditions.
3, 7	3, 8	3, 9	3, 10	3, 11	3, 12	3, 13
Demand for sales. Costs and other expenses. Cash position. General economic conditions. Controls. Objectives.	Surveys of plant and equipment; consumers anticipation surveys. Private organization forecasts; econometric model forecasts; general economic conditions. Turning points in economy.	R & D Selections.	Social attitudes.	Fiscal and monetary policies.	New products development.	Crops.
4, 7	4, 8	4, 9	4, 10	4, 11	4, 12	4, 13
Total sales. Costs and other expenses. Social and economic trends. Goals, objectives, and strategies establishment. New products.	Trend extrapolation. State and type of economy.	Areas of technological pursue. R & D selections. Available alternatives.	Social trends, Tastes. Areas of pursuance.	Trends in the rate of taxation, depreciation, and concept of free market.	Capital investment. New technologies. R & D selections.	General Environmental Constraints (pollution level, Availability of raw material, etc. . . .).

amount of data; for example, the sales for the coming day or week can be well determined by examining the number of orders received. The cash inflows can be estimated by looking at the magnitude of billings, and so on. Thus in forecasting for the immediate term a large number of deterministic events are generally involved whose prediction is often a trivial affair. For this reason immediate term forecasting is frequently done on an informal and implicit basis.

No matter how trivial it may be, however, the task of preparing immediate-term forecasts must as a rule be performed for a large number of situations, and these forecasts are needed as an input for planning purposes such as scheduling, assigning workers to activities, and providing materials. There are a number of reasons why the utilization of a formalized forecasting procedure can be more accurate yet cheaper than an informal procedure in such situations.

One aspect of immediate-term situations that makes formalized forecasting appropriate is the large number of times that forecasts must be made during a year. A weekly forecast will be required 52 times during the year, whereas a daily forecast may be required for each of 200 working days. This repetition, coupled with the fact that there is generally little uncertainty involved, implies that if a quantitative method is to be useful it must be cheap and easy to employ as an input to planning. Otherwise it will be of little value to the planner except in special cases involving high-valued items.

The forecasting methods that can be most appropriately used for immediate-term situations include the mean, smoothing techniques, and some of the decomposition and control techniques. Since all but the smoothing techniques require a large number of data points before they can be used, and thus are more expensive, in practice the smoothing techniques are the most appropriate method. This is especially true when each of a large number of items requires a forecast. When the number of items is small and the value of increased accuracy in a forecast is high, the possibility of utilizing decomposition or control techniques should be considered.

One procedure that makes possible the use of decomposition and control methods for immediate-term situations is that of aggregation. With one of these two methods a forecast can be prepared for an aggregated time period (such as one month) or an aggregated product group. This aggregate forecast can then be broken down into a daily forecast or product forecast as required. The results are often quite accurate because a more sophisticated approach can be used in making the aggregate forecast than would be worthwhile on individual forecasts. When there are large day-to-day fluctuations, however, or when the proportion of some product class attributable to each of the individual products fluctuates widely, this procedure may not be appropriate.

Time-series methods of forecasting are usually most useful for immediate-term situations because that is the only kind of data generally available. (Most economic data is not collected and reported so frequently.) An exception, however, could exist when an internal variable (such as orders received or the backlog) is used as the leading indicator to forecast another variable (such as the level of inventories). Similarly, it may be possible to use some independent variable as the basis for preparing a forecast of a dependent variable in immediate-term situations, but most methods that handle such causal models are also expensive to apply.

By their very nature technological or qualitative methods of forecasting are almost always inappropriate for immediate-term situations. Thus the manager faced with such a situation need consider only those quantitative techniques listed in Table 12-1. Some of the types of situation in the functional areas of business in which an immediate-term forecast might be needed are presented in Table 12-2.

Short-Term Forecasting (one to three months).   Short-run forecasting generally involves some form of scheduling which may be conducted on a monthly or quarterly basis and is usually related to a forecast of the level of demand. This demand is then translated by the manager into decisions relating to the commitment of human, material, and mechanical resources. Because of the longer time period involved in short-term situations, the planner generally has more control over the course of events following his preparation of the forecast. Thus in many cases he may decide to try to modify the expected outcome once he sees the value of the initial forecast rather than letting it run its natural course.

As is the case in immediate-term forecasts, in short-term situations the trend factor is generally not important. The cyclical and seasonal component in the forecast value can, however, be critical in these situations. Thus the kinds of forecasting technique most often used in short-term situations are those that can identify and predict seasonal and cyclical variations. Because of this, smoothing methods are generally not appropriate in these short-term situations. Rather, techniques such as decomposition, control, or multiple regression methods are much more useful. Because of the longer time span involved, short-term forecasts are usually less accurate (more uncertain) than immediate-term forecasts. This longer time span, however, also makes it possible to use causal models, since macroeconomic data is generally available on monthly and quarterly bases.

As in immediate-term situations, it is generally the quantitative forecasting techniques that are most appropriate, but there are some situations in which technological forecasts can be used. They include forecasting such things as the availability of money, various interest rates, and weather conditions.

Medium-Term Forecasts (from three months to two years).
Medium-term situations generally involve the allocation of resources among competing activities. These tasks are most often performed in connection with budgeting at either the divisional or departmental level. Forecasts are generally prepared for medium-term situations on a semiannual or annual basis and then updated periodically. Because of the longer time span involved and the importance of the resource allocation process, forecasting for medium-term situations must include predicting the general level of economic activity and the major factors, such as sales and costs, for the firm itself. This means that the cyclicality of the data must be understood, the occurrence of turning points in various patterns must be identified, and the trends in its history must be isolated. In such situations the seasonal factor is generally not important, since over the semiannual or annual time span it generally averages out. Although the trend factor is significant in medium-term situations because it determines the change on an annual or semiannual basis, it is the cyclical component that is most important.

The forecasting techniques that are most effective for medium-term situations are decomposition, control, and regression. Because of the importance of accuracy in most medium-term situations and the fact that a forecast is prepared only once or twice a year, it is generally worthwhile to employ more accurate and more elaborate methods than in short-term and immediate-term situations. Oftentimes it may even be wise to utilize more than one forecasting method so that the accuracy of the results can be checked on a comparison of the two techniques. Unfortunately, the medium-term problem of forecasting turning points cannot be handled particularly well by any of these methods. Predicting such turning points will generally require the personal attention of the manager or of some staff unit concerned with monitoring performance. Most practitioners have found that anticipatory survey publications which examine the outlook of the economy, the results of econometric models, government intentions, and similar published materials can be used effectively to predict the general level of economic activity and in conjunction with quantitative forecasting techniques in medium-term situations.

Long-Term Forecasting (two years or more). Long-term forecasts are used mostly in connection with strategic planning to determine the level and direction of capital expenditures and to decide on ways in which goals can be accomplished. Here the managers are concerned with more aggregate variables that are under their control or that may be important in influencing their decisions.

The trend element generally dominates long-term situations and thus must be considered in the determination of any long run decision. The term "trend" does not necessarily refer only to a linear extrapolation of history but also refers to the rate of change and increases or decreases over time. Thus part of the trend element involves predicting when saturation points will be reached and when the rate of change will begin to vary. Preparation of forecasts that will predict these saturation points are important to management so that they can plan to take certain actions that will minimize the effects of these points or that will actually modify their severity and the time at which they will arrive.

An important characteristic of long-term situations is that the time span is long between the point at which a forecast must be prepared and the actual occurrence of events. This means that forecasts can be modified as the time of certain events approaches and as more information relevant to that situation is obtained. It is in this area of strategic planning that perhaps the greatest value of forecasting lies. The uncertainties involved, however, are also much greater than in shorter term situations because the future is never exactly the same as the past. Few people could or did, for example, foresee the decline in railroad growth of the last few decades or the saturation in sales of the glass and aluminum industries. These are the situations and variables that must be predicted as part of strategic planning in long-term situations.

The forecasting methods generally found to be most appropriate in long-term situations are regression, input-output analysis, life-cycle analysis, and those that are technological or qualitative in nature. It is usually a combination of quantitative and technological techniques that can be used to give the best results in these situations. The quantitative techniques generally identify basic patterns and their extrapolation into the future, whereas technological methods examine possible deviations and the likelihood of changes in these trends. Both time-series and causal models are appropriate in long-term forecasts. The first type provides extrapolation of past trends and the forecast can be utilized to show how the natural course of events would run if constancy were present. On the other hand, causal models can express the future as an extention of several factors, such as GNP, prices, advertising, R & D expenditure, and capital spending. Since many of these variables can be controlled, the future or the extrapolated trend can be modified in a direction most beneficial to the organization. Again, Table 12-2 summarizes some of the long-term situations in which quantitative and qualitative forecasting methods are appropriate. Table 12-1 then indicates the methods that have been found to be the most useful in practice.

The Pattern of Data that Can Be Recognized

In Chapter 2 we identified four basic subpatterns, some combination of which usually exists in any business or economic series of data. These were

(a) trend, (b) horizontal, (c) seasonal, and (d) cyclical. By way of summary a trend exists when there is a pattern of growth or decline in the data over the time span referred to. A horizontal (or stationary) subpattern exists when the data are about evenly distributed over time, that is, when there is no apparent growth or decline over time. A seasonal subpattern exists when the data is influenced by seasonal factors such as the months of the year or the days of the week. Finally, a cyclical subpattern exists when the data are influenced by longer term economic fluctuations related to the general business cycle. (The time period involved in a business cycle is much longer than a complete seasonal cycle.) Unlike the seasonal subpattern, the cyclical pattern is of no fixed duration and it is generally much harder to predict than a seasonal pattern. The majority of practical situations consist of some combination of these subpatterns.

Identifying the type of subpattern that one would expect to find in a given situation is an important step in selecting the forecasting method, since many techniques are much more flexible and can deal with a much wider variety of subpatterns than others. Furthermore, some of the forecasting methods can be much more successful in handling a given subpattern than more flexible methods, since they are really adapted for that subpattern.

Starting with the simplest quantitative forecasting methods, the mean and simple smoothing techniques can deal only with horizontal subpatterns in the data. Higher order forms of smoothing can deal with correspondingly more complex subpatterns in the data. Regression methods with some adaptation can handle most subpatterns of data except for those that are strictly horizontal. Finally, the decomposition and control methods can handle all combinations of horizontal, trend, seasonal, and/or cyclical components. Since technological methods of forecasting do not seek to identify some past basic pattern in the data, the question of matching a technological method to a given subpattern is not applicable.

It should be clear from the preceding chapters that certain quantitative techniques are much more appropriate for some subpatterns than are others. It is generally true that all these techniques have difficulty in dealing with the cyclical component and in predicting turning points, whereas they generally do much better with seasonal factors, trends, and horizontal factors. Control methods are better in general with seasonal data and can handle cyclical variations quite well as long as the variations move in a manner related to the seasonal factor. However, it is hard for them to distinguish between seasonal and cyclical factors without a tremendous amount of work on the part of the person applying the technique. Decomposition methods, on the other hand, are stronger in dealing with the cyclical factor and can provide more information than any other method in predicting turning points due to that cycle. The Census II and the Foran system methods are particularly geared toward the task of identifying the cycle and its turns. Finally, multiple regression and econometric models are capable of dealing with both seasonal and cyclical subpatterns when they can be isolated by a causal relationship involving dummy variables and other economic factors. The fact that one must be able to predict the values of the independent variables before using regression analysis to forecast a dependent variable restricts somewhat its usefulness in practice.

Another dimension of the subpattern involved in the data is the existence or nonexistence of autocorrelation. As we have seen autocorrelation relates to the dependence among successive values of a given data set. This dependence or lack of it must be considered in the selection of a forecasting technique for most situations. Some methods, such as regression, are not only inappropriate for handling autocorrelated series but its mere existence is a violation of a basic assumption in that technique. Other methods, such as the Box-Jenkins approach and adaptive filtering, rely on autocorrelation as the basic means of discovering the underlying pattern in the data. The decomposition techniques are really neutral to the existence of autocorrelation. Finally, the smoothing and control methods utilize the very existence of this autocorrelation in the data in obtaining their forecasts.

In general it can be said that the higher the degree of autocorrelation (i.e., the further the autocorrelation value is away from 0), the more appropriate it is to use a control technique. On the other hand, when the autocorrelation is small, a regression method is likely to be appropriate. It should be mentioned that regression analysis can be applied to autocorrelated data when certain transformations are carried out. These transformations are aimed at eliminating the autocorrelation so that regression analysis can be applied in its standard form.

Table 12-1 not only shows the types of pattern for which various forecasting methods are most appropriate but also indicates the data points that are required in using each of these methods. The amount of data required actually to apply a technique is generally used only to determine the feasibility of alternative methods and only indirectly in selecting the most appropriate method for a given situation.

The Type of Model

Two dimensions can be used to identify the type of model associated with a given forecasting method. The first is that of time series versus a causal model. A time-series method uses time as an independent variable, whereas a more general causal model implies that other independent variables can be used in preparing a forecast. The advantage of a time-series model is that it provides a forecast for virtually any future time period once the model has been developed. Thus, if we have the model

$$sales_t = 30 + 2t$$

and we want a forecast for period $t = 20$, the corresponding sales forecast will be

$$sales_{20} = 30 + 2(20) = 70 \text{ units.}$$

In a causal model, on the other hand, we must specify the magnitude of each of the independent variables before we obtain a forecast. Thus, if GNP, price, advertising, and R & D expenditure were the independent variables in a causal model, their values would have to be known for period 20 before a sales estimate could be prepared for that period.

Among those quantitative forecasting methods we have discussed only regression and the Box-Jenkins approach can be used in the form of a causal model. All the other quantitative methods are restricted to time-series models. Even with the Box-Jenkins approach its application as a causal model involves a highly complex procedure that makes it extremely costly and difficult to apply in that form. This indicates the importance of regression methods, which can handle all types of data and both types of model, thus providing a flexibility not present in any other method. Its limitations, however, are its inability to deal directly with autocorrelation and the amount of data that is required before it can be applied to a particular situation.

The second dimension we have considered under the criterion of type of model is the statistical versus nonstatistical. Statistical forecasting methods not only provide managers with a single point forecast but also supply the information needed to develop a confidence interval or range of values around that point forecast. This range and the associated probabilities can be provided for any number of time periods into the future. Nonstatistical models, on the other hand, output only a single value and do not provide the information necessary to test its significance. It should be remembered that accuracy is independent of whether the method represents a statistical model or a nonstatistical model; for example, it may be that adaptive filtering or some decomposition method can provide the same or better (more accurate) results than a simple regression method, but since simple regression uses a statistical model it can provide measures for testing the goodness of fit and the range within which future values might fall. This can often be much more important than having a simple, slightly more accurate point forecast.

By their very nature technological or qualitative forecasting methods are nonstatistical. Some of them, however, can be used as causal models or with time-series models. Table 12-1 summarizes the type of model that can be represented by each of the various forecasting methods.

The Cost of Using Each Method

Three kinds of cost are associated with the development and utilization of a given forecasting method: development costs, storage costs, and running (operating) costs. Since most quantitative techniques of forecasting are applied by computer, the cost comparisons made in this section and summarized in Table 12-1 are based on its use.

Two portions of development costs are generated by a given forecasting method. The first d_1, is associated with writing and modifying the computer program needed to apply that forecasting method. This development cost includes manpower cost required for development and computer time for debugging the application. Once the program exists it is necessary to develop a working model based on data from the situation to be forecast. Its development may take only a few minutes, as it does with a simple smoothing method, or it may require several man-months as it does with an econometric model and an input-output method. We denote by d_2 the development cost associated with the working model, which includes both the manpower and the computer time cost.

To utilize the computer program of a forecasting method, we must have the program as well as the required data stored in the memory device of a computer. Thus the storage cost must be included in computing the total costs associated with a given forecasting method. We use s_1 to denote the storage cost of the program and s_2 to denote the storage cost of the data.

The third kind of cost in a forecasting technique is associated with each run that is made with the computer program to obtain a forecast or to modify the working model. Using the letter r to represent this cost, it can be seen that again it represents both the cost of the computer time and the man-power cost involved in making each computer run.

If we assume that the total cost consists of fixed, semifixed, and variable costs, we have

$$\text{fixed cost} = \frac{d_1}{i} + \frac{s_1}{i} + s_2,$$

where i is the number of items that use the same program for forecasting purposes. Further,

$$\text{semifixed cost} = d_2,$$

$$\text{variable cost} = r.$$

Thus, the total costs are

$$TC = \frac{d_1 + s_1}{i} + s_2 + d_2 + r.$$

It is only by the computation of all these costs that the manager can obtain a true picture of the total expenses involved in utilizing a given forecasting method for a specific situation. Using the three categories of cost given above, Table 12-1 compares the various forecasting methods on a scale of 0 to 10. For the qualitative forecasting methods only the development cost has been listed, since generally speaking it must be incurred again for each new forecast that is made with one of these methods. As can be seen from this figure, the cost associated with different techniques varies tremendously.

The Accuracy of Forecasting Methods

The value of a forecasting method in a given situation is a function of how accurately predictions can be made by that method. As described in Chapter 2, there are two basic ways of measuring the accuracy of forecast values. One uses the complete set of historical data to fit a method to that situation and then to measure the error between the actual and the predicted values. This error could be measured in terms of the mean square error or the mean absolute deviation. Either measurement will tell the manager how accurate the forecasting method is for that set of data. If he then assumes that there is constancy in the pattern of the data and in the amount of randomness that it contains, errors between predictions and the actual values that will be observed can be expected to be similar to the mean square error or mean absolute deviation computed in training that particular forecasting method.

An alternative way of estimating the accuracy of a forecasting method is to fit it to only part of the available historical data. Thus the data can be broken into two subsets. The parameters for the selected forecasting method can then be determined by using the first subset of data and then applying that method to the second subset of data to test its accuracy. Since this second subset was not used to determine these parameters, this is equivalent to an ex-post testing of the method's accuracy. The advantage of this approach is that the manager can gain two measures of accuracy, one based on the first subset of data for which the method was actually trained and the other based on the second subset of values, which are equivalent to future values. The disadvantage of this approach, however, is that all the historical data points are not being utilized to train the forecasting method. This deprives the method of much useful information that could otherwise be utilized in the training process. Following this procedure also involves the risk of making an incorrect judgment concerning the accuracy of a certain method simply because there is some chance that the data points in the second subset may not be representative of what may happen in the future. In spite of these shortcomings, many managers prefer to measure the accuracy of a forecasting method by using this approach.

As we have already pointed out, different forecasting methods vary in their ability to predict accurately the continuation of some basic pattern compared with predicting the turning points in that pattern; for example, simple regression, with time as the independent variable, is excellent for discovering long-term trends in the data but is completely unable to predict turning points, either due to saturation of the market or a cyclical factor such as a recession or a boom in the economy. Thus the accuracy of a given method must be related to its ability to predict the type of pattern that the manager believes to be present in his particular situation. Table 12-1 rates each of the different forecasting methods in terms of predicting a basic pattern and also in terms of predicting turning points in the pattern. As we can see from this table, some of the methods are completely ineffective in predicting turning points, whereas others are quite competent at handling both kinds of prediction.

The Applicability of Forecasting Methods

The final criterion that can be used to match a forecasting situation with available forecasting methods is the ease with which the method can be ▓▓▓▓▓▓ Two basic dimensions of this criterion can be identified. First is the amount of time available when the need for a forecast arises until that forecast can actually be provided and second is the intuitive appeal that the method has for the user in that situation. Both factors are straightforward to assess.

The time span required must be considered in relation to the total forecasting effort, for when predictions for a large number of items are required it can mean a considerable time commitment for the computer system. Thus, although the other criteria may indicate that a fairly sophisticated method would be worthwhile in a given situation, the amount of time available on a computer may lead to the application of a much less sophisticated method simply to economize on computer time. Another example of when this is an important factor is when a manager may have a limited amount of time in which to make a decision. Some forecasting methods require considerable time simply to develop the working model for that situation. It may be longer than the total amount the manager has available to make a decision, and thus he may select a less sophisticated method that is much easier to develop for his application.

The "intuitive appeal" factor relates to how well the manager can understand the method and how valuable its results are to him personally. Complex and highly mathematical methods generally have much less appeal than simpler techniques which he can understand without a tremendous amount of training. If a manager is to rely on the results of a given forecasting method, he must understand how it works and why it is appropriate to his situation. Forecasting methods that involve the manager more directly and provide him with the opportunity to modify and pass judgment on the forecast produced are much more likely to be applicable to his situation than more automated methods.

Using a scale of 0 to 10 similar to that with which the various methods on the criteria of cost and accuracy are evaluated, Table 12-1 rates the applicability of the methods. These ratios are based on experience reported in the literature as well as on our own tests and experience with these methods.

DESIGNING A FORECASTING SYSTEM

The first part of this chapter has outlined those criteria that can be used in evaluating alternative forecasting methods and in matching the most appropriate method to a given situation. Although they represent considerations that the manager must take into account in selecting a method for his own situation, we have yet to describe the procedure that the manager can follow in making those considerations. The remainder of this chapter examines the detailed steps in such a procedure and their application to a specific applied.

In the first step that must be taken the manager must commit himself to developing a set of procedures and identifying the technique that will be most helpful to him. Even in a large firm in which a specialist from an operations research or computer group may be doing most of the technical work of selecting a specific forecasting method, the commitment of the decision maker is essential if the result is to be useful to him. Thus he must be involved from the start and at each phase in the development of such a forecasting system.

As a starting point in the selection of a forecasting procedure in a given situation, the decision maker must determine whether sufficient historical data is available to use a quantitative method of forecasting or whether one of the qualitative methods is more appropriate. In the event that a qualitative approach seems most appropriate the establishment of a forecasting system involves selecting the particular qualitative method and the group of experts who will use that method. Since these techniques are less well developed than the quantitative techniques, it is suggested that the manager who is just beginning to use formalized forecasting procedures try to apply the quantitative methods first before undertaking the more qualitative type of forecasting requirements. For this reason the major emphasis in this section is on *selection of a quantitative method of forecasting*, with the assumption that the manager has already determined that this approach is more appropriate than one that is qualitative.

The task of selecting a quantitative forecasting technique for a given situation can be broken into three steps. First is the phase of becoming thoroughly familiar with each alternative technique that is to be considered. This is necessary in order to understand the real limitations and the power of each method and to develop an efficient and accurate procedure (computer program) that can be used when that technique is selected for forecasting. Second is the phase of comparing techniques to find the one that seems most appropriate for the given situation. This selection is then followed by the third plase of specifying the parameters associated with the technique and training it on available historical data.

Before proceeding with the detailed examination of these three phases one point needs to be mentioned. It concerns the use of artificial (synthetic) data in the various steps of testing alternative forecasting techniques. Although many practitioners seem to feel that they can examine alternative forecasting methods using only real data, this is not the case, and in many instances it can be argued that synthetic data (data generated by some simulation technique) is more useful than the real. Essentially the argument is that for any time-series forecasting the observed values represent the combination of the value resulting from some underlying pattern plus some randomness. The object of the forecasting method is to identify that true underlying pattern. Therefore, in studying a forecasting technique, we should like to know two things: how well can it represent different underlying patterns and how well can it distinguish between the true pattern and randomness? Synthetic data is obviously much better than real data in answering the first question, since a series can be generated that contains no randomness at all. Even in answering the second question synthetic data is often better than real data because the amount of randomness can be controlled and changed experimentally. The procedures for developing synthetic data by the use of simulation have been described by Brown (1963).

Phase 1. Understanding the Alternative Forecasting Techniques

Generally a number of things must be investigated if we are to understand fully a forecasting technique such that we can determine whether it is the appropriate technique for our specific situation.

1. Identifying guidelines that can be used in specifying values of the decision variables associated with the technique (e.g., how should a value of α be chosen for exponential smoothing?).

2. Determining the technique's ability to adapt to changes in the pattern.

3. Determining the technique's ability to forecast series that exhibit different patterns.

4. Determining the effect of randomness on the ability of the technique to distinguish the true pattern from such randomness.

5. Identifying and interpreting the assumptions of the technique in practical terms that are understandable to the manager.

6. Determining the effectiveness of the technique when there is a limited number of historical observations.

7. Understanding the adaptations that the technique goes through when trained on a specific set of data.

Although it is not possible here to discuss how these seven questions can be answered for each of the forecasting methods presented, it is possible to determine how this phase can be handled for at least one of the techniques. This is done for the technique of adaptive filtering which was discussed in detail in Chapter 4.

As a brief review, adaptive filtering is a method of forecasting which, like moving averages, exponential smoothing, and polynomial fitting (using the method of first differences), develops a forecast based on a weighted average of past observations. This can be written as

$$S_{t+1} = \sum_{i=1}^{N} w_i x_i, \tag{12-1}$$

where S_{t+1} = the forecast for period $t + 1$,
  w_i = the weight to be assigned to observation i,
  x_i = the observed value in period i,
  N = the number of periods (weights) used in computing S_{t+1}.

The basis of adaptive filtering is to start with a set of weights and then, in a number of iterations, train those weights to give forecasts that will minimize the mean square error. As has been shown elsewhere (Wheelweight and Makridakis, 1971; Widrow, 1966), this can be done by revising the weights after each iteration by using the simple equation

$$W' = W + 2keX, \tag{12-2}$$

where W' = the revised weight vector,
  W = the old weight vector,
  k = a constant referred to as the learning constant (k determines how fast the weights are adjusted),
  e = the error for the old set of weights,
  X = the vector of observed values.

The details behind the theoretical development of this equation are not important for purposes of this discussion. Suffice it to say that it can be proved that with a small enough value of k this approach of adaptive filtering will find the set of weights that will minimize the mean square error, assuming that some underlying pattern exists.

What is of concern to the manager who would like to understand adaptive filtering and who is considering its application in practice is finding out more about the technique, particularly in regard to the seven questions posed earlier. For adaptive filtering the decision variables are the learning constant k, the number of weights N, and the number of periods in advance that are to be forecast. (By default most forecasting methods simply forecast one period in advance.) Most important to understanding adaptive filtering are the effects of the size of k, the interaction between k and N, the number of iterations that should be run in "training" (adapting) the weights, and the ability of this technique to approximate a range of basic underlying patterns.

As a first step in gaining an understanding of the technique of adaptive filtering the manager is best advised to establish a computer program on an available computer system to help him with his investigation. This is essential with this technique because of the large number of computations it requires. Since the manager wishes to use the forecasting technique in several situations, it would probably be most convenient for him to have access to a time-sharing system so that he can interact with the program as he uses it.

At this point the manager needs to outline a strategy that will help him to investigate adaptive filtering and to understand those aspects of it with which he is most concerned. His strategy might consist of the following steps:

1. Ensuring that the method works as predicted by the theory.
    a. Generating a time-series without randomness.
    b. Computing the optimal set of weights by hand.
    c. Running the computer program and then comparing the weights it produces with those determined by hand computation.

2. Testing the ability of adaptive filtering to predict various patterns.
    a. Generating different patterns of data: trend, seasonal, constant, constant with periodic changes, and trend plus seasonal.
    b. Using adaptive filtering on each of these series and comparing the number of iterations required and the mean square error of forecast after a given number of iterations.

3. Examining the effect of randomness on the efficiency and effectiveness of adaptive filtering.
    a. Using the generated series (2a), adding three magnitudes of randomness (10, 30, and 50%) to obtain series that include varying amounts of randomness.
    b. Testing and comparing the use of adaptive filtering on these series with randomness.

4.   Examining k, N, and the number of training iterations.
    a.   Reviewing the results from the above test runs.
    b.   Providing an incremental analysis of changes in each of these factors for the series without randomness (2a).

Obviously these tests will not exhaust the possibilities for learning about adaptive filtering. They will, however, point out several of the most important aspects of the technique and enable the manager to develop guidelines that can be used in applying it to his own situation. Although this may seem like a tremendous amount of work simply to investigate a given forecasting technique, it is important that it be done if the manager is to have the confidence that is needed to base decisions on forecasts prepared with that technique.

As a final check on the manager's understanding of the usefulness of a given forecasting technique, it is recommended that the technique be applied to a real series of data with which the manager is familiar. This added test should help to verify earlier results and to strengthen the manager's confidence in that forecasting method.

Phase 2. Selecting the Forecasting Method

During the phase of learning about individual forecasting techniques the manager and forecasting specialists will undoubtedly become aware of some broad general characteristics that can be used in making an initial screening of available techniques for a specific application. These characteristics will include the time horizon involved in forecasting and the type of underlying pattern that probably exists in the true data; for example, in selecting the technique to be used in making monthly forecasts of something like U.S. auto sales for the next 12 to 24 months, the fact that an intermediate term forecast is required and that a visual inspection of the data indicates the presence of a seasonal pattern in the series allows the manager to narrow his selection process to a choice among four forecasting techniques: multiple regression, classical time-series analysis, adaptive filtering, and Box-Jenkins. (The other methods of quantitative forecasting we have discussed are not suitable for this type of seasonal series.)

If the manager has carried out the first phase of understanding the available techniques in a thorough manner, he will probably have a series of computer programs available, one for each technique, that can be used again during this phase of further comparison. After the initial narrowing of the possible alternative techniques each of those remaining can be applied to the existing series of data (or to some artificial data that is similar in nature) to compare their performance in terms of such things as mean square error, maximum error, the existence of any pattern in the sequence of forecasting errors, and the cost of using each of the alternative techniques. Using monthly auto sales data as an example, Table 12-3 shows how these four methods might be compared for that situation. At this point the manager must consider the six criteria outlined at the beginning of this chapter in selecting the most appropriate forecasting method. To further our illustration let us suppose that after due consideration the manager selects adaptive filtering for this situation.

Phase 3. Tuning the Selected Forecasting Technique

The final phase in selecting and utilizing a forecasting technique is to "tune" or fit the technique chosen in Phase 2 to the actual situation in which it is to be applied. This requires specifying the decision parameters associated with the selected technique; for example, if adaptive filtering has been chosen as the most appropriate method, the manager would need to determine and specify a value for k, the learning constant, a value for N, the number of weights, and a value for the number of iterations to be used in training the weights. This could be done by using adaptive filtering on historical data from the actual time series. Thus, if U.S. auto sales were to be forecast for the coming months, adaptive filtering could be used on the historical values of U.S. auto sales to determine the most appropriate values of these decision parameters.

The importance of properly identifying values for the decision parameters associated with the forecast technique cannot be overemphasized. No matter how good the theory behind the forecasting technique, if the parameter values are not appropriate for the given situation, the technique will never perform as it should and as the manager would like it to.

Once the manager has performed these three phases in the selection of a forecasting technique for his particular situation, he is then in a position to design a set of procedures that will result in its effective utilization. The first step that should be taken in developing these procedures is to outline in writing the current procedure that the manager follows in making his decisions in that area; that is, if a forecasting technique has been selected to prepare forecasts of monthly auto sales, the manager will need to outline his personal decision-making procedure for which this forecast will be an input. Thus, if he is trying to make decisions about advertising policy or some other aspect of marketing and the forecast of auto sales is to be one input in making this decision, the manager must outline his procedure for making that advertising decision. With this outline, he can then determine what the timetable is for having the auto forecast prepared, and he can also determine which individuals in the firm are properly located to give support in that area.

Table 12-3 Comparison of Actual and Forecasted Values for Passenger-Car Sales: Methods Trained on Monthly Data, 1964-1969

| | | Forecasted Values | | | | | | Percentages of Error (forecast over actual value) | | | | | |
| | | | | Regression-multiple | | Box-Jenkins Method | | | | Multiple Regression | | Box-Jenkins | |
Period Forecast (1970)	Actual Number (thousands of units)	Classical Decomposition	Adaptive Filtering	Time as One of the Independent Variables	Unemployment as One of the Independent Variables	Simple	With Decomposition	Classical Decomposition	Adaptive Filtering	Time as an Independent Variable	Unemployment as an Independent Variable	Simple	With Decomposition
January	619.15	681.46	619.29	669.11	662.11	727.3	698.6	10.60	.02	8.07	6.94	14.87	11.38
February	578.43	646.14	650.60	641.25	629.58	600.6	613.4	11.70	12.48	10.86	8.84	3.69	5.71
March	741.14	787.31	669.73	763.87	750.36	726.8	717.1	6.22	9.66	3.07	1.24	1.97	3.35
April	768.34	878.50	666.41	851.44	832.26	849.6	851.6	14.33	13.53	10.81	8.31	9.56	9.77
May	784.39	867.05	701.57	852.44	827.97	754.9	803.8	10.53	10.56	8.67	5.56	3.89	2.40
June	900.86	829.38	706.53	833.44	827.97	796.6	778.0	7.93	21.58	5.26	8.09	13.09	15.79
July	837.72	833.31	650.42	854.44	827.97	896.6	857.1	.52	22.46	2.00	1.16	6.55	2.27
August	683.15	745.97	625.47	755.13	728.93	715.5	743.3	9.19	8.44	10.54	6.70	4.52	8.10
September	612.14	602.59	621.14	649.76	625.99	691.3	609.9	1.56	1.47	6.15	2.26	11.47	.37
October	719.04	758.42	653.82	816.99	823.70	792.5	776.8	5.47	9.07	13.62	14.56	9.27	7.43
November	537.15	725.71	624.28	737.12	702.58	631.5	648.3	35.10	16.22	36.48	30.80	14.94	17.14
December	606.68	836.43	615.25	859.44	819.44	719.0	689.6	37.87	1.41	41.66	35.07	15.65	12.02
Average percentage of error (absolute values)								12.59	10.59	13.10	10.79	9.13	8.00

Eventually, the manager must decide who will gather the historical data to be used in preparing the forecast, who will actually apply the forecasting technique (most likely in the form of a computer program), and who will communicate the actual forecast to him in time to help him make his decisions. With these responsibilities specified, it is then much more likely that the forecast will be prepared appropriately.

The successful implementation of these new procedures will depend on the manager's working closely with those who will prepare the forecast so that they will feel the importance of carrying out their responsibilities and so that the necessary changes in their behavior will occur. These changes can generally be accomplished by the manager's personally following the preparations for the first few times. Once an individual has become familiar with the procedure and has used it repeatedly, the manager need no longer devote his personal attention to it. It is at this point that forecasting procedures can really begin to pay their way.

Obviously, the firm that is establishing its first forecasting procedure will be faced with many more problems than the firm that is preparing its thirtieth or fortieth forecasting procedure. This is to be expected. It is hoped that those firms that are just starting will realize the substantial benefits that will accrue as forecasting is used in a wide range of situations and thus not despair because of unexpected problems in the first application.

REFERENCES FOR ADDITIONAL STUDY

Brown, R. G., 1963. *Smoothing, Forecasting and Predicting of Discrete Times-Series*, Prentice-Hall, Englewood Cliffs, New Jersey.

Wheelwright, S. C., and S. Makridakis, 1971. "Forecasting with Adaptive Filtering," INSEAD Research Paper No. 41, Fontainebleau, France, INSFAD, May.

Widrow, B., 1966. "Adaptive Filters 1: Fundamentals," SU-SEL-66-126, Systems Theory Laboratory, Stanford University, Stanford, California, December.

CHAPTER 13

ORGANIZING AND IMPLEMENTING A CORPORATE FORECASTING FUNCTION

In Chapter 12 we examined those factors that should be considered in selecting a specific forecasting technique for a given situation. We focused on matching the situation to the method and said little or nothing about who would actually do the work. Clearly it is only in the smallest firms that the entire application of a forecasting method will be performed by the manager who will actually apply this forecast. In medium-sized and large firms there will generally be some staff support involved in the application of forecasting techniques. The purpose of this chapter is to examine those aspects of a corporate situation that should be considered in establishing a forecasting function within the firm.

The first section of this chapter examines some of the elements of an ongoing forecasting procedure to identify the skills and resources that are required within the firm to carry out that function successfully. The next section deals with the forecasting organization and its sponsorship within the firm. It includes an analysis not only of the staff support needed for forecasting but also the role in it of other parts of the corporate organization. The third section of this chapter deals with the behavioral aspect of forecasting. Since people are involved in the forecasting function, these behavioral aspects are important considerations in everything that we have discussed so far. In this section we focus on some of the more important considerations in this area that are essential to the successful implementation of forecasting systems. The final section examines some of the characteristics of successful forecasting applications and how a corporation might apply itself to getting started.

As in the preceding chapters the emphasis here is on those aspects of the corporate forecasting function that are most important to the manager. Clearly there are details associated with establishing a staff organization to support forecasting that must be known by the individual who will be in charge of that group. This chapter, however, does not deal at that level of detail but rather aims at covering the main points that are important to the manager (user) of that forecasting support group.

ELEMENTS OF AN ONGOING FORECASTING PROCEDURE

In any specific forecasting application six basic steps or elements will generally be followed. These six steps are important considerations in establishing the forecasting function within the firm because support must be made available for each of them. If any of these steps is omitted or not properly supported, the results of forecasting will not be completely satisfactory. To see just what skills and resources are required for the forecasting function we shall examine each of these six steps in turn.

1. Identification of Management Requirements for a Forecast. The starting point on any new forecasting application is an identification of management's requirements. Because of the nature of forecasting and the supportive role it plays in decision making, the forecasting staff group will frequently identify what they think is a need and then on asking management about it will naturally receive a positive reply; that is, since supplying a manager with a forecast does not require any explicit change in his decision making, he can always say he would like more information, whether or not that information is directly relevant to his problem. Following such a procedure in the development of new forecasting applications can be detrimental to the forecasting function in the long run. When the forecasting staff group identifies the potential needs, it is likely that the number of forecasts being supplied to management will increase rapidly, yet the effect on management's decision making will be only minimal.

What is needed at this stage is a procedure that will require the manager's participation in determining what forecasts would be most useful in his specific situation. Although it will clearly be harder to involve a busy manager in this identification process, those firms that have done so have found it much more profitable in the long run. One approach that has been used successfully has been to have the staff group initiate interest in forecasting by holding discussion sessions with small groups of managers. The purpose of these sessions is to introduce managers to some of the possibilities that exist in the application of forecasting. This is then followed with a procedure in which managers themselves will identify what they think may be appropriate situations for forecasting. A staff person can then meet on a one-to-one basis with the manager to discuss the possible applications and to identify the one or two that look most promising.

2. Competent Support Staff.   In any medium-to-large company it is attractive to have a specific staff group of one or more people to help in the development and application of forecasting. The main tasks of this group are to support each of the steps of forecasting as a catalyst and to be responsible for the actual data collection and the application of specific techniques in a given situation. It is imperative that its members be competent in their understanding of the available forecasting methods and that they also be competent in understanding management problems. In most cases their training will have been on the technical side, but it is still of the upmost importance that they be able to discuss with the manager his problems and situations in order to fit the most appropriate forecasting technique to that application.

The problems attendant on the development of such a staff group are similar to those that accompany the development of an operations research group or some other technical group designed to support management efforts. In general companies have found that it is better to trade understanding of the management task for technical expertise in setting up these groups; that is, one would much rather have a person who is of average competence in the various techniques of forecasting and very good at discussing these techniques and their appropriateness for different situations with management. It is important that management understand that this staff group has been established to support them in their work and that they can call on them when necessary. Whenever additional stumbling blocks appear in getting support from this group, managers will find other ways of acquiring the information they need (or go without it). Thus the firm must supply the staff support and make it available directly to those managers who can potentially apply forecasting.

3. Data Collection.   One characteristic of successful forecasting is that the manager who becomes involved in the development of a new application wants to see results. Whenever it takes several months or even years to obtain these results, the manager will tend to lose interest. In the data collection area this means that support must be available, either in the form of a data base or in terms of a willingness to acquire published sources of data so that new applications of forecasting can provide forecasts soon after they are identified. Although there are exceptions when a manager will be willing to wait a considerable length of time to initiate a new forecasting procedure, in general it is best when first applying forecasting with a given manager to select an application for which data can be collected rapidly.

The actual collection of data will generally be under the direction of the forecasting staff group and may be performed by them or by someone in the accounting group. The actual person doing the collecting of the data will be determined by its type and source. Clearly, if the data is related to the accounting system, it would be best to get the accounting people to collect it. If, however, it comes from a single outside source not currently being used by the company, it is generally more efficient to have the forecasting staff collect that data themselves.

Once the procedure has been established for the actual collection of the data, it must be put into form for applying the forecasting method. This will generally involve getting the data into the company's computer system or a local service bureau so that a computerized version of the forecasting method can be applied. The design of this data collection and formatting operation is one of the key technical functions of the forecasting staff.

4. Applying the Forecasting Method to the Data.   Once the data has been collected, the forecasting staff can then apply the appropriate method of forecasting to that data. Again, this is a technical problem and is best handled by the staff. It is important, however, that the manager understand the underlying features of the method that is being applied and recognize the strengths and weaknesses of that forecasting procedure.

At this stage it is generally essential that the corporation supply the necessary computer support needed to prepare these forecasts efficiently. This support will generally include not only computer time but also some initial time of a programmer to fit the forecasting method to the available data. Sometimes a member of the forecasting staff will be capable of doing the programming himself. In larger companies the importance of having a forecasting staff that can effectively communicate with management makes it more attractive to have such people spend a large portion of their time with the manager and his problems and use specialists in the task of programming.

5. Communicating the Forecast to the Manager.   In order for a forecast to be of maximum usefulness it must be given to the manager when he needs it and in the form that will fit his decision-making situation. This requires that the forecasting staff be fully aware of the time frame within which the manager will operate and have sufficient rapport with him that he will call them if that time frame changes. In terms of the format in which the forecast is presented it is always useful not only to supply the manager with the single forecast but also with some of the assumptions inherent in the data and the method used. Thus, if there were some special problem in getting the data for this forecast and if the staff had some doubts about the accuracy of that data, the manager should be made aware of it. One thing that should clearly be avoided is overloading the manager with information. It is not generally necessary to give him a complete listing of all of the data used in preparing the forecast but rather to highlight those factors of which he should be aware.

6. Feedback and Comparison of Actual Results to Forecast Results. To measure the effectiveness of a forecasting application it is necessary to compare the actual results with those that were forecast. This can generally be done by setting up a periodic review procedure. For these reviews the forecasting staff must analyze the errors in the forecast and any trends that may be apparent in the errors. It should be a staff responsibility to perform this initial analysis and then to sit down with the manager and reassess the usefulness of the forecast and the opportunities for improving it for that situation.

A good checklist for a company establishing a forecasting function or appraising an existing function is to consider the six steps outlined above and the level of support available in each one. It is easy for an ongoing procedure to treat one or more of these steps lightly and thus reduce the effectiveness of that forecasting procedure.

FORECASTING ORGANIZATION AND SPONSORSHIP

A good starting point in the development of a forecasting function is to analyze the firm's preparedness for such a function. Clearly some firms are in a much better position to initiate a formal forecasting operation than are others. The three factors that determine a firm's preparedness are top management's attitude, middle management's attitude, and the competence of the forecasting staff. If all three of these factors are considerably above average, the success of forecasting in that firm is much more likely. Even if these three factors are only average, there is still a good chance that forecasting can be applied successfully. If, however, any one of these factors is below average, the firm is best advised not to go ahead with a formalized forecasting setup.

In determining just where the firm stands on these three factors it is necessary to perform an actual analysis of the firm. In determining the attitude of middle management and top management toward forecasting, it is not enough just to ask them what their views are. Forecasting is like many other current fads and everyone feels that they should be interested in it. However, in performing an analysis on one's own company, it is necessary to ask specific managers why they think it would be useful and just what it would do for them. This kind of questioning frequently points up that everyone thinks it is a good idea but that for one reason or another it would not be appropriate in their own situations. When one management group is not sold on the usefulness of forecasting, an educational phase can often be undertaken to help management understand the value of planning and controlling the firm's operations and the usefulness of forecasts in this function.

When the firm identifies a problem of staff incompetency, the only solution is to bring in new blood or to wait the several months to a couple of years necessary to train the existing staff. Most firms have found that initiating a forecasting function in parallel with the training of a staff is not effective. It is much more appropriate to develop competence at the staff level before undertaking forecasting to aid management.

Avoiding the Common Mistakes

After the fact managers are always amazed at the extraordinary problems that can develop in getting a forecasting procedure initiated and working effectively. Overcoming some of them is often more than a matter of simply reorganizing the project. For one thing personalities can often be the cause and cannot be changed overnight. Simply redrawing the organization chart will not solve most underlying problems. However, a number of them seem to occur regularly in forecasting and an examination of the experience of several companies in these areas can help the new company establishing a forecasting procedure to avoid them. They include the following:

1. People make mistakes in recording data and thus the decision maker is understandably reluctant to base decisions on that data.

2. Those whose job it is to check a forecast may only rubber stamp it and simply pass it on without adequately verifying its reliability.

3. The decision maker may find that the forecasting data never seems to be available in time for his decisions.

4. The decision maker may not be committed to the forecast and to its use because he does not understand it.

5. Many of the individuals whose contribution is required to make forecasting successful do not feel any personal need for making those changes in their own procedures that are necessary to complete the forecasting system.

6. On occasion the wrong forecasting approach may have been adopted and thus the experts in the firm are reluctant to push for its implementation.

There are four general areas in which careful planning and support can be done to help eliminate problems such as the above. These areas involve the allocation of responsibility. They determine who will make decisions, specify who is to pay for forecasting applications, and determine who will do the work. Each of these areas is discussed in turn.

Who is responsible? A major mistake that companies often make in establishing a forecasting function is never to define clearly the responsibility and leadership for it. Oftentimes top executives just hope that this responsibility will find its own home in due time. This approach, however, can often cause tremendous misunderstanding and thus give a bad orientation toward forecasting right from the start.

The responsibility for developing forecasting applications and a forecasting function must be given to a member of the management team. This will generally involve the individual either in charge of accounting and control or of other systems activities within the firm. There is no set rule about the area that is most appropriate in general. Rather a company is well advised to examine its own experience in terms of how other parts of its organization have been patterned; for example, if a company has done well with projects in which a staff individual has been put in charge, then this same organization will probably work well in the forecasting area. If, however, the company as a general rule puts such staff responsibility under an operating manager, then they should seek to be consistent in this area as well. The key is to make sure that one person is responsible for the success of the function and that he has the authority to take the actions necessary to guarantee success.

Who Makes Decisions?   There are two kinds of decisions to be made in connection with the forecasting function in the firm. One, which was mentioned in the preceding paragraph, involves guiding the entire function in the organization. In this case a single individual must be given the authority to make the guiding decisions.

The other type of decision involves specific projects and applications of forecasting. The difficulty here is to decide which decisions will be under the control of the forecasting staff and which under the control of the manager, or user, of that particular forecast. One consideration is who will be available when they need to be made. Many of the smaller technical decisions clearly should fall under the direction of the forecasting staff. Major technical decisions, however, should at least be reviewed by the manager who will use the forecast. Thus it is not at all inappropriate to involve the manager in the choice of a forecasting method.

Some of the areas in which it is clearly the manager's responsibility to make decisions include determining the applications for which forecasts are to be prepared and the frequency with which they are needed. As a general rule, companies have found that the best division of this decision-making responsibility is to have the forecasting staff act as a catalyst in getting the decisions made, and to recommend what they think is best, but to let the user of the forecast have the final word on any major decision.

Even in ongoing situations, it is important that the decision-making responsibilities be agreed on by both the staff and the operating people. This can be viewed largely as an educational task of informing those involved just what constitutes acceptable behavior and what seems to have worked most effectively in other situations.

Who Pays for Forecasting Projects?   An easy answer to this question is simply to say that the company pays, but assigning the cost of forecasting applications to specific departments and organizational units is an important aspect in the forecasting function. There will generally be some overhead cost associated with the maintenance of a forecasting staff, but the majority of the expense should be assignable to specific projects. Experience has shown that it is important to allocate these costs whenever possible to the organizational unit making use of a forecast. The main advantage of doing this is that the operating manager will then be much more likely to evaluate the benefits of the forecast in contrast to its cost than he would otherwise. When an organizational unit does not have to pay for having a forecast prepared, it will usually justify any forecast as having value, even if it is only marginal.

As a part of the cost allocation process, the initial analysis of a forecasting application should include the development of a budget for that application and the user's agreement to cover its cost. The forecasting staff can then be evaluated in terms of their staying within the budget and accomplishing the objectives outlined for the project, and the user of the forecast can have a firm idea of what he will be charged for.

In those situations in which a forecast is being supplied to several different organizational units, as is often done at the start of the long-range planning cycle, most companies have found that the best procedure is to assign the costs of that forecast as they would the project as a whole. Thus, if the cost of long-range planning is simply charged to general corporate overhead, the forecasts supplied in connection with that planning project should be handled in a similar manner. On the other hand, if the costs are generally allocated to individual divisions, so should the forecasting costs.

Who Does the Work?   Three functions are involved in any forecasting application: the forecasting staff which identifies and carries out applications of forecasting, the management user who will apply that forecast to his own situation, and the computer group that will actually apply the forecasting method to the data. To coordinate the efforts of these different people, it is essential that one person have the responsibility for seeing that the project is completed on schedule and that procedures are established for coordinating the various units. Generally the individual to be placed in charge of the project will be a member of the forecasting staff. Since he has the technical background and the interface with the management user, he is in the best position to coordinate these activities.

Perhaps the most common problem in assigning the work is scheduling the computer support time. Since the computer group is also a staff group, it is often difficult for the forecasting people to get the kind of response from the computer staff that they need to be effective. One solution to this problem is to have both staff groups reporting to the same individual. An alternative solution is simply to set up procedures that state firmly when forecasting projects will be worked on and give the time schedule that must be met by the computer group in those applications.

One approach that has been used quite effectively in forecasting is the development of a project team. Although many forecasting situations are small and really require the support of only a couple of people, in other projects in which the forecast will be used by several organizational units it is helpful to have a team whose responsibility is the success of the project. This project team can serve as a communications system for progress being made in the development of the application and will ensure that the application will meet the requirements of the users. The project team also provides a means of exposing several different people in the firm to forecasting and its usefulness.

Locating the Forecasting Function in the Organization

The guiding rule to be used in locating the forecasting function in a given corporation is that the position of a staff group should be consistent with the rest of the firm's organization. Thus, if its staff groups are generally placed under each of the different cooperating divisions, with only a skeleton staff at the corporate level, a similar plan should be followed in forecasting. In another company in which all the staff support may be completely centralized that type of organization should be followed in forecasting.

Technically, the forecasting staff is most closely related to the work done by systems people and operations researchers. Thus it may be attractive actually to combine these groups. When this is done, however, it is essential that specific individuals in those groups have the responsibility for forecasting. Otherwise, a firm that has hired two or three additional operations researchers may find that after a year there is still no forecasting application because the new people have been working on other projects that the operations research group thought were more important. By setting up a separate subgroup the forecasting function is given considerably more emphasis and the chances of its being useful in the near future are greatly enhanced.

One of the similarities between forecasting people and systems people is that they are usually technique oriented rather than management-problem oriented. This can become a major problem if the staff people are not given good direction about their responsibilities and where there emphasis should be placed. It can often happen that these forecasting people will select one or two methods of forecasting and then look for situations in which they can be applied. It is much more useful if the staff people realize from the start that their prime concern should be with management and management's problems and only secondarily with the techniques of forecasting. This requires that the forecasting staff report to an individual who understands both the technical and management sides. Since these people are not abundant, most companies find that they have to pay a fairly high salary for such a person. In the long run, however, they have found it to be well worth while, since failure to have such a person in charge generally means ineffective forecasting applications.

Integrating Forecasting with Existing Procedures

As mentioned in the preceding section, an important consideration in organizing the forecasting function is to make it consistent with the rest of the corporate organization. This same rule applies to establishing forecasting procedures that are consistent with other procedures in the firm. Two areas that are particularly related to forecasting are those of budgeting and planning. Most companies have established procedures in these areas that have not included forecasting, but in setting up a forecasting function budgeting and planning will probably represent two of its initial applications. Thus it is instructive to determine how forecasting procedures can be integrated with at least these two existing functions to get an idea of some of the important considerations.

In the budgeting process followed in most firms an annual cycle is set up which usually includes the preparation of a budget for perhaps each of the next 12 months and each of the next three to five years. Forecasting can take on one of two roles in this budgeting process. In its major role the budget would be prepared for a coming time period by using a forecast based on historical relationships and costs. This forecast could then be reviewed by management and changes made as needed. In this role forecasting could save considerable time in the budgeting process, particularly in those areas that are not usually considered discretionary. In its alternative role it would serve as a backup to management's own estimates and would identify large discrepancies that need to be justified. One major difference between these two roles of forecasting and budgeting is who actually uses them. In the first case it would be the manager responsible for preparing the budget; in the second it would be the accounting department responsible for checking the appropriateness of the budget.

It is important in establishing a forecasting procedure to support budgeting that responsibility be assigned to the appropriate user. Clearly, the accurateness required by the manager in this situation would be different from that required by the accounting department. Thus the ultimate user must be identified and involved in establishing the forecasting procedure.

Another prime consideration is the timing factor. Budgeting procedures generally follow a tight time schedule and thus for a forecast to be useful it must meet its demands. In the long run it might be more efficient for the firm to adjust its timing of the budgeting cycle so that forecasting can fit more effectively. Initially, however, this is not a practical consideration. Rather, the forecasting application should be designed to fit the existing budgeting procedure. As discussed in the next section of this chapter, the fewer changes that are involved in the initial application of forecasting, the more likely it is that it will be successfully adopted.

The potential application of forecasting to formal corporate planning procedures can take on one of three major roles. Two are similar to the roles identified for forecasting in the budgeting process and involve using forecasts to verify the feasibility and soundness of a plan and as part of the plan itself. Again, in the first case the forecast is used by the corporate planning group and in the second it is used by the manager who is actually responsible for preparing the plan. A third role of forecasting in formal planning systems, and perhaps the one most often used, is in establishing a basis of assumptions on which plans can be prepared. In this situation a company might prepare a set of forecasts relating to the industry in which it operates and then distribute these forecasts at the beginning of the planning cycle. These forecasts can then serve as a basis for the development of the operating managers' individual plans. In this role forecasting supplies the managers with general information about the environment over the next three to five years.

Setting up a forecasting procedure that will serve as the basis for environmental information in planning is perhaps one of the most difficult types of forecasting application. The problem is that the forecasts are really being prepared for the corporate planning group and a number of different management users. This makes it much more difficult to determine exactly what forecasts are needed and the form in which it would be most useful to report them. In this situation the project-team approach described earlier is usually most effective. A project team, consisting of someone from the forecasting staff, a member of the corporate planning staff, a member of the management group who will use the forecast, and possibly a member of the computer systems group, can work effectively in defining those forecasts that would be most useful. Even in this situation, however, a single individual must be given responsibility for seeing that the forecasts are prepared and distributed in a timely manner. Many companies have found that a member of the corporate planning staff is the most appropriate person to take on this overall responsibility. This individual can ensure that the forecasting procedure will be consistent with the planning cycle and can obtain feedback from operating managers about its appropriatness and usefulness.

In any application of forecasting it is important that an evolutionary approach be taken. This means that the initial application need not be perfect in every respect but should be satisfactory and useful and serve as a starting point from which improvements can be made. Trying to second guess what all of the possible problems and possible considerations will be in a forecasting situation is impractical, if not impossible. Rather, it is much more useful to start with something that is satisfactory and feasible, and then, as managers learn about the possibilities of forecasting, to revise applications and improve the procedures.

THE IMPLEMENTATION OF FORECASTING REQUIRES CHANGING BEHAVIOR

To stress the importance of changing behavior when adopting a forecasting procedure it is fair to say that the resulting forecasts will have value only if in fact they do change behavior; that is, if the same decisions are made after a new forecasting procedure has been developed as were made before, then that forecasting procedure is of no value.

It is not only the behavior of the decision maker that must be changed in order to utilize forecasting successfully, but those who gather the data, those who select and apply a given forecasting technique, and those who evaluate the use of forecasting within the company: their behavior must also be changed. In some instances it may be that the decision maker performs all the steps and thus it is only his behavior that must be changed. In most cases, however, someone else will be involved in at least one of these steps and that person's behavior must be changed also.

A tremendous amount of work dealing with the problems of changing individual behavior has been done in the last few decades. One researcher who has made particularly useful contributions in this area is Edward Schein. Schein has developed a model of behavioral change that is most useful to the manager who is considering the changes necessary to successful forecasting.

During the 1950's Schein, a psychologist, made an extensive study of Communist brainwashing techniques used during the Korean War. From this experience he has developed a model that can be used in taking the steps that are essential to implementing behavioral change. Although many examples of coercion were used in the development of this model it can also be used by those wishing to direct changes in their own behavior and the behavior of others without coercion.

An example of the cases studied by Schein can serve as a basis for identifying the major parts in his approach. In this particular example, Schein examined the procedure used by the Chinese Communists in trying to brainwash a Catholic priest who had been taken captive as a prisoner of war. The procedure followed a three-step process. In the first the priest was put into a cell with several other people who, unknown to him, were stooges. These stooges would point out any time that the priest bothered them. They tried to show him that his self-concept was incorrect; that is, they wanted to convince him that instead of being helpful to people, as he had always thought, he was a bother to them. In the second step the priest came under continual interrogation in which he was asked to confess. His interrogators would not tell him what to confess because they wanted the *change* to be his own. After several months the priest finally did start to write his own confession, at which time the third step of the process was undertaken. The priest was again placed with stooges who pointed out to him how he could reconcile what he had written in his confession with a new set of beliefs. They tried to make him feel comfortable and accepted because of his new ideas.

From this and other situations Schein developed a conceptual model for changing attitudes and behavior that follows a similar three-step process and is applicable in a wide range of situations. The first step is what he calls "unfreezing" in which the individual must perceive a need for changing his behavior. This need can develop either because he feels some aspect of his behavior is inadequate or because he identifies the opportunity of improving his behavior.

The second step in Schein's model is the change itself. Here the individual must see the change as his own and incorporate it into his own behavior patterns. This requires that he be fully involved in developing the change and in implementing it.

The final step is what Schein refers to as "refreezing." The change made in the second step must be personally incorporated into the individual's everyday pattern of behavior. Effective refreezing ensures that the individual will not easily go back to his former behavior.

Some examples of how this unfreezing, change, and refreezing have been used will help to make its relevance to forecasting much more apparent. The first example comes from a course in speed reading called Reading Dynamics. This course advertises that the reader can triple the speed at which he can read in a very short period of time. To unfreeze the individual, Reading Dynamics Institute offers free introductory sessions to potential customers to demonstrate how easy it is to improve their reading speed and thus to convince them of the need for making such an improvement. The Institute then offers sessions that teach the technique of speed reading. It is in these sessions that the individual makes the changes necessary in his own behavior that are required to read much faster. Finally, for refreezing, the Institute offers "whip" sessions, or refresher sessions, that are aimed at reinforcing the individual's use of the technique to ensure that he will not go back to his old reading habits.

It is in the last step of refreezing that Reading Dynamics is weakest. This is often the place in which learning techniques are weak. In fact, in the earlier example of the priest who was being brainwashed refreezing was the downfall of those directing the brainwashing. One day the priest heard children singing outside his prison window. They were singing a song that he had taught them, and just this one experience was enough to awaken the old attitudes and he immediately reverted to them.

This three-step process of unfreezing, change, and refreezing can be used by the decision maker who wishes to change his own behavior or the behavior of those involved in making the forecasting procedure successful. Many of the problems that were outlined at the beginning of this chapter can actually be traced to a failure at one of these three stages of behavioral change; for example, the failure of the decision maker to use the forecast in making decisions could well be the result of weak refreezing following the change; that is, the manager might be aware of the need for forecasting and might feel that the change in procedure that would utilize forecasting is his own. The fact that he had not followed that procedure for a sufficient length of time to ensure refreezing may explain his failure to use the forecast effectively. Another example would be the problem in which the data never seems to be available on time because the person collecting the data feels no urgency to prepare it according to some schedule. This problem is typical of the failure of those implementing the forecasting system to make that person feel that the need for the data is personally important; that is, the secretary or clerk who gathers the data does not feel that the change his procedure required is worth the trouble because that change was imposed by someone else and does not represent a personal need.

Of course, before the manager can expect behavioral change to occur, he must have a clear idea of the steps that are required to utilize a given forecasting procedure successfully. These steps must be clear in his mind, and it is usually helpful to have them put down in writing so that each person's responsibilities can be checked from time to time and any failure in the application of the forecasting system can be easily analyzed and corrected.

CHARACTERISTICS OF SUCCESSFUL FORECASTING SITUATIONS

The preceding sections of this chapter have outlined a number of steps that can be taken by the manager and by individuals responsible for forecasting to improve the likelihood that it will be useful in a particular situation. Also a number of more general steps and simple problem attributes are associated with the successful application of forecasting. These deal with three areas: the type of manager involved, the general level of support within the firm, and the forecasting situation itself.

As we would anticipate, the level of success in applying formalized forecasting methods is closely related to the type of manager involved in the forecasting situation. Three things that generally characterize a manager who successfully implements forecasting are, first, that he understands the situation for which the forecast is being prepared and knows what is required for successful decision making in that area. This ensures that the forecast is in a meaningful area and that he will feel comfortable about using it in that type of situation. A second characteristic is that the manager must be interested in real improvements in decision making. A manager who simply implements a forecasting procedure because his boss thought it would be a good idea will never be so successful as the manager who adopts forecasting because he really wants to improve his decision making. The third characteristic is that the manager must understand the forecasting technique and its value. Even in a large firm in which adequate staff support is available it is only when the manager takes the time to become familiar with the forecasting technique and its strengths and weaknesses that the forecast will have significant value.

The second aspect of a successful forecasting application is the environment within the company. There are several things that a company can do to support formalized forecasting applications. These include communicating successful applications to others in the company, which indicates that the company is concerned with forecasting and takes note of those who are successful in using it. Another is training its managers on various forecasting techniques and the general procedures for adapting them to their own situations. Top management in the company also needs to give their support and encouragement to such applications. Finally, the company must give the manager access to those resources that are required to utilize forecasting. These resources include historical data (and manpower to update the data), specialists in the area of formal forecasting techniques, and computer support to help in the actual preparation of the forecast. All these things can help to make the company a more likely environment in which forecasting will be successfully used.

Finally, the situation itself is important to insure the success of forecasting. Situations must be chosen that are helpful to the manager, that provide the opportunity for reducing uncertainty, and in which the value of improvements in decision making is substantial. Although it may be easier to use forecasting on well-established problems in which historical data is available, it is often the case that the firm's decision-making procedures in such areas are also well developed, and thus there is little room for improvement even with formal forecasting. What is needed are situations in which the opportunity for improvement exists and in which the manager involved is the kind of person who would like to improve the decision making in that area.

SUGGESTED REFERENCES FOR ADDITIONAL STUDY

Brown, R. G., 1963. *Smoothing, Forecasting and Prediction of Discrete Time Series*, Prentice-Hall, Englewood Cliffs, New Jersey.

Chisholm, R. K., and G. R. Whitaker, 1971. *Forecasting Methods*, Irwin, Homewood, Illinois.

Krauss, Leonard I., 1970. *Computer Based Management Information Systems*, American Management Association, New York.

Schein, Edgar H., 1961. "Management Development as a Process of Influence," *Industrial Management Review*, Vol. 2, No. 2 (May).

INDEX

Accuracy, 9, 13, 195, 198
A. C. Neilson Company, 150
Adaption cycles, 55
Adaptive filtering, 48, 207, 214
  in practice, 55
A/F ratio, 172
Aggregated data, 157
Aircraft speed example, 184
Alpha, 37
  selection of, 39
Applicability, 26, 198
Autocorrelation, 111, 126, 207
  coefficient, 126
Automobile production, 101
Auto regressive (AR), 129
  moving average (AEMA), 129
Ayres, Robert U., 181, 194

Barton, Richard F., 176
Bayesian statistics, 174
Behavioral aspects, 26
  change, 231
Bonini, C. P., 82
Bootstrap approach, 26
Box, G. E., 143
Box-Jenkins, 62
  method of forecasting, 123
Brookings Institute, 135
Brown, R. G., 47, 213, 219, 235
Budget forecasting, 3; see also Forecasting, for finance
Budgeting process, 229
Building contracts awarded, 101
Butler, William F., 161
Burch, F. W., 161
Brown, R. G., 235

Calibrating a forecaster, 171
California Plate Glass example, 100
Cash flow forecasting, 3; see also Forecasting, for finance
Casual relationships, 113
Causal model, 23, 64, 208
Cement bidding example, 165

Census II, 97
Centralized economies, 141
Cetron, Marvin J., 179, 194
Chambers, S. K., 181, 194
Champagne sales forecasting, 56
Chisholm, R. K., 235
Christ, C. F., 143
Clarke, Arthur G., 178, 194
Classical decomposition method, 84
Coefficient of determination, 79, 105
Communicating forecasts, 223
Computers, 5
Computer time, 135
  usage, 140, 209
Conceptual model of change, 232
Confidence interval, 74, 106
  levels, 24
Constant variance, 110
Control algorithm, 125
  methods, 202
  versus planning, 7
Corporate environment, 234
Corporate forecasting function, 220
  planning, 230
  sales example, 115
Correlated variables, 77
Correlation coefficient, 77, 119, 126
  multiple, 100
  significance of, 78
  simple, 63, 77
Cost, 9, 198
Cost allocation process, 227
Cost of forecasting, 209
Criterion, decision making, 168
Cumulative probability graph, 172
Cyclical factor, 84, 132
  pattern, 18, 56

Data, 3, 9, 11
  acquisition, 144
  aggregates, 152
  base, 144
  base system, 153
  categories, 157

collection, 144, 147, 222
collection errors, 151
handling, 144
level of detail, 154
patterns, 15; *see also* pattern
sources, 144, 147
storage costs, 25
updating, 160
Decision analysis, 6, 163, 167
limitations and extensions, 174
steps in, 170
Decision making, functional tasks, 1
need for explicitness, 1
Decision making characteristics, control
versus planning, 7
existing procedures, 7
level of detail, 6
number of decisions, 7
stability, 7
time horizon, 6
Decision making process, 163
responsibilities, 226
situations, common elements of, 3
Decision point, 167
Decision tree, 167
Decomposition, 204
evaluation of, 95
forecasting, costs of, 97
limitations of, 96
method, 83
Degrees of freedom, 118
Delphi Method, 188
Demand forecasts, 30
Dependence, 102
Dependent variables, 26, 100
Deseasonalized data, 88
Designing a forecasting system, 212
Development costs, 25, 209
Deviations, 68
Dispersion, 172
Durbin-Watson statistic, 111, 118

Ease of application, 9
Econometric forecasting, 135
Educational task, 226
Endogenous variables, 139
Envelope S-curve, 182
Environmental information, 230
Error, 14
analysis of, 12
comparison, 224
measurement, 20
minimization, 52
Event description, 156
Evolutionary approach, 231
Exogenous variables, 139
Expected value, 169
Experts, 5
judgment, 180
use of, 178
Explained variation, 77, 79, 105, 107
Exploratory methods, 179
Exponential relationship, 66

Exponential smoothing, 49
double, 44
simple, 36

Feedback, 224
First-order smoothing, 30
Fisher, F. M., 143
Folding back, 169
Foran, 97, 206
system, 99
Forecasting, annual sales, 100
characteristics of successful, 233
common mistakes in, 225
costs of, 24
developing a procedure for, 10
different from planning, 3
economic, 3
environmental factors, 3
feedback in, 12
for finance, 2
function, 228
horizon, 58
in the firm, 10
means and not an end, 1
manpower, 2
for marketing, 2
methods, accuracy, 9, 20, 210
applicability of, 211
characteristics of, 8, 15, 198
costs, 9
ease of application, 9
pattern of data, 8
time horizon, 8
type of model, 8
organization, 224
procedure, elements, 221
for production, 2
range of problems, 2
relationship to decision making, 2
short-term, 17
sponsorship, 224
staff, 228
system, 144
techniques, comparison on six basic
criteria, 198
evaluation of, 15
overview, 4
tuning of a, 217
Freund, 99
F-Statistic, 79, 107
F-test, 79, 118
Function, 65
Functionally false data, 153

General Electric TEMPO Center, 185
Gerstenfeld, Arthur, 179, 194
Goldberger, A. S., 143
Gordon, R. A., 99
Gordon, T. J., 194

Hadley, G., 99
Helmer, Olaf, 194
Hidden information, 151

Hillier, P. S., 176
Honeywell Corp., 190
Horizontal pattern, 17
Hypothesis testing, 73

Ijiri, Y., 161
Immediate term, 26
    forecasting, 197
Implementation, 219, 220, 231
Independent variables, 26, 100
    choice of, 113
Information, 3
    amount of, 49
    overload, 175
Input-output tables, 141
Integrating forecasting, 229
Interdependence, 138
Internal audits, 160
Interval, 134
Intuitive appeal, 211
Inventory control theory, 143
Inventory forecasting, 3; see also Forecasting,
    for production
Iterations, 215

Jantsch, Erich, 179, 194
Jenkins, G. M., 143
Johnson, J., 82, 122, 143
J. Walter Thompson Company, 150

Kavesh, Robert A., 161
Klein, L. R., 122, 143
Krauss, Leonard I., 235

Lead time, 25, 197
Learning, 47
    constant, 53
    squares, method of, 67, 103, 139
Level of accuracy, 147
    of detail, 146
    of support, 234
Lieberman, G. J., 176
Life-cycle analysis, 205
Likelihood, 73
Linearity, 109
Linear trend, 63
Logistic curves, 180
Long range planning, 179
Long term, 26
    forecasting, 204

Mail order house example, 64
Maintenance costs, 25
Management participation, 221
Management requirements, 221
Man-made illumination example, 181
Mathematical notation, 12
McLaughlin, R. L., 99
McRae, T. W., 161
Mean, 69
    absolute deviation (MAD), 21, 33
    squared error, 14, 21, 52
Measurement errors, 151

Medial average, 89
Medium term, 26
    forecasts, 204
Model, 8, 22
    types of, 22
Monte Carlo simulation, 175
Moore, G. H., 161
Morgenstern, Oskar, 150, 161
Morphological research, 185
Moving averages, 48, 85, 129
    double, 41
    limitations of, 34
    mathematics of, 34
    simple, 30
Multicollinearity, 112
Multiple regression analysis, application of,
    103
    assumptions inherent in, 109
    practice usage of, 113

Naive forecasting, 17
National Bureau of Economic Research, 150
Noise, 51
Nonstatistical model, 24, 208
Normative forecasting, 191
Null hypothesis, 106

Observed values, 12
Office of Business Economics, 148
Operating costs, 25, 209
Overspecified, 140

Pacioli, 155
Parameters, 56, 67, 104, 139, 217
    estimation of, 125, 217
Parsimony, 81
Parvin, R. H., 190, 194
Pattern, 190
    changes, 5
    cyclical, 17, 206
    data of, 8, 198
    horizontal, 17, 206
    linear, 63
    recognition, 15
    relationship, 15
    seasonal, 17, 206
    time series, 15
    trend, 17, 206
Planning, interaction with forecasting, 4
Planning procedures, 7
Pointers, 157
Point forecast, 163
Polynomial fitting, 49
Price deflators, 149
Primary trend, 184
Porter, W. T., 161
Probability, 162, 164
    laws of, 166
Problem formulation, 113
Production planning, 29
Profiles of the future, 178
Project management, 226
Propulsive powerplants example, 186

Qualitative curve-fitting, 180
Qualitative forecasting, 177
  recent experience in, 193
  technique of, 4
    acceptance of, 5

Raiffa, Howard, 176
Ralph, 179
Ramp change, 35, 41
RAND Corporation, 188
Randomness, 20
  effect of, 214
Random variable, 81
Reading dynamics, 232
Refreezing, 232
Regression, 204
Regression, multiple, 100
  simple, 63
Regression analysis, equations for, 69
  error distribution, 81
  steps in applying, 113
Regression coefficients, 72
  significance of, 106
  standard error of, 73
Regression equation, as a model, 80
  significance of, 72
Regression forecasting, 70
Relevance tree method, 190
Relevant errors, 155
Residuals, 81
  independence of, 111
  normally distributed, 111
Retail sales of passenger cars, example, 131
Responsibility, assignment of, 225

Sales forecasting, 3, 16; see also Forecasting, for marketing
Sample size, 79
Sampling methods, 151
Schein, Edgar H., 231, 235
Schlaifer, Robert, 176
S-Curve, 180
Seasonal factor, 18, 84, 132
Seasonal index, 85
  adjusted, 88
  unadjusted, 88
Seasonal pattern, 18
Selecting a forecasting method, 195, 216
Serial correlation, 111
Shiskin, J., 97, 99, 161
Short time, 26
Short term forecasting, 203
Sigford, J. V., 190, 194
Significance, 104
  tests of, 72
Simple correlation matrix, 105, 114
Simple regression, 211
Simple smoothing, 30
Simultaneous equation, 139
Simulation trials, 176
Smoothing, higher forms of, 39, 47
  methods, 48
    comparison of, 39

Smoothing constant, 37
Smoothing techniques, 29
Specification, 139
  of variables, 145
Spurr, W. A., 82, 122
Stability, 7
Standard deviation, 73, 172
  of estimate, 118
Standard error, 73, 106
  of estimate, 74
  of forecast, 74, 108
Stationary, 17
Statistical control theory, 98
Statistical model, 24, 174, 208
Statistical significance, 72
Steckler, H. O., 161
Step change, 35
Straight line parameters, determining of, 66
Subjective estimates, 162
Subjective probability, obtaining, 171
Subjective probabilities, 166
  analysis, 6; see also Decision analysis
Successful forecasting situation, 233
Supermarket sales, 16
Support staff, 222
Survey of current business, 148

Technological forecasting, 5, 177
  methods, 24
  see also Qualitative forecasting, techniques of, 177
Telecommunication engineering, 51
Tests of significance, 106
Time horizon, 6, 8, 197, 198
Time independent technological comparisons, 183
Time-lagged variables, 127
Time series, 4, 13, 123, 203
  model, 23, 208
Tinter, G., 143
Total variation, 77, 105
Trading-day differences, 98
Training cycle, 56
Training iteration, 59
Training phase, 52
Transformation, 66
Transportation speed example, 181
Trend, 17, 205
  factor, 84
T-test, 73, 106
Turning points, 5, 9, 98, 177; see also Pattern, changes
Type of manager, 234
Type of model, 198, 207

Uncertainty, 3
  in decision making, 162
Uncertain event, 167
Underlying pattern, 16
Understanding forecasting techniques, 213
Unemployment insurance claims example, 84
Unexplained variance, 79, 107

Unfreezing, 232
U.S. Census Bureau, 97
Unit of measurement, 147

Variable, 13
Variance, 79, 107

Weight adjustment, 52
Weight vector, 56
Weighted average, 48
Weights, 14

Wharton School of Business, 135
Whitaker, G. R., 235
White-nose, 81
Widrow, Bernard, 61, 219
Wilde, D. J., 61
Winters, P., 47

Y intercept, 65

Zwicky, 185, 194
Zachau, E. V. W., 161